THE
VANISHING
OF
VIVIENNE
CAMERON

Also by Vikki Petraitis

The Phillip Island Murder (with Paul Daley)
Victims, Crimes and Investigators
The Frankston Murders
The Great John Coleman (with Wayne Miller)
Rockspider (with Chris O'Connor)
Cops: True Stories from Australian Police
Forensics: True Stories from Australian Police Files
Crime Scene Investigations
Salvation: The true story of Rod Braybon's fight for justice
The Frankston Serial Killer
True Stories from Australian Police Files
The Dog Squad
Once a Copper
The Frankston Murders: 25 Years On
Inside the Law
Cop, Drugs, Lawyer X and Me
Police Stories
Forensics
The Unbelieved
The Stolen

THE VANISHING OF VIVIENNE CAMERON

FORTY YEARS SEARCHING FOR THE PHILLIP ISLAND MURDERER

VIKKI PETRAITIS

SIMON &
SCHUSTER

London · New York · Sydney · Toronto · New Delhi

THE VANISHING OF VIVIENNE CAMERON: FORTY YEARS SEARCHING
FOR THE PHILLIP ISLAND MURDERER
First published in Australia in 2026 by
Simon & Schuster (Australia) Pty Limited
Level 4, 32 York St, Sydney NSW 2000

10 9 8 7 6 5 4 3 2 1

New York Amsterdam/Antwerp London Toronto Sydney/Melbourne New Delhi
Visit our website at www.simonandschuster.com.au

A catalogue record for this
book is available from the
National Library of Australia

ISBN: 9781761820830

Cover design: Luke Causby/Blue Cork
Cover image: main (Phitchaya/Adobe Stock), photo of Vivienne (Sue Chadwick)
Typeset by Midland Typesetters, Australia
Printed and bound in Australia by Griffin Press

The paper this book is printed on is certified against the
Forest Stewardship Council® Standards. Griffin Press holds
chain of custody certification SCS–COC–001185. FSC®
promotes environmentally responsible, socially beneficial
and economically viable management of the world's forests.

For Vivienne Cameron and Beth Barnard, may your stories always be told. And to truth-seekers everywhere; if we don't seek the truth, it will remain buried and will never be known.

CONTENTS

KEY CHARACTER LIST (IN ALPHABETICAL ORDER)

Beth Barnard (murder victim)

Beth Barnard's friends
Denise
Jacquie
Mandy
Maree
Michael

Family members
Ian Cairns (Fergus's brother-in-law)
Marnie Cairns (Fergus's sister and Ian's wife)
Donald Cameron (Fergus's older brother)
Fergus Cameron (Vivienne's husband and Beth's boyfriend)
Pam Cameron (Donald's wife)
Vivienne Cameron (missing, presumed dead)

Police

Sergeant Cliff Ashe (Phillip Island)

Detective Sergeant Kevin Casey (Victoria Police)

Detective Sergeant Ronald Cooper (Wonthaggi CIB)

Sergeant Geoff Frost (search and rescue)

Senior Constable Brian Gamble (crime scene examiner)

Detective Senior Constable Garry Hunter (homicide squad)

Detective Senior Constable Graeme Inch (homicide squad)

Detective Senior Constable Alan McFayden (Wonthaggi CIB)

Senior Constable Peter McHenry (Phillip Island)

Detective Senior Constable Rory O'Connor (homicide squad)

Sergeant Hughie Peters (crime scene examiner)

Vivienne Cameron's friends

Sue Chadwick

Anne Davie

Glenda Frost

PROLOGUE

A CRIME WRITER'S ORIGIN STORY

I began writing the Phillip Island book back in 1991 when my daughter was four years old. Every parent has that moment when you realise you have to be careful what you say around your kids. One minute they're too young to understand; the next, they're not, and you've missed the transition. As a budding crime writer, my moment was more horrifying than most. When the phone rang one day – the old landline type with a cord – my daughter raced to answer it. I could hear the one-sided conversation, typical of kids that age. 'Good,' she said. A pause. Then, 'Mummy's writing.' Another pause. Then, 'She's writing a book about Beth, and Vivienne who jumped off a bridge.'

Oh dear.

Note to self: *Stop telling people about the book when your daughter's listening!*

Up till that point, my life's trajectory had gone something like this: married at 20, baby at 22, diploma of teaching at 23, job teaching primary school at 24, and at 26, writer investigating a murder.

1

I heard about the Phillip Island case from an unlikely source: a professional development day for school teachers. A woman came to tell us about a new program designed to support children from families of divorce. The program was sponsored by the family of Vivienne Cameron. Vivienne came from a broken home; her father had left when she was eight years old and she never really got over it. In time, she married a man named Fergus, moved to Phillip Island and had two boys. One of her sons had just turned eight when Vivienne found out Fergus was having an affair with a young woman called Beth.

At that point, according to the speaker, Vivienne just 'snapped'. All the hidden rage and sorrow from her parents' broken marriage – as well as her own failing one – came crashing down on her. She broke into Beth's home, killed her and then jumped to her death off the Phillip Island bridge.

I guess the other teachers in the room that day heard the story and thought, *Wow, that's proof right there that we need a program to help kids!* But I was thinking, *Wow, that's just the story I've been looking for!*

Right from the start, I was mesmerised by the case. I could see all of its complexities and facets and sorrows. Of course, back then I assumed – like so many others – that it was a simple story of love, betrayal and murder. But nothing is ever as simple as it seems. I also felt sure the families would welcome a book which would get their message out to more than just a hall full of teachers. I was wrong about that too. But by then it was too late for me *not* to write the book.

The story took up a *lot* of headspace – and still does. Stories that speak to the common experience are compelling. They invite you in and ask you to think about what *you* would do, how *you* would feel, and how *you* would react. So sometimes you're Vivienne, filled with rage or sorrow that your husband is having an affair with a 23 year old and the pair are flaunting it under your nose. Sometimes you're Beth, falling hard for the charismatic older boss and letting your heart rule your head, believing the my-marriage-is-over, my-wife-doesn't-understand-me line because you're too young to know it's a cliché. And sometimes you're Fergus, laughing and joking with the fresh-faced young woman full of life and desire for you, and you compare her with the wife back home, who demands things from you like time and understanding and help with the children – one knows you all too well, and the other looks at you with stars in her eyes. And sometimes you're just a young teacher, juggling work and family, trying to get your head around something that seems impossible.

True crime cases without a resolution are enthralling. They have a haunting siren's call. They trick you into believing that somewhere within the pages of scientific and police documents lies a solution. Something unspoken happened that night, and all you have to do is crack the code to find out what it is. It's like a monkey puzzle tree – so-called because there are too few low branches for even monkeys to climb. But monkeys and authors won't be stopped simply because they can't get a grip. They will always find other ways.

Back in the early 1990s, I would write long into the night, carving out time for the book between my family and my teaching. People asked how I managed to do both, but for me, crime writing and teaching were a perfect balance. By day, I delighted in watching children in my class learning and laughing and playing; by night,

I wondered how long a knife blade would have to be to collapse a lung. After days of childish innocence, my nights reminded me the world had teeth.

'Why did this case get under your skin?' one of Vivienne Cameron's relatives once asked me. 'It was so long ago, why do you still care?'

The question stopped me in my tracks.

Why, indeed?

Maybe it was seeing the pictures of Beth Barnard, lying on her bedroom floor, so brutalised. Maybe it was because of Vivienne, lost and alone, having given her love and trust to a man ill-deserving of either. Maybe it was Vivienne's two little boys, growing up without their mother, being told that she was a murderer. Or maybe it was because in death, Beth was cast as 'the mistress' and Vivienne 'the murderer' and then, after they were both blamed and shamed, they were covered in a veil of secrecy and silence. But mostly, I cared about this case because it was a matter of justice. No one had ever been brought to justice over Beth Barnard's murder. It was still technically an open case, but it felt shut. Slammed shut.

As much as I couldn't let it go, the case wouldn't let me go either. I moved on. Wrote other books. Lots of them. But always, just when Phillip Island began slipping from my mind, I'd get a letter or an email or a phone call from someone who, just like me, had let it get under their skin too. It was a never-ending game of Chinese whispers, leads that went nowhere, or added a gossamer thread to the story.

Maybe my dogged pursuit was something deeper. Maybe the dead can't rest till the truth comes out. And maybe I can't either.

Note: This case can be complex, with information coming to light over the course of 40 years. In this telling, I'll make things easier where I can. Sometimes, I'll add something before it's known to those on the scene, just to give you a heads-up. For example, when the detectives see a drop of blood, I might whisper in your ear and say, *It's Vivienne's,* while the men looking on remain in the dark.

CHAPTER 1

THE MURDER

Phillip Island sits in Western Port Bay off the southern coast of Victoria, just under two hours' drive from Melbourne. Most people get there by crossing the bridge that runs from San Remo on the mainland to the town of Newhaven in the island's southeast. While one side of the island is protected by the bay, the southern side faces Bass Strait, a treacherous body of water. There are rocky outcrops and koalas and pelicans; and snakes too, dangerous ones, usually too cold or too lazy to bite, coiled under fallen tree branches. And of course, there are penguins.

It's a strange place. Maybe it's because it's an island. Insular. Cut off. Once you cross the bridge, the rules change. There are old families and old alliances. Landed gentry. Rippling beneath the surface are power structures that outsiders don't understand. You're not considered 'local' unless you can count several generations on your family tree.

It's worth keeping this in mind.

*

Make no mistake. The murder of Elizabeth 'Beth' Barnard was a brutal one. Crime scene photographs taken in the cold light of day on Tuesday 23 September 1986 show her lying diagonally across her bedroom floor, covered from the nose down by a doona. Of course, the photos show only two-dimensional images of what must have been a hundred times worse in real life. Even though we can see very little of her, we know she's dead because blood has soaked into the carpet around her head like a halo. Her eyes are open but unseeing; they're vivid blue but all the spirit and spark they once contained has fled. As long as Beth stays covered, the atrocities beneath the doona stay hidden.

Let's rewind the clock to before the police and crime scene photographers arrive; let's imagine that we're here in the hours when Beth's body lay undiscovered. While it's quiet, let's look around.

Beth's bedroom shows signs of a struggle. Blood is spattered on her white chest of drawers. There is blood on her bed, where she was attacked, perhaps disturbed while sleeping, a knife tearing through blanket and sheet and into her body. There's a haunting handprint on the wall – an echo in blood – like she has grabbed at the knife and then smacked her hand against the wall in the struggle. The killer has set the blanket to rights, rather than leaving it hanging like it surely must have been after Beth was dragged or fell from the bed.

Aside from the body, the rest of the room is achingly normal; jumbled with clothes, and knick-knacks on the chest of drawers separating the two single beds. A toy cow next to a toy penguin. A little pink cocktail umbrella. A glass of water next to a lamp. A watch. Family photos. A sun hat on a bedpost.

On the floor beside Beth's bed are a box of tissues, an open magazine, a bloodstained pair of jeans and a white pillowcase spotted with blood. Leaning against the other single bed is a poster-sized picture of Beth at the Phillip Island Penguin Parade. In the picture she is holding two of the small fairy penguins that tourists flock to the island to see each evening as they wobble like drunks through the breaking waves to return to their burrows. The joy on her face is evident. Beth works there. *Worked* there. Past tense now.

It is peaceful in her bedroom. The violence is over and nothing can hurt her now.

She has gone to her rest.

Let's leave Beth there for the time being and take a look around her house for clues as to who might have hurt her. Because somebody did. They came, by the looks of things, in the dead of night, to end her life. When a woman is stabbed through her bedclothes, the point of the interaction is clear. Someone wanted her dead because that's what happens when you aim a knife at a person's chest, then strike the blow. You're aiming to kill. A stab to the heart, so to speak. Let's move gently through the house so we don't disturb any evidence.

Outside Beth's bedroom a hallway runs from the back door to the kitchen. It's a sea of beige, in carpet and wall. On the floor by the back door is a yellow Dolphin torch and a set of keys marked 'Barnard'. Are they always left there like that, lying on the carpet? Or is there something sinister about their position-ing? Because if the killer came in the dead of night for Beth, they might have used the torch and dumped it there when they entered through the door to leave their hands free. Is it the killer's torch? Or does it belong to the family?

We don't know. We are just onlookers.

The back door is a puzzler. It's ajar, but the brown Lockwood lock is in the un-snibbed position. Everyone had these sorts of locks back in the 1980s – you could snib them in and the door wouldn't lock, or you could un-snib them and the door would lock when closed. It's probably understandable that the killer left it un-snibbed. You'd want to get the hell out of there once you saw what you'd done. But if Beth shut the door when she went to bed, it would have been locked, surely. In the cool of September, you'd hardly leave your door ajar at night. So how did it come to be open? And who opened it? We don't know.

Beyond the back door, the outside light is on to illuminate the concrete porch. Did Beth leave the light on when she went to bed? Or might the killer have flicked the switch as they were leaving to light the way home?

You can feel the questions mounting and we're only in the hallway.

Let's move away from the back door – and the torch and keys that might be a clue or might be nothing – and head up the hallway to the kitchen and dining area. There's a big, long table with bench seats on either side. It's a reminder that Beth had a big family: two brothers, two sisters, two parents. They live in the Melbourne suburb of Kew and this is their holiday home and farm. They visit on weekends. During the week, Beth is mainly here on her own.

In the kitchen, there are the usual cupboards and drawers. In the second drawer down are wooden-handled knives, each with three brass rivets in the handle. Although the police would later suggest the killer brought their own weapon, the knife lying under the doona next to Beth in her bedroom looks a lot like these other knives in the drawer. If we were of a suspicious mind, we might wonder if the knife that killed her came from this drawer. And if it did, it might raise all sorts of questions such as: how did the killer sneak into the house in the dead of night, then creep down the hall to the kitchen, select a weapon, then creep back down the hall to attack a sleeping woman? And all this creeping round under the nose of Beth's kelpie, Minty, who didn't bark. Because we can't forget the dog.

On the kitchen floor are two containers: one full of water and the other full of dog food. Minty is with pup, belly swollen, ready to deliver. She's more pet than farm dog. But she's nowhere to be seen. And from our bird's eye position, we know she hasn't been in the house since Beth was laid out on the floor. We know this because dogs are loyal and they stay by your side. Dogs – and I don't want to sound indelicate here – lick. One can imagine a loyal companion, whining with heartbreak and sorrow by her human's side, licking to comfort, licking to clean, like she will do to her pups soon to be born. But Beth still has smears of blood on her face; in fact, all over her body. Minty must've been put or taken or kicked or dragged outside, depending on whether she attacked Beth's killer or not. We'll never know because she is not mentioned in any police statements.

There's an ashtray near the phone on the kitchen bench. I always thought Beth was a non-smoker, but someone recently told me she smoked when she was a teenager, so I'm not sure if she came to her senses or still smoked when she was murdered. There are two Claridge cigarette butts in the ashtray. No traces of blood or DNA would ever be found on them so we don't know who smoked them, or indeed if they were props, placed there in order to 'stage' the scene.

There's another cigarette butt in the bathroom so let's move there and take a look. Next to a cup holding five rag-tag holiday toothbrushes, the butt sits in a little clear glass ashtray. This one won't retain any forensic trace of its smoker either. Now, looking closely at the basin, you can see there's blood. Not a lot, but traces of it. If you bend over a little, you can see a red drip on the side of the cold-water tap. You can see it's been diluted – like a bloodied hand turned on the tap, then a wet and dripping hand turned it off and made the watery drip. There's a towel there too – maroon Myer Heritage brand. There are traces of blood on it as well. Not a lot; just a dot and two small lines. Later, we will find out this blood is type A, not Beth's blood type which is O.

With all of that blood throughout the house, it's two little smudges on the concrete path outside the back door that will set the tongues on Phillip Island forever a-wagging. Two little smudges of blood, belonging not to Beth Barnard, but to Vivienne Cameron, the wife of Beth's boyfriend, Fergus. Two little smudges of blood that might have dripped or might have been walked in on someone's shoe. We will never know because the fact they were *there* would always be seen as more important than how they *got* there. Vivienne smoked Claridge cigarettes: the blood on the towel would turn out to be hers.

The case against her is building.

Hush now. Someone's coming to discover the body. We've loitered here long enough. Let's step aside and let things play out.

CHAPTER 2

THE NIGHT BEFORE
THE MURDER

We don't want to get ahead of ourselves: the night *before* the murder is when all the players step onto the stage and take their positions. By the time the curtain falls, one woman will be dead for sure, another one will be dead for not sure.

What's this story about? Well, it's about a married man who has an affair. His wife finds out. Then in the blink of an eye, the girlfriend is dead, and the wife has vanished. But what is it *really* about? I hear you ask. This story is really about violence, jealousy, rage, possession, family, freedom, love and hate. Just who was feeling which of those emotions is a job for jigsaw puzzle experts with psychology degrees.

There's no doubt that Beth Barnard loved Fergus Cameron. She hadn't really fallen for a man before. The first fall is the hardest. The first love, the one we'll never forget. At university, her friends watched as guys fell for her, but Beth never reciprocated; she wanted to be one of the gang, not someone's girlfriend. She sailed through uni maintaining friendships, but never relationships. She was level-headed. She was smart. And this is why, when she told her friends about her relationship with a married man – a married man with two young sons no less – they were surprised. It was so unlike her.

Mandy and Jacquie were Beth's closest friends at university and Beth and Mandy were going to be Jacquie's bridesmaids at her wedding that December. In all their giggling and laughing and planning, the three never imagined that only two would make it to the big day. They felt young and invincible with their whole lives ahead of them.

After university, Beth moved to her family's farmhouse in the small town of Rhyll and got a job as a park ranger at the Phillip Island Penguin Parade. The island is around 140 kilometres from Melbourne, but it might have been a world away. It was cocooned, with its own set of rules. You weren't considered local for several generations and could still be a newcomer after decades living there. And there were some families that mattered more than others. It was a power thing. Families united and stuck together.

Mandy knew the island: she and other university friends had been down there for barbeques and Mandy had stayed at Beth's family's farm to do some work experience as part of the agricultural science degree they'd all studied. When Beth confided she was having an affair with Fergus, Mandy told her she didn't approve – these things never ended well. Beth got angry and after that, the affair became the elephant in the room; present and heavy, but never discussed.

On the night of Monday 22 September 1986, Mandy rang Beth's parents' house in Kew. Beth was supposed to have been there, but she wasn't. Mandy wanted to finalise the arrangements for the next day, when she planned to pick up Beth and go meet

Jacquie at Jacquie's sister's pub in Fitzroy. But when she couldn't get a hold of her, Mandy waited till after 9 pm to try Beth at the Barnards' farm on Phillip Island. Long distance calls – as they were known back then – were cheaper after 9 pm. Beth answered the phone but sounded tired. She wasn't well, she said. She'd seen the doctor on Sunday and that's why she'd delayed her return to Melbourne. She said she'd just had some visitors over but they'd gone. Mandy didn't ask who the visitors were. And because Fergus was a name left unspoken between them, Beth wouldn't have said it was him, even if it had been.

Over the years, when Mandy has let herself go there, she has wondered: *Why Fergus?* In trying to make sense of it all, she imagined Beth would have loved his lifestyle and his two boys, Dugald and Hugh. But more than that, Beth was convinced that Fergus loved her and that he was going to leave Vivienne. It was a Cinderella dream, except while in the fairytale, Prince Charming was single and available, Fergus had a wife and two young children and was only available in snatches of time.

That night on the phone, Beth and Mandy firmed up their plans to catch up the next day when Beth came to Melbourne. 'I'm tired,' Beth said again. 'I'm going to go to bed. I'll see you tomorrow.'

'Okay, see you tomorrow,' Mandy echoed, never imagining she wouldn't.

That wasn't the only phone call Beth got.

Earlier that evening, Beth's friend Jacquie had also called and they too discussed their Melbourne catch-up. One of their favourite cover bands, Dean and Carruthers, was playing at Jacquie's sister's pub. Add a bunch of uni mates, and it promised to be the perfect gathering.

Jacquie was worried for Beth. She'd watched her friend agonise over a married man for nearly two years. It was love, Beth had declared. Beth was normally so sensible. Mates with everyone. Guys liked her, but until Fergus, she hadn't liked any of them back in that way. (For a while it was called friend-zoning until people started to realise that friend-zoning is simply having friends that you didn't want to sleep with, which when you think about it, is all your friendships. I reckon guys who complain about being friend-zoned never wanted to be 'just friends' because that would mean they wasted all that time for nothing. You know the type . . . and if you *are* the type, stop it!) Beth just wanted to be herself, hang out with everyone, not have to fend off constant demands for her affections. Probably figured it was easier to keep them all at bay. But then Fergus had broken through her normal reserves. Beth told Jacquie that Fergus's wife, Vivienne, knew about the affair and hated her.

Jacquie was flummoxed. 'Come on,' she said. 'You really want to raise two little kids?'

'I love them,' Beth said, 'but I don't know if I could take them on. Besides, Vivienne would never let them go.'

It hadn't been easy hearing about all the times Beth had almost made a break, only for Fergus to reel her back in. Beth had described going for a job at Werribee on the mainland only for Fergus to talk her out of it. And Beth was worried people would find out about the affair. It was bad enough that Vivienne hated her; she didn't want the rest of the island hating her too.

As far as Jacquie could see, Fergus had Beth trapped. Fergus had pursued Beth, but as a married man with two jobs, two children and a wife, what could he possibly offer her? He definitely couldn't offer her time or support or even public acknowledgement. What he could do was turn up for sex a couple of times a week.

It was a hopeless situation – and it was stopping Beth from living her best life. Jacquie decided to stage an intervention of sorts and was going to take Beth aside and help her find a pathway out of the mess. If Jacquie's plan worked, Beth would come home to Melbourne permanently. Beth had taken two weeks' leave from the Penguin Parade and the Cameron farm, which meant Jacquie had a fortnight to convince her friend to leave Fergus.

That night on the phone, Jacquie and Beth talked about Jacquie's upcoming wedding. While they were in Melbourne, maybe they could settle on a pattern for their bridesmaids' dresses? Jacquie was going to wear an off-white dress that had belonged to her mother-in-law. Her sister was going to make the dresses for the bridesmaids. Sleeveless? Off the shoulder? The popular dropped waist? Jacquie didn't mind. At least they'd settled on a colour. Apricot. That was a start.

After Beth's murder, her two friends waited for the police to contact them, certain that they were the last people who'd spoken with her. But no one ever did. The police said they couldn't check the phone records from the night of Monday 22 September 1986 because local calls on the island didn't show up. But Mandy's and Jacquie's calls weren't local, they were long distance. Phone records would solve this case. I've come to think the police never checked them at all, local or otherwise.

*

Meanwhile, on the other side of Phillip Island, in the town of Ventnor, Fergus Cameron got home a little after 9 pm. What follows is his account to the police, interspersed with his sister Marnie's story. In piecing this case together, we must tread carefully. Like making a delicate soufflé, we must gently combine the ingredients – in our case, statements and forensic evidence – and see what comes out in the end. But like a soufflé, don't bang the oven door in case it all falls flat.

Fergus told the police that Marnie and Vivienne were sitting at the kitchen table when he got home. Their two boys, Dugald and Hugh, were asleep in their bedroom. 'Marnie looked very agitated and Vivienne was visibly trembling, and as I walked in, the phone rang,' he said. 'I could see Vivienne was drinking a glass of wine and Marnie might have been as well.' Fergus read the room and was saved by the bell – he answered the phone.

Note: I recently spent an unpleasant hour on the phone myself with the man who claimed to be the caller that night. The man didn't want his name mentioned in this book, and I'll also refrain from giving him a pseudonym in case it ends up being Mr Cranky-Britches. He remembered the phone call as being earlier – not after 9 pm, but rather, between 7 and 8 pm. Said the police never followed up with him either. Never asked him about the call, about Fergus's demeanour, or what they spoke about. Nothing at all. If I were a detective, I'd be more curious, because Fergus is a man about to lose his girlfriend and his wife in one fell swoop.

'I spoke on the phone for 15 to 20 minutes and I could see that Vivienne was very upset but was not showing it to Marnie,' Fergus said. It turned out Marnie had phoned the Penguin Parade at

8 pm and was told Fergus had left work for the day. 'She thought she would come up here to help me sort out some of my business and personal problems. She went on to say that she hadn't picked the most appropriate time to come and left almost immediately.'

If this was a hashtag, it would be #awkward. So there was Fergus, home an hour late – evidently having thought he could sneak off to see his girlfriend Beth – only to find his agitated sister and shaking wife sitting at the kitchen table.

'After Marnie left,' Fergus went on, 'I shut the back door and walked back into the dining room, picked up my glass of wine . . . Vivienne followed me in. She pulled the plug out of the phone and screamed, "Where have you been?" I just said, "I've been talking to Beth." She then raced at me with the glass of wine and screamed, "I knew you were with the little bitch!" I think she hit me with the wine glass which broke on the left side of my head and cut my left ear. I turned my back, away from her and she hit me two or three times with the broken glass.'

Ouch.

The three cuts to Fergus's back were close together. Vivienne was either lightning fast, or Fergus didn't move while she attacked him. He's a better man than I am because I would have leapt out of the way after the first one. Note: I am not a man.

What did Fergus do after sustaining a cut to the ear and three to the back? 'At this stage I was standing between the dining room and a hallway in the doorway itself,' he said. 'I turned and walked to the [spare] bedroom at the top of the house and sat on the bed.' Note: The police photo of the bed shows it covered in papers and folders. If Fergus did sit on the bed, he must have moved these because they are not bum-crumpled. He must've also straight-ened the bedspread when he stood up again, because it too shows no sign of being sat on.

Sorry to interrupt, Fergus. Please, do go on.

'Vivienne was still following me and . . . pushing me. She was screaming out things including, "I knew what was going on! I've been watching the number of hours you've been working! I suppose everyone out there knew what was going on!"'

At some point, the spare bedroom floor – covered with that straw matting floor, so common back then – became spattered with blood. I blew up the police photo and counted 98 drops, clustered freckle-like, between the door and the bed, with more on the white bedspread.

'Her rage would have lasted no longer than a minute and a half and quickly changed to concern as there was blood everywhere and she wanted to take me to hospital immediately,' Fergus said.

Here's one of those times I'm going to whisper to you about the blood: the 'blood everywhere' later turned out to be Vivi-enne's, not Fergus's, except, that is, for one of the papers on the bed, which had Beth Barnard's blood on it. Go figure. It was an instruction sheet for a pesticide – maybe Beth cut herself while working on the Cameron farm and bled on it. Still, weird. (Also weird that a couple of drops of Beth's blood at the Cameron house meant nothing while a couple of drops of Vivienne's blood at Beth's house meant everything. But enough of that. I don't want to sound like a negative Nelly just yet. I'm saving that up for later.)

'I refused and she shouted that she was going to start making some decisions around here,' Fergus continued. 'At that point I went and poured myself a whiskey . . . Vivienne kept insisting that I had to go to hospital. These comments were interspersed with that she knew all along what was going on between Beth and myself.' And then, it seemed, after all Fergus's bedsitting and whiskey drinking and bleeding and bed straightening, Vivienne's response changed from shouting and accusations to worry. 'Her only concern at that point appeared [to be] to get me to hospital as I was making some attempt to staunch the flow of blood from my ear and I also knew my back was bleeding fairly badly. She was saying repeatedly, "Why couldn't you talk to me?" and I was in tears saying, "I don't know. I don't know." At this point I was holding her and she was holding me.'

Vivienne must've avoided his bleeding bits in the holding, because when they did eventually get to the hospital, no one noticed any blood on her.

Finally, Fergus relented. 'I agreed to go to hospital and we agreed that we must ring Marnie to come and look after the children. To the best of my knowledge this would have been about 10.15 pm.'

One of them must've plugged the phone back in to call Marnie.

Marnie's statement fits Fergus's like a glove. She told the police, 'I hadn't been home very long, in fact I still had my jacket on, and I received a phone call from Vivienne. She asked if I could go back and look after the children as Fergus required a couple of stitches. I could tell by the tone of her voice that there must have been some form of altercation which was probably due to his late arrival home from the Penguin Parade or even the lengthy phone call. I didn't actually ask her what had happened, but I said I would look after the children.' Here's a whispered aside: Pssst!

Marnie was a nurse. Is she the only nurse in the world who wouldn't ask what happened when told her brother needed to go to the hospital? Because that's the natural response, right? *I need to go to the hospital for stitches . . . OMG! What happened?* My daughter is a nurse, and I reckon if I rang her and said I needed to go to the hospital for some stitches, she'd totally pepper me with nurse questions. *What happened? What did you do? What needs stitching? How bad is it? Have you had your tetanus shot? Do you need me to call an ambulance?* There's no way she wouldn't ask what happened. Note: She takes after her mother.

Fergus then said they left straight away for the hospital. 'We did not wait for Marnie to arrive, but I changed my shirt and jumper and went into hospital with Vivienne driving and me in the front passenger seat. We went in my Holden sedan.'

The police would later find blood in the Holden; a big smear on the right-hand side of the passenger seat. We're not sure if it was Fergus's blood because firstly, his injuries were on the left, and secondly, while analysis would conclude it was human blood, the type was unknown.

According to Fergus, Vivienne talked all the way to the hospital about how she knew what had been going on between him and Beth.

'When we arrived . . . Vivienne parked outside and [as] she was turning off the ignition, she turned to me and said, "I'm just going to get the little bitch." I didn't take this threat seriously as these threats are often made by persons in anger and I thought that her physical anger had been vented on me and the subsequent concern would stop her doing any more acts of violence.'

What, I wonder, did Fergus imagine his wife would do – or not do – to Beth? What did he think 'get' meant, even if it wouldn't happen? And who are the 'persons in anger' who often make threats that Fergus is drawing from? So many things to ponder. Including: *Did she really say that?*

But let's leave the questions and Vivienne and Fergus, and slip back across the island to the Cameron farm in Ventnor for a moment to take a look at what Marnie and her husband Ian Cairns said they saw when they went to mind the children. Apparently, the little ones slept through all the yelling and screaming and attacking going on in the small weatherboard house – but we'll never know for sure, because the police never spoke to them.

'I then went straight back, and Ian said he would follow me,' Marnie said. 'When I arrived, I checked the two boys who appeared to be asleep, and noticed that the small fan heater had been tipped over.'

Marnie then took more of a look around. 'I went into the toilet and noticed a pile of blood-soaked clothing consisting of a singlet, T-shirt, a pale blue shirt from the Penguin Parade, a face washer and a towel. There were also some tissues in the basin which had blood on them.'

Before we go on, I want to point out here that while Marnie says she saw these blood-soaked items in the laundry, there was no mention of a singlet or T-shirt in the items collected the next day by the crime scene examiners, nor a face washer and towel. But a face washer would later turn up in the Camerons' Land Cruiser, and a towel in Beth's bathroom. Forensic examination would find Vivienne's blood on both. Sorry to interrupt, Marnie. Please go on with your story.

23

'Ian arrived shortly after and I showed him the clothing. He suggested that we leave it where it was and not touch it.'

Note: We are not sure why Ian was also required to look after two sleeping children – and needed to such a degree that he makes a separate trip, but I'm fascinated here how Ian seems to treat the house like a crime scene, despite the fact no crime has yet been discovered, let alone a body. Like, why wouldn't you put a load of washing on rather than leave blood-soaked stuff everywhere? I'm totally an A type personality. Note: I don't actually know what an A type personality is, but when I've heard people speak about being one – a little bossy, kind of exacting, single-minded, a lot bossy – I always think: *That's totally me*. So I would have snapped on a pair of rubber gloves and given the place a once-over. I also don't know what the opposite of an A type personality is – B type? Z type? – but maybe those are the type of people who can walk into a relative's house and not wipe up the blood. Marnie and Ian had a good old sticky-beak around the house though. Maybe they were onlookers, not cleaners.

Marnie would later tell police, 'I had a look around the house and saw blood on the bed in the spare room and also on the bench in the kitchen.'

Note: The blood in the spare bedroom (aside from the piece of paper) as well as the blood on a sponge in the kitchen sink were all Vivienne's A type. Second note: This is no relation to my suspected personality type. All this blood, according to Marnie and Ian, was present when Vivienne and Fergus left the house. This blood that they didn't clean up. This blood that told a story of Fergus being attacked with a wine glass and going into the spare room and bleeding. But of course, their story matched the blood, and no one had heard of DNA back in 1986.[1] Back then, blood was blood and anyone could point to a spillage or a droplet and say, 'That's mine,' and no one would know they were lying.

Marnie and Ian said they found broken glass on the dining room floor. We only have their word for it because that broken glass was never found. They also noticed a glass of whiskey and a glass of claret, even though when Marnie was there earlier, she said she and Vivienne were drinking white wine. Fergus corroborated they were drinking wine and mentioned getting a whiskey when he spoke to the police. The claret is anyone's guess.

Now, sleuths, back to the hospital!

*

Nurse Lisa Price was on duty at the Warley Hospital in Cowes the night of Monday 22 September 1986. Warley, now long closed, was a 15-bed facility with a small casualty department. If people arrived after hours, a nurse let them in through a glass sliding door. When the doorbell went – around 10.15 pm – Lisa saw Vivienne and Fergus Cameron standing outside, Fergus holding a cloth to the side of his head and obviously bleeding. She let them in and led them down to the casualty department.

Things turned odd when Lisa asked them what had happened. As she later told me, 'I was asking questions like: *What's actually*

---

1   Yes, yes, true crime fans, don't shout me down. We all know that Dr Alec Jeffreys *knew about it*, and two years and 13 days earlier, on the other side of the world, had made a breakthrough in his lab, and that a couple of months before the events on the island, Colin Pitchfork had killed his second victim and was about to be pursued by DNA technology and ultimately convicted. But it wasn't *common* knowledge.

happened here? and they would look at one another; there were very long intense looks between the two of them but they never said anything. I certainly didn't think there had been an argument . . . they looked very close during this time and she looked quite concerned about him and he looked concerned about her.' Lisa thought she'd make them a cup of tea. 'But then as I got up, I happened to walk behind Fergus and I could see blood coming through his shirt. And so I pulled up his shirt and saw what appeared to be puncture marks. And then I got a little bit annoyed and said, "Guys, you've gotta tell me what's gone on because I can't assess the injuries."'

After a lot of prompting, Vivienne said, 'There's been an accident and Fergus fell through a plate glass door.'

Naturally, Lisa didn't believe them and suspected there had been an altercation, perhaps between the brothers. This would account for their caginess. She knew the Camerons. They were a very private family. Lisa hoped that the doctor on call that night, Allan Powles, might have better luck working out exactly what had happened. She briefed him on their reticence.

The hospital visit was the last time Vivienne was seen outside the family, so Lisa's impressions are important. Lisa told me, 'She was very quiet . . . she looked concerned. They looked very deep in thought. I think Fergus was crying. He was certainly the more emotional of the two. And she was certainly playing a caring-type role towards him . . . that's why it never occurred to me that she would be responsible for those injuries because it just didn't read that way.'

Fergus would later recall that while they were waiting for the doctor to arrive, Vivienne had said, 'Beth is obviously very special to you.' According to Fergus, she then added something like, 'I didn't mean what I said before,' which Fergus 'took to mean that she didn't have any intention of doing any harm to Beth'.

While Lisa thought Vivienne was calm and Fergus was upset, Dr Powles saw it quite differently, as men often do. 'While I was treating Fergus,' he said, 'I noticed that Vivienne seemed upset and tense.' At one point, Dr Powles asked Fergus whether his injuries hurt. Fergus said that they didn't, and Vivienne said, 'Well you're luckier than I am.' While he couldn't remember all of their conversation, Dr Powles did recall Vivienne saying something like, 'I'm better inside, but no good with this shit.'

According to Dr Powles, Vivienne wanted Fergus to stay in hospital overnight, but the doctor didn't consider this necessary. The only time Vivienne left the room was when she went with Lisa to the office to phone Marnie. By this stage, Lisa was nearing the end of her shift and had handed over to nurse Susan Bishop. Lisa brought her colleague up to speed and explained that Vivienne and Fergus refused to be clear about what had happened.

Susan too sensed something was amiss the moment she saw the couple. 'Fergus was lying on the table being attended to by Dr Powles and Vivienne was standing next to the table,' she told the police. 'I know Fergus and Vivienne and they were obviously embarrassed. Lisa then left and went home and I checked on the other patients. I then remained in the office until Dr Powles came out and asked if there was a male bed available. I informed him that there was, and he then went back to Vivienne and Fergus. There was some discussion about whether Fergus should stay in hospital or go home . . . It was then decided that Fergus would go home, and I assisted Dr Powles with bandaging Fergus and dressing the wounds.'

I told Lisa Price that I'd always wondered if it was so obviously embarrassing for Fergus and Vivienne to go to the hospital, why didn't they ask Marnie for help because she was a nurse. Lisa felt that if the injury needed stitches, it might have been beyond Marnie's experience. She also may not have had the supplies to clean and dress the wounds. But even so, Vivienne and Fergus decided to go to the hospital without even giving Marnie the chance to see if she could help – which seems a little strange.

When Dr Powles left the hospital at 11.45 pm, Susan finished cleaning and dressing Fergus's ear.

Since Vivienne was soon to vanish, what she was wearing that night is important. These were the last clothes she was seen in. According to Susan, 'Vivienne was wearing a pink mohair jumper with a round neck. She may have had a skivvy or something underneath because I remember something around her neck, blue faded jeans and black ankle boots and a scarf around her hair . . . I did not notice any blood on her or her clothing.'

About 15 minutes later, around midnight, Vivienne and Fergus Cameron – wounds dressed but still maintaining a veil of silence – left the hospital and headed home.

CHAPTER 3

THE END IS NIGH

Whenever I give author talks on this case and repeat what Fergus Cameron told the police about the conversation he and Vivienne had after they got home from hospital that fateful night, the women in the audience typically burst into incredulous laughter. I'll give you a heads-up when I get to that bit. See if you laugh, too.

It's important to remember in the Phillip Island case that we don't have the full cohort of people involved to tell us what happened. One of them didn't last the night, and the other one vanished into thin air, leaving behind only her blood, which meant nothing to the investigating officers. It was peripheral. White noise or a red herring. We know it meant nothing because nowhere do the police try to find out *why* her blood was there. It's almost like they didn't notice. Or didn't read the scientific report when it came back months after the event, on 10 February 1987 to be exact.

'When we arrived home, Marnie wanted to go home straight away, and we asked her to stay and talk to us,' Fergus told the police. 'Marnie still believed there was still time to have marriage counselling, but Vivienne and I didn't. Vivienne and I discussed

29

our marriage for an hour and a half and the following suggestions all came from Vivienne: that we separate immediately; that she resign from her job and move to Melbourne; [and] that I have the custody of our children. I agreed to this and she said that I was an excellent father. She [said she] wasn't a very good mother and I disagreed and she gave me two warnings . . . not to be too stern with the children and not to take it for granted that Beth was going to make an excellent mother.'

Yes, Dear Reader, that's the bit that invariably elicits laughter from the women in the audience.

Sure honey, I'll move out and leave you my precious children so you can move your girlfriend in, said no woman ever.

In other parts of his statement, Fergus admitted to working 90-hour weeks and being largely absent from the family home. When he wasn't working on his family's farm or at the Penguin Parade, he was sneaking in time with Beth. And if, as he said in his statement, he lied about his finishing time at the Penguin Parade so he could snatch an hour with Beth, he would have missed the chaotic dinner, bath and bedtime routine with his two young sons. And then there's something that I hadn't realised before, even though it's right there in his statement. Fergus said that Dugald was born in September 1978 and in December that same year, he started working nights at the Penguin Parade. I had this image of Vivienne alone all day with a newborn and then he waltzes in (Note: There is no evidence to suggest actual waltzing) and tells her he will be gone at night too. This meant Vivienne, separated from her own family, was alone and isolated with a baby because her mum, Marjorie, lived in Warrnambool, and her brother Keith and sister Deirdre lived in Melbourne.

By his own admission, Fergus had grown distant and uncommunicative and flaunted his affair under Vivienne's nose. Vivienne, on the other hand, was by all accounts devoted to her two boys. She also worked hard on the Cameron family farm. Earth mother. Tiger mother. So, does this fit? That Vivienne would suddenly tell him what an excellent father he was? I'm not seeing it. Neither do the women at my author talks. It's like we've all grown weary and cynical in our middle age.

According to Fergus, Vivienne even helped him prepare to leave to go to Marnie's. I've never understood why he would have decided to go to Marnie's in the middle of the night, especially after his description of Vivienne's generous offer to walk away. Why go to your sister's when you just got everything you wanted? Why leave Vivienne to clean up all the blood left behind? Why leave if you're such an excellent father and you know the kids will be up in five hours, needing to be washed and dressed and fed and driven places? Why leave your wife to do all of that while you get pampered at your sister's place? Whoops, I think I just answered my own question. Just kidding. I'm not sure any of this account rings true. Anyway, let's let Fergus keep talking.

'She helped me pack a bag and talked about what I would need the next couple of days, and I said that I would give her a ring in the morning to see how she was getting on . . . At Marnie's place we sat in our car . . . and I said to Vivienne, "I wish we had done it differently." She said, "I'll give it a good bash but I don't think I'll make a very good divorcee." I then said goodbye to Vivienne, and Marnie kissed her goodnight and Vivienne left . . . and I haven't seen her since. To the best of my recollection, she left about 1 am on the Tuesday morning.'

31

The timing here is wrong. Fergus said they got home around midnight, talked to Marnie about their marriage and then, after Marnie left, talked for another hour and a half. So by his own calculations, if Vivienne dropped him at Marnie's, it would have been closer to 2 am. Much later, the coroner would add this mistake to his verdict and say that Vivienne was last seen at 1 am. Is it only authors that go through this stuff with a fine-tooth comb?

I've never understood why Marnie stayed up and waited for Fergus. She had to be at work at 8 o'clock the next morning. If it were me, I would have gone to bed. But in this story, Marnie waited until her brother and sister-in-law arrived, gave Vivienne two Mogadon tablets in an envelope, told her to take one and said goodbye. It would have been handy for Fergus in the long run that his sister stayed up to bear witness to the departure of Vivienne, unscathed. Handy for him too that she was at his place earlier to witness his arrival home from his visit to Beth's, unscathed. Her statement gives him neat alibi bookends.

Marnie told the police, 'Fergus said, "Well, it's all over, Marnie," and was very upset. He told me that they had had a long, rational talk and Viv seemed determined that that was the only solution. We spoke very broadly and went to bed at about 3 am.'

Years later, a man would come forward with an entirely different story. He claimed he was with Vivienne the night of Monday 22 September 1986, waiting for Fergus to come home from the Penguin Parade. But since I'm doing my best here to stick to a chronology, I'm going to make you wait to find out when I did. Just flagging it here, though, so you're not too surprised later on.

CHAPTER 4

THE PHONE CALL IN THE MIDDLE OF THE NIGHT

A couple of things happened that night that cemented Vivienne Cameron as the killer in the minds of many people on the island, not least the police. The first was that someone purporting to be her phoned some family friends of the Camerons – Robyn and John Dixon – around 3.10 am to ask them to come and collect the two Cameron boys. But it was a quick call and when John Dixon answered the phone, he was likely half-asleep. It therefore begs the question: what if it wasn't really Vivienne on the line?

The second thing occurred 20 minutes later at around 3.30 am, when Margaret McFee, one of Beth's neighbours on McFees Road in Rhyll, heard a vehicle drive by her property.

Verdict: Vivienne rang to get the kids minded, then drove to Beth's to kill her. Case closed. Slam dunk. Guilty, Your Honour!

*

Let's examine these events one at a time. When John Dixon answered the phone at 3.10 am, this is how the call went: Vivienne

33

said she was phoning from the hospital and her kids were at home alone. Could the Dixons go and get them? John would have been half-asleep when he answered. It was a quick phone call. Was it actually Vivienne who made the call? I hope John got it right because that was the call that made her a killer.

But what if it *wasn't* her?

What if a couple of sentences spoken to a man newly roused from sleep were *not* spoken by Vivienne? What if someone else made that call? What if sleepy John focused on the words, not the voice? *We're at the hospital. Can you go pick up our children?*

What if? What if?

Let's leave John to hang up the phone and hurry with his wife to collect the two boys. I suppose it's not overstepping the mark to wonder if the Dixons tumbled out of bed at that ungodly hour and cursed Vivienne for not ringing someone in the family to pick the kids up. After all, Fergus's brother Donald lived just across the road and Marnie and Ian were a couple of minutes down the same road. Why call the Dixons, who lived ten minutes away and would have to leave their own sleeping children to go and collect Dugald and Hugh?

But getting the Dixons to pick the Cameron children up meant they would be well out of the way for whatever happened next. It was always assumed that the Cameron children slept through the dramatic events that night at the farmhouse, as if they were not attuned to the barometric shifts that happen when peace turns to violence in your own home.

Now let's look at the second thing that happened that night. At 3.30 am, Beth's neighbour Margaret McFee woke up to go to the bathroom. She heard a car go past, up to the end of McFees Road, then turn around again. It sounded like her son's Toyota ute. Go back to bed, Margaret, and sleep tight. Tomorrow the police will be on your doorstep with some very bad news about your lovely young neighbour, Beth.

Recently, I heard a story I'd never heard before that needs to be included. After my podcast, *The Vanishing of Vivienne Cameron*, came out in 2020, people began writing to me with more leads and tips about the case. One day I received an email from a woman who said she had some pertinent information about the night of the murder:

> My family and I lived on the island at this time. We had been visiting friends in Melbourne on Monday. We were driving home to the island when we crossed the bridge and saw the Camerons' farm ute with hay on the back heading in the opposite direction at approximately 1–1.30 am in the early hours of Tuesday morning . . . My dad thought it was odd that the Camerons' farm ute was driving around at this time. He did report it to Cliff Ashe.

Cliff Ashe was the local cop at the Cowes police station on Phillip Island. We will meet him soon. Naturally, I wrote back to the woman and asked how she could be sure what they'd all seen, given that the events took place some 35 years ago. And here's the extraordinary thing: the woman said her dad knew the Camerons and was very familiar with their Land Cruiser. The reason the family had never forgotten was because the following day, when word got around that both Vivienne and the Camerons' Land

Cruiser had vanished, the woman's dad did the right thing and went straight to the police station and made a report.

When I spoke to retired homicide detective Rory O'Connor (who, in this story, is just about to head to the island to investigate the events of this dreadful night) he told me he had no recollection of this information being passed on to him. This information was important. As you'll remember, according to Fergus, at 1.30 am, he and Vivienne were at their place talking about what a great father he was. So who was in his Land Cruiser leaving the island?

That Land Cruiser would play a small but crucial role in the Phillip Island murder mystery. It and its hay bales would be found the next afternoon, parked fairly close to the Phillip Island bridge. The coroner would later make much of that.

The curious thing about hay is that it's not something farmers generally use in September. Hay is for when animal food is in short supply. In September, on the island, food is plentiful. The rain of the winter gives way to the sun of spring, and the fields are awash with green. In other words, the grass is greener on all sides of all the fences. So who got the hay out of storage and put it on the back of the Land Cruiser? And why? That is the question.

CHAPTER 5

THE SMALL HOURS OF TUESDAY MORNING

Just before sunrise on Tuesday 23 September 1986, bakery delivery driver Wayne Hunt turned into Forrest Avenue in the town of Newhaven. Forrest Avenue is the first street on the right after you come over the Phillip Island bridge. There's a park on one corner with play equipment for children and a public toilet block. On the other side of the road is the bakery. Wayne didn't take much notice of the vehicle parked in the small parking bay – just enough to remember one was there – but nonetheless his vague statement turned into gospel truth in the eyes of the police.

The Land Cruiser was eventually found by Pam, the wife of Fergus's brother, Donald Cameron on Tuesday around 4 pm but we're not there in our story yet. So yes, it *was* there at 4 pm, but *when* it was put there is the big question, although, clearly not for those listening to Wayne Hunt and making a leap of faith.

Timeline spoiler alert: if Vivienne called to get the kids minded at 3.10 am, and Beth was killed sometime after Mrs McFee heard what sounded like a Toyota at 3.30 am, then the Land Cruiser ended up parked half a kilometre from the bridge at 5 am, then this made the men who decide these things hop, skip and jump to conclusions: Vivienne must surely have killed Beth then suicided off the bridge.

What? I hear you say. *Big leap?* Yes, clever reader, you are absolutely correct.

It will be.

So given that, later in this book, a coroner will also make this big leap, I imagined when I finally got my hands on Wayne Hunt's statement, it would be a thing of beauty and precision. The Land Cruiser was in situ, waiting to be driven past by police all day. But it wasn't like that at all. If the term *WTF* had been coined back then, I might have used it.

'I cannot say what type of car it was or colour,' Wayne said, 'all I can say is that there was a car parked there. I just glanced and kept on going, but thought it was strange for it to be parked there at that time because normally there is nothing there. I thought it must have been someone using the toilet and didn't think any more about it.'

Considering how much weight was put on what Wayne saw, the mind boggles.

Wayne Hunt saw a car. And that is it.

Another local, Maurie Duffy, was also out and about that morning. He didn't see the Land Cruiser. He saw an ag bike (or agricultural bike for the city folk). Maurie was up before dawn to go feed the horses at a local stable. He would later tell police, 'I recall that at about 5.30 am on the day that young Beth Barnard was found murdered, I was coming out of my road which was at the time Sunderland Bay Road. When I got to the inter-section of the Cowes Tourist Road which also intersects at the

Rhyll-Newhaven Road I heard a two-stroke motorbike coming from the direction of San Remo/Newhaven way which was on my right.

'I stopped my car at the intersection and let the bike go past. I saw that it was a two-wheel agricultural bike with no head or taillights on. At the time it was dark, pitch black, and all I saw was the bike go past with a rider on it. All I saw of the rider was that he or she was wearing an oil skin type of coat. At the time, I believe that the bike [was] headed along the main Tourist Road. After I turned left, I headed along the Back Beach Road. I didn't see the bike after this, but I presumed that it possibly headed up the Tourist Road . . . Certainly, it's not uncommon for bikes to be riding around with the lights off because most of the ag bikes in the area have their lights broken and they are hardly ever used on the road. A couple of days later I heard that the Cameron ute was found at Newhaven. At the time I put it together that I had previously seen an ag bike on the back of the Cameron Land Cruiser. I don't know who was driving the ag bike on the occasion I am talking about, and I am not able to say whether it was the Cameron bike or not.'

It was eight years before Maurie Duffy came forward and gave his statement. At the time, he may or may not have felt his observations were significant. Word quickly got round the island that Vivienne Cameron was the killer and because the Land Cruiser was found 500 metres from the centre of the bridge, everyone assumed she must've jumped. No one on the island really talked about the case until 1993, when *The Phillip Island Murder* book that I wrote with journalist Paul Daley came out. The case was featured in the newspapers and on television. The homicide squad sent a detective to the island and people came forward with their pieces of the story. By then, men like Maurie Duffy, who'd perhaps spent the intervening years with the niggling feeling that they might have important information, decided to speak.

Wendy Orchard, an island local who knew Maurie well, said, 'If Maurie knew something or saw something, that would be him. He would tell. He was that sort of a person . . . Maurie was a mechanic . . . and he did a lot of the mechanic work around on farms like he would go to your farm and service your car or your motorbike or whatever. So he may well have known the bike.'

After the book came out, police took more statements and sent select pieces of evidence to be DNA tested. And then nothing happened.

But more about that later.

We don't want to get ahead of ourselves again. It's becoming a habit.

CHAPTER 6

THE MORNING AFTER

Tuesday 23 September 1986 dawned bright and sunny. Marnie Cairns left for her 8 am nursing shift at the Warley Hospital, the same hospital Fergus and Vivienne had attended the night before. Fergus's sister-in-law Pam Cameron tried to call Vivienne but got no answer.

About ten minutes from the Cameron farms, Robyn Dixon and her husband John were getting ready for work. They had collected the Cameron children after the 3.10 am phone call as requested and they still had them. Robyn was a school teacher and the children presented a bit of a problem. What was she supposed to do with them? She hadn't heard back from Viv and Fergus after the call to say they were at the hospital, and she needed to return their children so she could get to work. The clock was ticking. Robyn tried calling at 7.30 am. No luck. She then called Fergus's brother Donald Cameron. His phone was engaged. She tried again and again. Eventually Donald answered. By this time, Robyn might have sounded a little testy. 'Who's sick?' she asked.

Donald said he didn't know what she was talking about. When Robyn explained she had Vivienne and Fergus's two sons and needed to go to work, they agreed that Robyn would put Dugald on the school bus with her own kids and Donald would come and collect Hugh.

Robyn's phone call set off a domino effect. Where were Fergus and Vivienne and why were their children with the Dixons? Donald and Pam tried calling too. They had no luck. Pam later told the police she had tried to ring Vivienne before she got the call from Robyn Dixon and she too had wondered why no one answered the phone.

Pam called Ian and Marnie's place and finally tracked Fergus down. She would later tell the police, 'Fergus answered the phone and was not able to say very much and put me onto Ian. Ian informed me that there was a problem with Fergus and Viv, and that Fergus was staying with him, and that he'd tell me more later. I then informed Ian of my conversation with Robyn Dixon, and that Donald was going to pick up Hugh. At that stage I was very cross with the response I got from Fergus and Ian and was very short to them both and hung up.'

Ian Cairns seemed oblivious to Pam's anger. 'I took a phone call from my sister-in-law Pamela at approximately 7.45 or 7.50,' he told the police. 'She asked, "What's going on?" and I told her that Fergus and Vivienne had had a difference of opinion last night and that Fergus was at my place and Vivienne was at home with the children. I then told her that I would talk to her when I saw her.'

Pam Cameron said she felt sorry for her short tone with her brothers-in-law and called back. 'While Donald went to pick up

Hugh, I decided that I should apologise to Ian and Fergus for my shortness. I phoned again and Fergus answered. He informed me that he and Viv had a terrible argument which resulted in him having to go to the hospital, but he was all right now. He then became very emotional and said that he was worried about two people – and on me inquiring who, he said Vivienne and Beth. I know Elizabeth Barnard who worked for us on the family properties . . . I inquired of Fergus why he was concerned for Viv and Beth, but he did not give me an answer. I then formed the opinion at that stage that Viv and Fergus's argument had concerned Beth. Fergus didn't take the matter any further, and during that conversation, Donald had come home and stated that Fergus's car was in the garage. I tried to reassure Fergus that Viv was probably still at home and informed him of what Donald had just told me.'

After this, Ian Cairns went to Fergus and Vivienne's to pick up the Land Cruiser. But it was gone. Even though Pam had just told him that Vivienne had rung the Dixons to collect the children in the middle of the night, Ian would later tell the police, 'When I arrived, the Land Cruiser wasn't there and I presumed Vivienne had used it to take their eldest child to the school bus which comes about 8.10 am.'

Maybe he forgot that bit.

When Ian got back to his farm with the news the Land Cruiser was missing, Fergus told the police, 'My anxiety was further increased when I was told that Vivienne had taken the Land Cruiser which was parked in the shearing shed. On hearing the Land Cruiser, Beth would automatically think it was me and open the door. The two people who drove the Land Cruiser were either Beth or myself.'

Not technically correct, though. Ian Cairns said he had gone to get the Land Cruiser, so that meant *he* drove it. When it was gone, Ian assumed Vivienne was in it, so she must have driven it too. And Beth didn't open the door; she was attacked in bed. Or if she did open the door and went back to bed – she's hardly likely to do that if it was Vivienne at the door.

As soon as he heard the Land Cruiser was missing, Fergus assumed Vivienne had gone to Beth's. He didn't think his wife had left for Melbourne after their fight, even though she told him she was leaving, and he didn't rush back to the farm to check. Did he see her as a killer even then? Before Beth's body was discovered? Whatever he was thinking, his leap of logic put his wife in the cross-hairs well before the family knew anything was wrong. If Fergus was so worried, it's a wonder he didn't race over to Beth's right then and there.

And here's another thing that never made sense: if Robyn Dixon had the two Cameron boys, then surely the most pressing issue would have been finding Vivienne. At this stage, Fergus, Ian, Pam and Donald all knew she was missing. Yet none of them looked for her. Instead, Fergus told Donald and Ian to drive across the island to tell Beth about the argument the night before. But why didn't he just pick up the phone and call her?

CHAPTER 7

THE DISCOVERY

What time Donald and Ian left Fergus to head over to Beth's place is disputed. Over the years, I've asked the police about it – some involved in the investigation and others I randomly corner when they're alone and unarmed. They provide a counter argument. People aren't checking their watches, they say, and time is one of those things that is hard to be exact about. And I get it. Some have even suggested in this case that the times things happened the morning after the murder aren't important.

I beg to differ. Timing is *everything*. And if it doesn't add up, we want to know why. When I say 'we', I'm referring to those interested in finding a solution to this case, not the police. Sorry if that sounds snarky, but considering that the police have a murder on their hands that no one has been convicted of, you'd think they would be more interested in finding out. Note: If there are any lone-wolf police detectives out there who are driven by the desire to catch bad guys and solve mysteries, please come round to my house. I'll have the kettle on and some scones in the oven.

Anyway, back to the story.

At some stage, Fergus or Donald – stories differ – called Marnie at work. By this stage – around 8.30 in the morning – Marnie had started her shift at the Warley Hospital and was changing beds in the ward with Lisa Price. Lisa described that morning to me.

'The normal routine . . . is to go round and start making the beds and getting people up having their showers . . . the phone rang and I remember it was quite early in the shift because we hadn't done many of the beds . . . I went to the office, answered the phone and it was Donald. I know Donald and Fergus well enough to know them by the sound of their voice. I don't know whether Donald announced himself or not but I certainly knew it was Donald and he said, "I need to speak to Marnie." I went back and got Marnie and Marnie answered the phone and I left the room. And after a few minutes, Marnie came out and she said, "There's been a family emergency and I have to go, I have to go immediately." And she left.'

Marnie gave a different version of events. She said it was *Fergus* who had phoned the hospital, not Donald. She put the time much later than Lisa. 'At about 9.30 am, I received a call at work from Fergus telling me that Vivienne had phoned Robyn Dixon at about 3.15 am and asked her to look after the children as they were by themselves in the house, and that he was concerned about Beth. He then asked me to ring her number and let her know. I phoned Beth but there was no answer, so I then rang Fergus back and told him. He was obviously very concerned and worried, and asked me to come home. I then arranged this with the matron. I drove straight home and found Fergus sitting at the kitchen table looking out the window. He said, "I know something terrible's happened," or words to that effect. We waited, and I kept trying the Barnards' number but there was no answer. Fergus told me that he had asked Donald and Ian to go over and see if Beth was all right.'

Another woman working at the hospital, Anne Davie, remembers Marnie leaving earlier too, somewhere around 8.30 am, and doesn't recall Marnie making any phone calls. I never believed Marnie's account anyway. Fancy ringing your sister at work, calling her off the ward to ask her to ring your girlfriend then ring you back – all while you are sitting by a phone yourself. It always seemed weird to me that Fergus said he asked his family to check on Beth and he didn't, especially if he thought 'something terrible's happened'. In fact, given that the night before, Vivienne had apparently green lit his relationship with Beth, it's a wonder he wouldn't have wanted to ring her right away and start planning the rest of their lives together. Or drive right over to her house and tell her. And even if he didn't do that, surely, he would have been up with the roosters to drive over to Beth's the next morning like he said he was going to so he could give her the good news. Why was he suddenly getting his family to do his bidding? And why was his focus on Beth when his wife was missing?

So Donald and Ian set off for Beth's property on McFees Road in Rhyll, I suppose because they must've agreed with Fergus that it was more important for Beth to be told of Vivienne's disappearance than it was to look for Vivienne. Donald's account has him at Beth's open back door, stepping inside, and discovering Beth in her bedroom. He then called to Ian, 'Come here quick! The worst has happened!' Ian Cairns, who had a good decade on his brother-in-law, hadn't gone in first. He'd been beckoned in by

Donald. But if talking to Beth was a two-man job, why wasn't Ian standing by Donald's side?

We know exactly what they'd find inside, but standing at the back door, *they* allegedly didn't, so you'd think they would have approached it like visiting any other neighbour: rapping on the wire door frame, seeing the door beyond ajar, singing out in a friendly way, 'Beth! Beth? Are you there?' And automatically removing their boots at the door like farmers might do when they've come a-calling and there's beige-coloured carpet. They would have assumed Beth was home because her car was there. And you'd imagine them both going in like they go into anyone else's house, like Beth would enter their houses or Fergus's house, because they'd expect to find her inside, alive, having a cuppa, reading the paper. If no one answered and they waited at the open back door, wouldn't they have thought she might have been out in a paddock, perhaps feeding the cows? But no. The way Donald told it, the men seemed to approach with trepidation. And when there was no answer, only Donald entered, then called out: *Come here quick! The worst has happened!*

Odd, when you think about it.

CHAPTER 8

INTERVIEWING CLIFF

When my co-author Paul Daley and I first interviewed retired sergeant Cliff Ashe in 1992, he was happy to talk. Happy to be in the limelight, to be part of the story. Even though he was out of the police force, he still had the air of the quintessential no-nonsense cop. Cliff Ashe entered the story when Donald Cameron and Ian Cairns arrived at the Cowes police station the morning of Tuesday 23 September 1986.

When Ashe described the scene where Donald and Ian arrived to report the murder, he left me in no doubt who held the position of power within the confines of the small police station. Ashe did.

Ashe had settled into his role as a country copper after years in the city and a stint at the vice squad. Phillip Island was a peaceful place, by and large. In the off season, policing involved traffic control, drunks misbehaving, and the occasional accident. The station closed at midnight and anything later than that went to the on-call officer. Summer was different. Holiday makers swelled the numbers for a couple of months and police

49

reinforcements came down from Melbourne. The station was open 24/7 and the jobs became more urgent: drownings, sea rescues, boating accidents. But summer or winter, murder was unheard of.

I imagined Ashe did the big-fish, small-pond thing with all the confidence of a veteran of almost 30 years. If you listened to him, he was a good copper. And back then, I hadn't heard anything to contradict this.

By the time we interviewed him, he was running a small supermarket in Cape Woolamai in the south-east corner of the island. He was expansive and generous with his time. We spent a long while talking about that Tuesday back in 1986. Ashe told us he'd just returned from holidays. First day back, in fact. The old police station – since replaced by a new brick one – had a wire door that creaked open as Donald Cameron and Ian Cairns entered. It was a strange visit, Ashe said, because for ten minutes, the pair just talked about family fights and conferences. Finally, Ashe interrupted and, in the retelling, he sounded impatient. 'Donald, exactly what are you trying to tell me?'

Donald Cameron, the man who had been – or would be – a farmer, Grand Prix racetrack owner, councillor, mayor and Order of Australia Medal recipient – a man known to be forthright – stumbled over his words. 'Um, it's Beth,' he said, leaning forward. 'I think she's not well.'

Beth was indeed 'not well'. Donald would later tell the police he had just come from the Barnard property in McFees Road where he had found Beth lying on the floor, covered by a doona, a pool of blood around her head. The 'not well' thing must've been a euphemism because, I suppose, if Donald truly thought she was 'not well', he would've checked for signs of life, tried to help her, and phoned an ambulance from her house. But he had done none of those things. Instead, he and Ian had got back in their car and made the 15-minute drive from Rhyll to the police station in Cowes to report it. Beth was dead. And Donald knew it. So why bury the lede?

When Ashe told me this story, he sounded more annoyed at their dithering than anything else. Like they were wasting his time with their roundabout account.

This story is not just about the Phillip Island murder, it is also a glimpse into my process writing the story, so I want to take you all to a moment years after I wrote the original book to the day I met a forensic linguistic expert. The expert talked about a study that had been done on 911 calls in the United States. Given that it was sometimes the guilty person who made the 911 call, linguistic analysis found that instead of a cry for help, the first utterance of a guilty person might be establishing a back story or an alibi. So instead of the first utterance to the emergency operator being: *Oh my god, my husband's been attacked! Send an ambulance . . .* It might sound more like: *I've just got home from shopping the entire afternoon and when I got home, I discovered my husband's been attacked.* While it's not an exact science, and nor could it be used as firm evidence, nonetheless, when I heard this, my mind spun back to the ten minutes Cliff Ashe described when Donald and Ian talked about 'family fights and family conferences' and didn't get to the 'cry for help' bit until they were prompted. It's like this case sits in my head, waiting for connections. And then the thought wriggles in like a worm and burrows deep: *Their first utterance was not a cry for help.*

Anyway, enough about me and the wriggly thoughts in my brain. Now, back to the story.

At the same time Donald and Ian were talking to Cliff Ashe, Senior Constable Peter McHenry was heading to the island aerodrome; the police air ambulance had run into difficulty on the runway and he was on his way to give them a hand. Years later, when I was sitting at Peter's kitchen table with a cup of tea, he told me how Cliff Ashe had radioed him and told him to come back to the police station. He tried to tell Ashe that he was needed at the aerodrome, but it was pointless arguing.

'You've got to come back,' Ashe said and that was that. Peter reluctantly did a U-turn and headed back to Cowes. It was 9.15 am when he arrived, which meant Donald and Ian must've arrived around 9.05 am, since they'd been there for ten minutes by Ashe's account. At first, Peter didn't see the urgency. Donald Cameron and Ian Cairns were standing at the counter. All eyes turned to Peter when he entered, then he and Ashe headed for the police car and Donald and Ian headed for their car. McHenry drove out to McFees Road and on the way, Ashe shared the scant details with McHenry that he'd managed to prise out of the two prominent Phillip Island citizens.

'Something's happened out there,' he said, nodding towards Rhyll.

McFees Road is a long, unmade road with just seven properties on it, a couple of McFees still counted among them. The road has the kind of corrugations that judder vehicles. Shakes things loose. To the left, you can see the water of Western Port Bay, calm and peaceful. To the right, there are a lot of trees, broken by the occasional driveway.

Following Donald and Ian, the two cops pulled into a property called Pleasant Point. Parking at the start of the driveway, the men got out. Peter McHenry stayed with Donald and Ian at the front gate while Cliff Ashe walked up the driveway. Given the vague description of what was wrong with Beth, Ashe went around the back of the house and opened the screen door. The back door was ajar. It only took a couple of steps inside the house to come to the first bedroom on the left.

Beth Barnard lay on the floor in the middle of the room. Her blue eyes were half open, staring at the ceiling. While Ashe could see blood and Beth looked dead, there were no visible injuries. He pinched a corner of the doona, lifted it up, and saw straight away that she had been brutally murdered. Her throat had been cut, and a knife wound to the face had taken out one of her front teeth. Ashe dropped the doona and backed out of the room.

The whole place had become a crime scene.

Outside by the gate, Peter McHenry didn't know what had happened inside because the silence had already begun. Normally something like this would swell the conversation, peppering it with regret and loss and disbelief and the shaking of heads at the tragedy of it all. Donald and Ian talked about anything else *but* the dead girl. Years later, Peter wouldn't remember what they had said, only what they *hadn't*.

When Cliff Ashe returned looking pale and upset, McHenry gathered that something terrible had happened. He could see that while Ashe appeared distressed, Donald and Ian didn't. Were they not affected by what they had seen? Or were they hiding their emotions? It's impossible to see a dead woman – especially one you claimed to know and like – and *not* react. In the grand scheme of things, a lack of emotion doesn't mean much, nor does it prove anything. And certainly, the slew of detectives that arrived at the McFees Road property on Tuesday 23 September weren't looking to gauge just how upset everyone was. They had more important things to think about. They had a murder on their hands.

The Wonthaggi detectives got there first. Sergeant Ron Cooper, Senior Detective Alan McFayden and Senior Detective Alan Lowe all met Donald and Ian when they arrived at the gates of Pleasant Point. The detectives gathered enough of the story to know that Donald and Ian had been asked by Fergus Cameron to check on Beth. Fergus and his wife Vivienne had had an argument the night before over Beth. An affair, apparently. Fergus stayed the night with his sister Marnie, who was married to Ian. Vivienne had called a friend, Robyn Dixon, in the middle of the night to come and collect their two sons, and Robyn still had them that morning. Vivienne was missing and Fergus wanted Beth to know.

In a nutshell, that's how they came to be there.

If any of the men at the gate that day wondered why Donald and Ian checked on the newly revealed girlfriend that morning rather than trying to find the missing sister-in-law of ten years, they didn't raise it.

Because lately, I've been wondering about this. If your brother suddenly revealed a clandestine young girlfriend then told you that your sister-in-law had left her small children and vanished in the middle of the night, what would you do? Wouldn't you be worried for your sister-in-law? Wouldn't you ring her family, go to places you knew she liked to visit, check cafés, phone her friends, check with her work? Would you rest until you found her? How likely is it that you'd prioritise the girl you just found out your brother was having an affair with over the woman you'd known for ten years?

The men at the crime scene that day didn't wonder about any of that.

Detective Alan McFayden and his colleagues from the Wonthaggi CIB were briefed. Cliff Ashe made special mention of the time it had taken Donald and Ian to tell him that something had happened. McFayden was given a broad-brushstroke story out of earshot of the two men. When he spoke to them himself, he described them as 'very composed'. He made a mental note of it before entering the house. While Ashe had pinched the doona and lifted it enough to reveal the damage to Beth's face and neck, McFayden went one step further and lifted the doona all the way up.

He was the first to see the large letter A carved into the dead woman's chest.

McFayden was a stoic cop, not easily moved to emotion, good at keeping his feelings at bay so he could get on with the job. Even so, he told me, 'It was really a very nasty sort of scene.' His voice was sad when he described how he felt the intrusion of the cops in Beth's bedroom, that they had to go through her things in the invasion of privacy especially reserved for murder victims.

He noticed that Beth's curtains were fully drawn and a dim light from a bedside lamp cast shadows. There were two single beds with jeans, underwear, jumpers and shoes strewn around. There were photographs of Beth, her sister and her parents, and her chest of drawers was cluttered with perfume and make-up, more photos and two stuffed toy animals. A bottle of cough medicine, some cold and flu and pain-relief tablets and a glass of water were also on top of the chest of drawers. McFayden noticed the large photograph, mounted on board, leaning against the other bed. Beth, alive, strong and attractive, smiling broadly as she held two baby penguins. Now her blood was splattered across her jeans and a pair of old sneakers on the floor.

He checked the rest of the house and found nothing out of the ordinary. As he joined the growing group of police and onlookers outside, he heard a detective say, 'Whoever did this didn't leave unscathed.' The detective pointed to two smudges of blood on the concrete path outside the back door.

Once McFayden confirmed that a crime had occurred, the homicide squad were called in from Melbourne and the investigative machine kicked into action.

*

Back in 1992, when Paul Daley and I returned from interviewing Cliff Ashe, we wrote up his chapter. It was important to me that anyone we interviewed would get to read what we'd written and check that it accurately represented what they wanted to say. After I gave Ashe his chapter, I said I would call later that day to see if he was happy with it.

When I rang him that evening, our conversation went something like this.

'Hi Cliff. It's Vikki Petraitis. Just checking to see if you liked the story.'

He said gruffly, 'I don't want to talk to you.'

And then he hung up.

I scrambled for a copy of the story and read through it. What could he be so angry about? I rang Paul and told him what had happened. He was as surprised as I was. We had both sat with Cliff Ashe, spent hours with him. What had happened in the meantime? Grasping at straws, we wondered if it was the story's first line. 'Phillip Island is the perfect place for an ageing police officer to finish his professional days.' Maybe Ashe thought we called him *old*.

In my defence, back then, I was 26, so anyone over 35 was old.

But over the years, people have given me alternatives possibilities for Cliff's reaction. He ran the small supermarket, they said. All it would take was for someone to whisper in his ear, 'If you talk to her, your customers will stop coming.'

Yes, the island is *that* kind of place. There are many who reinforce the silence, even now.

CHAPTER 9

THE UNRAVELLING

When a murder is committed, cops start at the body and work their way out. Beth Barnard was dead and so the story began with her. Crime scene officers, a police photographer and fingerprint experts were called in from the Victoria Police forensic science laboratory. The scientific examination of a crime scene means that everyone else has to stay away while evidence is photographed, documented and collected.

Detective Alan McFayden thought it prudent to get Donald Cameron's account right from the get-go. So while detectives from the homicide squad were making the two-hour drive to Phillip Island, McFayden and Donald reconvened at the Cowes police station.

When I wrote *The Phillip Island Murder*, there was something I didn't understand; it would take first-hand experience for me to learn the difference between giving a statement and being interviewed about an event. When you give a statement, you give your version of events. While the interviewer might help or coax the narrative from you, you basically give your story, they write it down, type it up, then you sign it. It's the job of the detective to document everything. Investigating its truth comes afterwards. Well, that's the theory, anyway.

It's an entirely different kettle of fish to be a witness in court and have wily legal folk trying to trip you up on the statement you made. As I imagine it would be when you are actually interviewed by the police. We've all seen it on TV crime shows. The detective sits on one side of the table, questioning and challenging the responses of the person sitting opposite. Giving a statement is not like that at all. You just give your version of events. The end.

So when Donald Cameron sat opposite Alan McFayden to give his statement, it was the detective's job just to get it down on paper. McFayden liked to keep an open mind. At this stage, all he knew was that Beth Barnard was dead and she hadn't killed herself. Therefore, there was a killer out there somewhere.

Donald began by telling McFayden about his younger brother Fergus Cameron, who was 36 and married to 35-year-old Vivienne. They had two sons, Dugald and Hugh, aged eight and five respectively. It all began that morning at 7.45 am, when Donald got a phone call from a close family friend, Robyn Dixon. Robyn was worried because she was minding the two Cameron boys, but had to get to work and couldn't reach Vivienne or Fergus. She said she could put the older boy on the school bus with her kids, but that left five-year-old Hugh.

McFayden noted all this down. At no point did Donald express any curiosity about why the Dixons had the children in the first place. 'I said, "Don't worry about Hugh. I'll come straight away and pick him up", Donald said. 'I handed the phone to my wife and drove directly to [the] Dixons.'

Stepping back and looking at this, it's a wonder none of them rang the local hospital at this stage. When Robyn Dixon first told them Vivienne called her in the middle of the night and hadn't been in touch since, why didn't they ring the hospital? Donald's sister Marnie worked there, as did family friend Lisa Price. They wouldn't have been ringing a big city hospital, but rather one where, chances were, the phone would be answered by a friend or relative.

Sorry. Where was I? Oh yes, Donald.

Donald went on, '. . . [Robyn] was in a hurry to meet the school bus, and we didn't say very much at all other than that we were both at a loss as to what was going on. Robyn told me that if necessary Dugald could come off the school bus that night. I said that I would look after Hugh and get him to kindergarten.'

McFayden was perhaps more interested in finding out about the dead girl rather than Donald's exact movements that morning, and so the statement doesn't contain much in the way of precise times, but we can extrapolate. If Robyn Dixon rang Donald at 7.45 am and he promised to drive straight to her place, he would have met up with her some ten minutes later – a little before 8 am. He said he collected Hugh. This was all taking place around Ventnor on the western side of the island.

I'm going to deviate from Donald at the police station here, because this isn't just about what members of the family told police. My work on this case has always been about collecting the stories of everyone who wanted to tell them.

So.

A prominent local would later tell me that 15 minutes after Donald Cameron said he picked up Hugh and took him back to his place, Donald drove past her on the *eastern* side of the island, on the Back Beach Road, heading towards Rhyll. This local and her husband had put their kids on the bus around 8.15 am and were heading off to the Royal Melbourne Show. They stopped to give way to Donald who – as far as they could see – was alone in his car. They waved, but he didn't return the greeting. They knew him well and this lack of acknowledgement was unusual. They thought he seemed 'extremely focused'.

The couple would later give a statement to a detective about what they saw that morning. But it was years after the event. The woman told me the detective tried to pin them down as to the precise time but the best they could do was to say they always dropped their kids at the bus at 8.15 am, so it would have been around then. They said the detective seemed to lose interest when they couldn't be more exact – which is weird, because 8.15 is pretty exact. They never heard from him again. The woman's story is one of many that came to light after the first book was released in 1993. I'm guessing here, but I think people read the book and heard what the family had told the police and then thought: *Hmm, that's not what I remember,* then came forward.

Donald's statement to McFayden was different – it did not put him on the road to Rhyll, but instead, on his way home. 'I then drove home to my place noticing on the way that Fergus and Viv's car was parked in the driveway in the garage at their place.'

Looking through the crime scene photographs, I wondered about this. In the one photograph of the outside of the Cameron property shared by Fergus and Vivienne, the driveway seems to curve around the house. There are lots of trees and no garage is visible. That's not to say the car's not there. Donald didn't say he drove up the driveway, he said he noticed a car was parked there while driving past. Maybe there's an obvious garage out of the line of sight in the photo and visible from the road.

'There were no other vehicles in the driveway but there is nothing unusual about this because the green Holden is the only vehicle that is parked in this driveway,' Donald said. In the crime scene photo, the driveway is empty and the green Holden is parked in what looks like a big shed.

I want to say here that from this point on, five-year-old Hugh vanishes from the narrative. Donald said he collected him, but that's the last we hear of it. It wouldn't be the last *they* heard from him. We have a five-year-old boy in my family. They're loud. But in this story, Hugh goes quiet.

When he returned with Hugh, Donald told McFayden he rang Marnie and Ian's place again. 'Fergus my brother answered the phone and seemed very distressed and did not particularly want to communicate at this stage and handed the phone to Ian.'

When Ian diplomatically hinted that something had happened and they would speak later, Donald told the detective that his wife insisted on knowing because they had Fergus's son. Possession of the boy gave them the right to know.

'With some reluctance Fergus told Pam that there had been a row and that he had been injured,' Donald said. 'He said that the row had been between he and Viv, and he had to go to hospital for treatment.'

But Pam wouldn't let it go. 'What had caused the row?' she wanted to know. She asked if it was about 'the workload that he [Fergus] was under re the racetrack development program taking place on the property we all own at Lukeys'. Donald, from his vantage point of hearing one side of the conversation, was able to gather that 'the row was of a domestic nature implicating Beth Barnard but I can't take the matter further'.

It's unclear from his police statement whether Donald couldn't 'take the matter further' because he didn't know about the affair, or because he didn't want to talk about it. If he didn't know about it, he must've at least suspected something. Beth and Fergus and their flirting and giggling had been noticed by others when they worked together on the Cameron farm. One farmhand would later tell the police, 'Beth was working as a roustabout . . . and I saw Fergus had her on a wool bale and he was tickling her. She was laughing . . . Fergus's brother Don told them to steady down acting like that in front of the shearers.'

Donald was seven years older than Fergus. I wondered what the tickling and giggling between his 36-year-old brother and a 23-year-old farmhand looked like to a man in his early forties. Folly, I imagine. And a bit embarrassing too, having to ask your brother to stop misbehaving in front of the shearers.

But Donald Cameron mentioned none of this to Senior Detective Alan McFayden. He estimated that when Marnie's husband Ian called him back a while later to tell him that the Land Cruiser was not parked in its usual spot in Fergus's machinery shed, it would have been around 9.05 am. Whether this was noticed or not by McFayden, he never said. But this is the first mention of the time discrepancies. If Peter McHenry returned to the police station at 9.15 am, as his statement suggests, and Donald and Ian had been at the station for at least ten minutes according to Cliff Ashe, then Donald can't have got the phone call from Ian at 9.05 am because by then he was at the police station.

Again, you can see why timing is everything.

For the moment, what's important is that both Vivienne and the Land Cruiser are missing.

And then came the bit that I find more difficult to understand as the years go by.

Donald told McFayden, 'Ian also told me that Beth Barnard should be told of the domestic that had taken place the night before between Fergus and Viv. This was told to him by Fergus and he was relaying the message to me from Fergus. At that point Ian suggested that we both go to Rhyll where Beth lives.'

Why, why, why didn't they prioritise looking for Vivienne over telling Beth? And why did *both* of them need to go? How many farmers does it take to change a lightbulb? Apparently two – the same number it took to check on Beth Barnard.

On a busy farming morning when, by Ian's account, he was up with the roosters with sheep to feed or fields to work, why didn't Fergus just ring Beth? She was supposed to be heading off to Melbourne that morning – so if Fergus did try to call her and she didn't answer, why didn't he assume she'd left? Why didn't he go tell her himself? Why send *both* Donald and Ian? And what were they going to say to her when they got there? 'Er, hello young Beth, we're here to tell you Fergus and Viv had a fight last night and she's left him.'

Er. Okay.

And another thing. They *know* Vivienne had rung John and Robyn Dixon in the middle of the night, asking them to collect the two Cameron boys. They *know* Vivienne's car is parked in the garage at her home. And they *know* she's not answering her phone the morning after a violent row with her husband that ended their marriage. Why didn't they rush over to the house to check on her as soon as Robyn called them at 7.45 am? Why didn't Fergus? It's just down the road. Marnie would say later that Vivienne had been so upset by Fergus's affair with Beth that she had called Lifeline. Putting two and two together, might they first have wondered if she had harmed herself? Why didn't they all hurry to look for her? But it was almost an hour after Robyn's phone call before any of them set foot in the Cameron house.

Donald continued, 'A couple of minutes later I picked up Ian at his home and saw Fergus at the back door . . . he appeared to be very distressed almost on the point of tears. We had no other further conversation with Fergus other than that we would call in at his place on the way to Beth's.'

Even though Donald doesn't expressly mention it, we assume he handed little Hugh over to his father at this point. Beth's house was hardly the place to take a child. He then described driving straight to Vivienne and Fergus's house. Donald said he and Ian walked up the passageway, looking in every room. But there was no one there. 'We drove immediately to Beth Barnard's farm in McFees Road and saw that the farm utility was parked in its usual spot in the garage and that Beth's own private car was parked in the carport at the rear of the house. I walked to the door and knocked, and I was aware that the lights were on in the porch. There was a flywire screen door shut, but the door immediately behind was open some six to eight inches.

'I called out and there was no response and pushed the door further open and there was no response . . . I took one step inside and saw that the door to my left was wide open and inside in the door I saw Beth lying on the floor with a doona over [her].

Her face was almost covered but I still recognised her, and she appeared to be dead ... I yelled out, "Come here quick! The worst has happened!" or something like that. We immediately left the house, and both reported the matter to Sergeant Ashe at the Cowes police station.'

And that concluded Donald Cameron's statement. Alan McFayden told me how when he had said to Donald that he would be in touch, he noted a look of surprise on his face. It was as if he was wondering what more the police could possibly need from him. Donald Cameron read through his statement and signed it.

McFayden duly noted the time. It was 12.50 pm. Remember this time, because it is going to become important when we hear from someone who saw Donald doing something odd later that afternoon.

There's one more thing in Donald's statement which is important. He gave the make and model of the missing Land Cruiser. He had first mentioned it at the gates of Beth's place when all the detectives were arriving. This information would have been put into a police alert and broadcast to all cops in the area via police radio. So if not before, by 1 pm at the latest, cops in the area would have been keeping a look out for the missing Vivienne Cameron and the missing Land Cruiser.

Senior Constable Peter McHenry was told to keep a look out for it as early as 9.50 am when he left the crime scene. He's not sure if there was an official alert out that early, but he was certainly instructed to keep an eye out for it.

While Donald gave his version of events to Alan McFayden, his brother-in-law Ian had left with Senior Constable Peter McHenry.

They had only stayed long enough at the start of Beth's driveway to await the arrival of the CIB detectives and brief them. By 9.50 am, Peter McHenry and Ian Cairns were on their way to pick up Dr Paul Flood. Detective Alan McFayden had called ahead to arrange to collect the doctor, so when Marnie Cairns rang Dr Flood to ask about getting Fergus's stitches checked – stitches that weren't even 12 hours old – the doctor said he was heading over to her place shortly in the company of a police officer and Ian.

Talk about a spoiler alert.

When Peter McHenry picked up Dr Flood, the drive from the Newhaven Medical Centre was a sombre one. The doctor asked Ian how he was going and that was about it. Years later, Peter McHenry recalled, 'I remember how he [Ian] sat very quiet . . . I don't think he spoke at all . . . he really didn't show a lot of emotion . . . I believe Paul Flood was more upset than he was.'

Once Marnie found out that the police and Dr Flood were on their way over, one can only imagine what she might have thought. Her husband had set off with Donald but was now on his way back with a police officer and a doctor. Of course, this meant that what McHenry saw when he got there was not surprise at the death notification, because the doctor had ruined the element of surprise. They *knew*.

Years later, Peter McHenry told me, 'I don't know why I was sent out there first. But I was instructed and that's what I was to do – go out and check on Fergus with Dr Flood. It seemed a strange way to go about it. I would have thought that first off, we should have taken the doctor out to the house where Beth was, just to confirm everything, but that wasn't until after we'd been out to see Fergus Cameron at the farmhouse. In my statement, it's after lunch. It struck me as strange, but as a junior senior constable, I just went with what I was told to do.'

And that was a theme with Peter McHenry that day. He was a junior and did what he was told. Didn't stop him from noticing things though. I've always been interested in this moment, when Peter, Ian and the doctor arrived at the house. It's easy to assume that Fergus would have been on edge – he'd sent Donald and Ian to Beth's house to check on her because Vivienne had called the Dixons in the middle of the night to collect the children.

'Was Fergus upset?' I asked him.

Peter wasn't in the room when Dr Flood broke the news – but he did describe Fergus as being 'very quiet, very ashen'. At this stage, Fergus knew Vivienne was missing, so perhaps a doctor and a uniformed police officer arriving at Marnie's place was indication enough that things had turned out very badly.

Peter didn't stay with Fergus for very long. Instead, he went to the kitchen and waited with Ian Cairns. Ian had been quiet on the ride over and nothing changed now.

Peter may have been a junior at the time, but in the ensuing years, he'd had a long career in the police force and had seen a lot. 'Usually if something like that happened, people are almost explosive . . . They are either angry or very visibly upset. I can't remember that at all. Thinking back on it, it was very strange.'

Once Dr Flood emerged from the bedroom, Peter McHenry drove him over to Beth's house on McFees Road. He walked the doctor up the driveway and around the back. Peter took him to the back door but didn't go inside. He knew Cliff Ashe had been in there earlier and every cop knows you have to keep the traffic at a crime scene to a minimum. The doctor went in alone.

After he pronounced life extinct and formally identified the body, the two men returned to the police car.

Peter McHenry couldn't help noticing Dr Flood was upset. 'That is a scene I never want to see again,' he said. Peter drove him back to the medical centre and took a statement of identification from him. Dr Flood signed it at 2.06 pm. On the formal document, the doctor declared that he had identified the body of 23-year-old Elizabeth Catherine Barnard, whom he had known for a year and had last seen on Sunday when she had visited him as a patient.

*

Over the years, I've spoken to a lot of Vivienne Cameron's friends. Not one of them said they got a phone call from anyone in the Cameron family that morning to see if they knew where she was. Vivienne's sister Deirdre and brother Keith didn't get any calls either. The first they heard that their sister was missing was on a radio bulletin later in the day. When they contacted the Camerons, the answers they got were evasive, much like Pam described when she tried to talk to Fergus.

So why the silence? Why the evasiveness? And why weren't they all out looking for Vivienne?

*

A woman contacted me recently wanting to add her story to the narrative. The woman's family all knew Vivienne's mother, Marjorie Candy, from Warrnambool. There was perhaps some sympathy for Marjorie when her husband left her with three small children, but she thrived. She supported the Liberal Party and was a member of the local gardening club. A lovely woman by all accounts, Marjorie was overseas when her daughter went missing and Beth Barnard was murdered. Shortly after the murder, this woman's father got a phone call from Marjorie, asking him to go and check her house. She was worried and a little scared her missing daughter might have been there.

The man drove to Marjorie's house and took a look around. Nothing seemed disturbed and there were no signs anyone had been there.

When Marjorie got back from her trip, her daughter Deirdre had a doctor and a minister meet her at the airport because she was frail with a bad heart.

CHAPTER 10

THE INVESTIGATION BEGINS

Detective Senior Constable Alan McFayden was a veteran cop. He was also a canny operator. He told me stories about the way he caught bad guys during his policing career that showed out-of-the-box thinking. Once, he called for a wanted man over the PA system at the races and when the man showed up at the office, saying 'Who wants me?' Alan stepped forward with his handcuffs and said, 'Me.' His stories were usually accompanied by a deep throaty laugh whether he got the upper hand or not.

Except for one.

He told me a story so haunting, it was almost beyond belief. He'd been called to an accident on a country road where a car had collided with a truck. The car's passengers were dead, but the driver was alive and trapped in the vehicle. People began to gather around, trying to free him, when suddenly the truck burst into flames. As the fire engulfed the truck – and crept towards the car – the driver screamed for someone to kill him. A man from the crowd leapt forward and told Alan he had a gun and would do it.

The cop was faced with the ultimate ethical dilemma: shoot the man or watch him burn alive. While his cop's common sense won out in the end and he prevented the bystander from shooting the trapped driver, he never stopped wondering whether he made the right decision. But he also knew that if the driver appeared on the autopsy table dead from a bullet wound before the flames got him, the shooter would be charged with murder.

The story ended with the crowd of onlookers driven back by the flames, watching in horror as the man burned to death, screaming as fire engulfed him.

Sometimes the law trumps compassion.

And when it does, no one wins.

*

After hearing Donald Cameron's story in the small Cowes police station interview room, Alan McFayden followed the next logical trail. If the road to discovering Beth's body began with the phone call from Robyn Dixon saying she had the two Cameron boys, then the next person to speak to was her. How did she come to have the boys? And most importantly, *where was their mother?*

Robyn Dixon was a teacher at a school in San Remo, off the island on the other side of the bridge. It was there that Alan McFayden headed after speaking to Donald Cameron. If McFayden took the Phillip Island Road, he would have driven past Forrest Avenue on the left. He would have passed the Camerons' Land Cruiser with the hay bales on the back that Donald had just described to him.

I remember Alan telling me about visiting Robyn Dixon at school. At that stage, I too worked in a primary school and disturbing a teacher from her class was done only in a dire emergency. Teachers just can't walk out of class. Someone has to take over from them because kids can't be left alone. Schools are all consuming, and breaks are rare. Once that morning bell goes, the outside world ceases to exist. With a teacher's solidarity, I imagined what it must have been like for Robyn. She would have been tired from the night before with the collecting of the Cameron children, and perhaps worried about Vivienne and Fergus. But the very nature of working with children means that your own feelings take a back seat.

When McFayden got to Robyn Dixon's school he explained the urgency of his visit at the front office and asked to see her immediately. I suppose whatever innocent explanation she might have formed to explain Vivienne's absence was dispelled the moment she saw the police officer. And what he needed from her was too urgent to wait another hour till the bell sent the children home.

The detective and the teacher found a quiet place to talk. Robyn told him the phone had rung at 3.10 am, waking her and her husband, John, who answered. It was Vivienne. She said she was calling from the hospital and that the children were alone at her place. She asked the Dixons to go and get them and take them home for the night.

'We agreed to this and John asked if everything was all right, but I can't recall what she said. John didn't want to go on his own in case Vivienne's children got a fright and he didn't want me to go alone so we both got dressed and went and picked them up.'

McFayden nodded and wrote down her words.

'We got to Vivienne and Fergus's place about ten minutes later, went into the house, woke up the children and took them home to our place for the night.'

'Was their car there?' McFayden asked.

Yes. Robyn had noticed their Holden Kingswood in the garage and had wondered how Vivienne and Fergus had got to the hospital. But she knew that the Cameron clan lived along the same road, so she assumed they'd been driven by a relative, or maybe an ambulance. If she wondered why Vivienne had called *her* to collect the children rather than one of the relatives who lived at the adjoining properties, she didn't share that with McFayden.

'What was it like when you got to the house?' McFayden asked.

'The back porch light, the bathroom light and a little room light were on . . . and everything appeared normal.' If Robyn checked the bathroom, she didn't notice blood on the floor. The linoleum was brown with swirls of darker brown; streaks of blood would have blended in. But of course, the Dixons were looking for children, not blood. Robyn told McFayden that she saw a handbag on a table inside the back door. 'I assumed it was Vivienne's . . . although I'm not sure. I know it was of black suede. This made me think she left in a hurry.'

So the Dixons collected the two sleepy boys and took them home.

Robyn had to work the following day, and waking in the morning with two extra children was a problem. At 7.30 am, she tried ringing Vivienne but there was no answer. I can imagine her rising anxiety. Teachers can't be late for school. Regardless of what is happening in your life, come 9 am, those 30 children are waiting for you at the door. Robyn told McFayden how she had tried calling Donald Cameron, but his phone was engaged. She waited, tried again, then tried a third time.

McFayden wondered who Donald had been talking to while Robyn was trying to get through to him. He hadn't mentioned any phone calls before Robyn's.

On the third try, Donald answered. In her statement, Robyn was blunt. 'I more or less asked him who was sick.'

But instead of an explanation, Donald said he didn't know what she was talking about.

Even though Robyn doesn't say it in her statement, I imagine there would have been a quick recapping of the middle-of-the-night phone call from Vivienne at the hospital, the picking up of the children, and not being able to get on to Vivienne.

'Donald . . . arranged to pick up Hugh who is five years old,' Robyn said, 'and I was to take Dugald with my children to the bus. This in fact eventuated and I met Donald at Hell Hill in Ventnor Beach Road.' Robyn concluded her statement by saying she hadn't seen Fergus or Vivienne in the last week.

McFayden got her signature and thanked her for her time. By this stage it was 3 pm.

It's easy to imagine McFayden driving back to the police station, wondering where on earth Vivienne Cameron was. For the second time in a matter of an hour, he would have driven past the Camerons' Land Cruiser, parked on the corner of Forrest Avenue and the Phillip Island Road in full view of anyone coming across the bridge.

I want to add a context here that I didn't understand at the time. If the Land Cruiser *was* parked there from the early morning, all the police coming and going never saw it. I didn't think much about this until I did a ride-along with the police at Frankston in 1993. Midway through the shift, a report of a stolen car came over the radio. It sounded like a bit of a wreck with mismatched gold and brown panels and dents. Hours later, I had forgotten all about the stolen car when we turned a corner into a suburban street and both officers said in unison, 'There it is!' For them, it was simply spotting a stolen car. For me, it was a lightning bolt.

Cops spot cars. It's their superpower. I might add here that it's not my superpower because from the back seat, I'm like, 'What are you talking about? What car? Oh *that* car?' And of course, that lightning bolt made me wonder how all the cops that day drove straight past the bloody big obvious Land Cruiser with hay bales on the back.

CHAPTER 11

THE HOMICIDE BOYS

As soon as Sergeant Cliff Ashe lifted the doona and saw what had happened to Beth Barnard, he called in the CIB detectives. Then, when Detective Alan McFayden lifted the doona and saw what had happened to Beth Barnard, he called in the homicide squad. There's a hierarchy in law enforcement when it comes to who calls whom.

Detective Senior Constable Rory O'Connor from the homicide squad got the call around 11.35 am. Along with Detective Senior Constable Garry Hunter, he was to attend McFees Road, Rhyll regarding the body of a female discovered at the premises. The drive from the homicide squad offices on St Kilda Road in Melbourne to Phillip Island took around two hours. They would have arrived in the early afternoon. They drove straight to the crime scene and, like Alan McFayden, right past the missing Land Cruiser on Forrest Avenue. By this time there would have been an alert for the vehicle broadcast over the police networks.

Like the CIB detectives before them, the homicide detectives were briefed at the gates of Pleasant Point. Dead woman inside.

Brutal attack, throat cut, the letter A carved into her chest. Person of interest identified as Vivienne Cameron, the wife of Beth's married boyfriend, Fergus. Vivienne and Fergus had fought the night before and both ended up at the hospital. After dropping Fergus at his sister Marnie's house up the road from their place at 2 am, Vivienne Cameron had called friends at 3.10 am to collect the kids. Now Beth was dead and Vivienne and the family's Land Cruiser were missing.

Briefing done, it was time for Rory O'Connor to look at the crime scene for himself. He and Hunter followed Detective Sergeant Ronald Cooper up the driveway to the side of Beth's house. By then, investigators had put markers on the two drops of blood on the concrete path. The men were careful to walk around them. O'Connor noticed the porch light was on. In the days before sensor lights, you either left your outside lights on, or you turned them off. If Beth was killed during the night, the killer could have turned on the light as they were leaving, or Beth could have left it on all night. There was no way of knowing.

Entering the back door, the men from homicide could see along the hall leading from the door to the front of the house. In the first room on the left, O'Connor saw a doona on the floor, covering the body of a woman. He carefully lifted the doona and would later report, 'I observed the deceased lying on her back. There was a severe cut across her throat.' He also saw a stab wound to her upper lip that had knocked out one of her front teeth, and cuts to the inside of her fingers on both hands. 'There was also what appeared to be a large letter A carved into her chest.' On the carpet beside her body was a blood-stained knife with a wooden handle. Not far from the knife, also lying on the carpet, was her front tooth.

At that stage, Rory O'Connor was mid-career. It would only be later, after he retired, that he could say for certain, 'This was the worst murder I would ever see.'

For such a ferocious crime, there wasn't much evidence of it in the rest of the house. A couple of faint blood stains in the bathroom basin where perhaps the killer washed up, and that was about it.

The less traffic through the house, the better, and as the crime scene crews arrived to begin their examination, the men from the homicide squad joined the local detectives in canvassing the neighbours. It was such a lonely dirt road, perhaps the killer had been seen by someone.

Working outwards from Pleasant Point, Rory O'Connor and Garry Hunter knocked on the door of Beth's immediate neighbour, Dianne. Dianne and her friend Joyce had noticed all the police cars and activity next door. While they no doubt suspected something bad had happened, they were shocked to hear young Beth Barnard had been murdered. Murder just wasn't something that happened on the island. And not to someone like her.

Had they seen anything?

Dianne told them that the night before, she had seen a car drive up McFees Road. She remembered because she thought it was going to turn into her driveway, but it went into Beth's driveway instead. The car came to a stop and Dianne watched through the tall row of trees separating the two properties as the car sat there with its headlights on for several minutes. She wondered what the driver was doing. Dianne was due to go out;

she checked the time on her watch. It was 7.50 pm. When she left her house half an hour later, she didn't notice the car.

Further down McFees Road, the detectives visited the house that belonged to Margaret McFee. The elderly woman was devastated to hear that the girl who lived up the road had died. She liked Beth. Shared a pot of tea whenever her young neighbour wandered over for a visit and a chat. Margaret told them how she had heard a car in McFees Road, but it was much later than the one Dianne heard. 'I had just woken up as I usually do in the middle of the night to go to the toilet and I heard a car drive past,' she told the police. 'It was a loud one and the lights shone right into my bedroom window. It sounded a bit like my son's Toyota.' She thought the time was 'about 3.30 am'.

There was a reason deeper than curiosity that made Margaret take notice.

'I was a bit worried, you see, because my sister-in-law lives at the end of the road by herself and I'm very conscious of vehicles going to the end of the road. I waited for it to come back and within a few minutes it did, so I didn't think anything of it, and I went back to sleep.'

As the homicide detectives O'Connor and Hunter left Margaret McFee's place and headed further down the road to visit her sister-in-law, Eileen 'Cherry' McFee, they discussed the information Margaret had given them. If Vivienne Cameron phoned Robyn Dixon around 3.10 am, and Margaret heard a car driving past her house around 3.30 am, then maybe it was Vivienne driving the missing Land Cruiser. If this was the case, thought O'Connor, the evidence was mounting against Vivienne Cameron, who still hadn't been found.

Cherry McFee had taken her dog for a walk shortly after 8 o'clock that morning. When the detectives asked her if she'd seen or heard anything out of the ordinary, she told them she had. 'As I walked through the front gate, I noticed tyre skid marks on the front lawn area. I noticed that it was fresh because I am conscious of keeping everything nice because I am having a wedding at the house on the weekend coming.'

Cherry McFee told the detectives that Margaret had stopped by soon after her walk to tell her about the car she'd heard in the early hours of the morning. 'I realised that the skid marks must have been made by that vehicle. The skid marks were definitely not there the night before because I mowed ... I like to keep everything nice.'

In speaking with the neighbours, the picture that began at the gate of the murder scene took shape. Vivienne Cameron had called to get her children minded in the middle of the night, then had driven the family's Land Cruiser to Beth's, and it was this vehicle Margaret McFee heard at 3.30 am. Vivienne was shaping up as a pretty good suspect. It was a matter of urgency that they find her.

Apropos of nothing, I'm going to toss a definition into the mix here because who doesn't love a random definition.

Confirmation bias: the tendency of people to favour information that confirms or strengthens their beliefs or values and is difficult to dislodge once affirmed.

As far as I can tell, none of the detectives paused to ask: *Was this the crime of a woman?* No one questioned the level of brutality. I wondered if these men, who had seen man's inhumanity to women over and over again in the course of their policing, ever stopped to ask if a *woman* could have done this.

O'Connor and Hunter then drove to the Camerons' house in Ventnor to get a photograph of Vivienne to circulate with the missing person bulletin. The photo they were given showed a version of Vivienne that even her closest friends would say didn't look like her. It was black and white for starters, so her auburn hair just looked dark. A thick pair of glasses reflected light, so it made it hard to see her eyes, and her eye colour wasn't discernible. She was wearing a turtle-neck top and smiling. In the photo, she bears a resemblance to Velma from *Scooby-Doo*. O'Connor's statement doesn't mention who met him at the Cameron farm or who gave him the photo.

The detectives took the photo and drove to their new temporary headquarters, the Cowes police station, to plan their course of action. They met Alan McFayden there.

I never asked them if they knew each other before the Phillip Island case, but they probably did. Alan spent years at the crime department in Melbourne and was well known and respected around the traps. The homicide squad and the crime department detectives were both housed at Russell Street, then both moved to St Kilda Road.

'What do you think?' O'Connor asked McFayden when they all sat down.

'I've never seen a bunch of people so cool, calm and collected,' McFayden said. 'You'd think these blokes discovered bodies every day of their lives.'

CHAPTER 12

THE CRIME SCENE EXAMINERS

With homicide detectives on the scene, the other services – crime scene examiners, photographers, audio-visual and fingerprint experts – are never far behind. The whole kit and caboodle, as my dad used to say before he had a bastard stroke that took away his words. The crime scene examiners in the case were Sergeant Hughie Peters and Senior Constable Brian Gamble. When they arrived, they were told that the prime suspect, Vivienne Cameron, had disappeared and that the police were searching for her.

Brian Gamble was one of the first police officers I ever interviewed. I remember he was a kind and patient man and allowed me my novice questions like, 'What's it like to see a dead body?' Back then, I imagined the first reaction would have been horror. Brian patiently explained that when crime scene examining was your job, you had to train yourself to see the deceased as *evidence*. If police stood around crying, they wouldn't be able to do their job.

Made sense, Brian. Thanks for that.

So then I understood that professional law enforcement people could look at a dead 23-year-old woman with a huge A carved into her chest and look beyond the horror for clues.

Once the doona had been removed and the police photographers had done their job, Brian studied Beth's body carefully. Aside from the A carved into her chest and the nasty throat wound, the thing that stood out most to him were the swirling smears of blood on her legs, arms and torso. In Brian's opinion, they were too prominent to have been caused accidentally during the attack. It looked more like the killer had done it on purpose. The worst-case scenario was that they had rubbed their hands all over her, revelling in what they had done.

Brian looked at the stab wound to Beth's upper lip and chin and the front tooth that had been knocked out and lay on the carpet. When we spoke, he shared his theories about the destruction of beauty in crimes such as this. He thought it suggested someone not only wanted to kill Beth, but to destroy her physical beauty as well. The theory made sense with what Brian had been told when he arrived – that the homicide detectives were looking for the wife of the man Beth was having an affair with.

Back in 1986, the reason this theory made sense was because it wasn't questioned. Before we demanded evidence-based conclusions, we could throw around theories of jealous murderous women even though there was virtually no supporting evidence, and virtually no precedent. Today we know a lot more about who is more likely to want to destroy beauty in a woman. Think acid attacks, setting women alight. We've seen it over and over again. It's not women doing it to women. In a late-night writing session,

I put the question to Copilot: *If a woman is attacked to destroy her beauty, who is statistically most likely to be the culprit?* Note: I put the question to Copilot because I already knew the answer, but I wanted a succinct reply. Here's what Copilot had to say:

> Statistically, when women are attacked – especially in ways that target their appearance or identity – the perpetrator is most often someone they know, rather than a stranger. According to global and Australian data, intimate partners or former partners are the most common perpetrators of violence against women. In many global case studies, intimate partners or rejected suitors are the most common perpetrators, particularly when the attack is motivated by jealousy, perceived betrayal, or attempts to control a woman's independence or sexuality.

So not usually a jealous wife. Now, back to Brian.

'The deceased was a female lying on her back,' Brian wrote in his notes. 'She was wearing a blood-soaked pink T-shirt and a pair of white and blue striped underpants. The T-shirt was pulled up at the front exposing her stomach, chest and right breast. Heavy blood smears were apparent on the deceased's arms, face, neck, chest and abdomen and thighs. On the carpet between the deceased's left shoulder and the left side of her head, was a pool of congealed blood.

'I observed the following wounds to the deceased. Her throat had been cut. She had a cut in her top lip and cuts on the inside of her fingers on both hands. What appeared to be a large letter A had been carved into her chest.'

What Brian described on Beth's fingers and hands are what every true crime reader has read about: defence wounds. These are the injuries sustained when people try to grab the weapon from their attacker or raise their arms to ward off blows. They are sad to see in crime scene photos because they are the echoes of a fight-back that ultimately proved futile. They speak of the last-ditch effort to cling to life, to live, to survive. But their presence on the dead shows it didn't work.

Looking around the room, Brian saw that nothing had really been disturbed. He reckoned that the ornaments on Beth's cluttered chest of drawers would have been knocked over without much difficulty and the fact they were all still standing made him think the struggle had been brief and contained. He noted that even the small bedside lamp, still switched on, appeared undisturbed.

Brian's job was to collect evidence samples. Eventually, he and his team would send off 70 items for testing. These had to be carefully numbered, labelled, bagged and photographed. They included the doona, the knife found next to Beth on the floor, every blood-splattered item from her bedroom, the cigarette butts and towels, and even the bathroom tap with the blood on it.

Brian also examined the points of entry to try and find out how the killer got into the house. He checked every window and door. Aside from the open back door, all the other windows and doors were locked. He also noted undisturbed dust around the windows which meant it was highly unlikely anyone had climbed through. Still, there was no way of telling whether Beth had invited the killer in, or if the killer had come in anyway.

Even though Beth had come to rest on the floor, Brian took notes of the place of origin of the attack. The evidence pointed to Beth being in bed when she was stabbed. 'Bedroom untidy, but no obvious signs of a struggle,' he wrote. 'Heavy blood staining apparent on the folded part of the top blanket and the bottom sheet.'

Not that it was necessarily part of his job, but Brian Gamble was not immune from putting two and two together. If the killer came in through the back door and attacked Beth in bed, she either let them in and got into bed while they were there – like one might with a sexual partner – or she was in bed and the killer attacked her there before she had a chance to jump up and confront them. With the lamp on and an open magazine on the floor near the bed, she could have been reading when the attack happened. Or she could have been sleeping and the killer turned on the lamp, before or after.

Outside, Brian took scrapings of the two smudges of blood on the concrete path near the back door.

Police fingerprint experts dusted surfaces in Beth's bedroom and around the back door as the suspected entry point. They labelled any prints they found and photographed them. They also dusted Beth's body, since it appeared the killer had wiped their hands on her arms, legs and torso, but they found no distinguishable prints. None either on the knife found next to Beth's body or around the basin in the bathroom.

The forensic team worked late into the night. When I interviewed him five years after the murder, Senior Constable Brian Gamble told me that the isolated farmhouse felt eerie as darkness descended.

Their work complete, the forensic team packed up, left the island and stayed the night at a motel in San Remo.

CHAPTER 13

THE LAND CRUISER

While the police were meeting to coordinate their investigation, in the middle of the afternoon on Tuesday 23 September 1986, Pam Cameron was on her way home from her job as a physiotherapist. She'd been at home that morning for the exchange of phone calls. She knew Vivienne was missing and that Fergus was worried about Beth. But then she'd gone off to work. At lunchtime, two things happened. Pam went to Newhaven to a pottery store and saw police there. In her statement to the police, she doesn't mention the route she took, but the first road on your right when you come over the Phillip Island bridge is Forrest Avenue, where she would later spot the Camerons' Land Cruiser. But during her lunch hour on the way to the pottery store, she failed to notice it.

When Pam got back to work, a colleague told her a woman had been found murdered in McFees Road. Pam knew that was where Beth Barnard lived and put two and two together. She would later say, 'I thought it was her and immediately rang Donald. He informed me that it was Beth and that Vivienne and the Land Cruiser were missing, and the police were searching for her.'

Phew, glad he mentioned the Land Cruiser was also missing because the next bit would be weird if he didn't. I wonder why Donald didn't ring Pam when he got home. Seems like the thing a husband would do. The fact that he was home meant he can't have been up the road at Marnie and Ian's with Fergus. Maybe they weren't the kind of family to come together when a tragedy happened.

Pam stayed at work and didn't leave until just before 4 pm. I've wondered what could have kept her there so long when she knew her husband had just found the body of a well-liked family friend, and her sister-in-law was missing. What would be so important at work that she couldn't leave? In contrast, Marnie had gone to work at the hospital that morning, but had raced home at the first sign of the family emergency. I wonder why Pam didn't do the same.

It was Pam's *second* trip over the bridge when she finally noticed the Land Cruiser – the vehicle that everyone had been both looking for and driving past all day long.

'As I was crossing the bridge onto the island,' she told the police, 'I noticed what appeared to be our Land Cruiser angle-parked opposite the fast-food outlet in Newhaven. I made a U-turn and went back to the vehicle and found that it was our Land Cruiser. I saw that the driver's window was open about two inches; it was unlocked, and the keys were still in the ignition. I also noticed that there was a gold Oroton purse, a black handbag and a brown hand towel on the seat. On the dashboard I noticed a full packet of cigarettes, also an open packet and a cigarette lighter. The cigarettes were a Claridge brand and were in a maroon and gold packet. The racetrack keys were also on the dash.'

Pam then spoke about her earlier trip to the pottery shop. It was relevant, she said, because when she drove past, she saw police. 'I forgot to mention that earlier in the lunch hour prior to me hearing the news from my colleague, I had driven to the pottery shop in Newhaven and on my return to San Remo I had noticed a police car parked by the bus stop near the bridge. Because of seeing the police car earlier, and it being in close vicinity to where I found the Land Cruiser, I assumed because of what Donald had told me, that Vivienne had been located by the police, and that the Land Cruiser had been left unattended.'

So we know Pam was looking in that direction on her way back from her lunch-hour trip to the pottery shop, but that she failed to see the Land Cruiser. Instead of driving to the police station at Cowes like her husband had done earlier, she took the keys out of the ignition and took the gold purse and went back to work, where she rang her husband.

'Donald then told me to report the finding of the Land Cruiser to the San Remo police and to lock the Land Cruiser. I then went to report it to the police, but the station was unattended. I then returned to the Land Cruiser. I removed the racetrack keys, wound the driver's side window up and locked the driver's side door. I then went around to the passenger's door which was also unlocked. I opened this door, and I immediately saw a black-handle carving knife on the passenger side floor, sitting on top of a pair of Driza-bone trousers. The knife was clean, and I recognised it as one of Fergus and Vivienne's kitchen carving knives. We also used to have a set the same. I then opened the glove box to see if there was anything else valuable and shut it again and then I locked the passenger's door.'

We are not sure where Donald was by the time Pam finished with the Land Cruiser, because she didn't go to her house. Instead, she went to Marnie and Ian's. 'I then went to Ian's place and told him what I'd done and he then contacted the police.'

I've always wondered why Pam went to see Ian and not her own husband. Had Donald gone to Marnie and Ian's by then, and that's where she called him? I would get an answer to this question years later.

'When I took the gold purse,' Pam went on, 'I opened it to see what was in it. I found loose change [and] two plastic type cards, one of which was Viv's licence.' Pam said there was no other money in the purse.

Pam gave her written statement to the police on Thursday 25 September 1986, just like Fergus, Marnie and Ian. At the end of her statement, the cop taking it, Detective Senior Constable Graeme Inch, asked her about the dynamic between Beth and Vivienne and Fergus.

'Because of the close working environment of the farm,' Pam said, 'Beth formed a close friendship with Fergus but there were no overt signs of any sexual relationship, and I was totally unaware of any serious affair going on between them.

'Over the 11 years that I have known Vivienne, whilst she has been married to Fergus, I am aware of problems existing with their marriage, which has resulted in arguments in front of family members.'

If I was Detective Graeme Inch, I would have asked loads of follow-up questions: When there were arguments in front of family members, who started them? Because everyone I've spoken to described Vivienne as quiet and not one to speak up. She'd joined

Toastmasters, perhaps to find her voice. Here's how other people described her: a thinker. A strategist. Gentle. Earth mother, a woman who didn't want to rock the boat, a mediator. So does she change when she's at home? Were they both fiery together? Did one argue and one placate? What did they argue about? All of these things are important and would have illustrated the power dynamic between Fergus and Vivienne.

I also would have asked Pam why she locked the Land Cruiser when she found it. In those days, no one locked their cars on the island. If you came across a car parked near the local shops, you assumed the driver would be shopping. It could have been someone in her family buying something for dinner in the takeaway across the road. If you locked a car, you'd lock them out. And given that, earlier in her statement, Pam said she tried to call Vivienne first thing in the morning, before the murder was discovered, I would have asked *why* she was trying to call Vivienne. What did she want to talk about at 7.30 on a school morning? Who else were she and Donald talking to, since Robyn Dixon couldn't get through to them when she was trying to call?

And one final question in my question palooza: lately, I've been wondering if Marnie would have called Donald and Pam the night before. The families all lived on the same road and worked their farms. If one family member was taken injured to the hospital, would the others be called? Even if it was to alert them to tread lightly the next time they saw Fergus and Viv. So, another question I would have asked would be: *Was Pam trying to ring Vivienne because she already knew something had happened the night before?*

92

Yes, Graeme Inch, I would have asked all those questions. I am much more of a busybody.

And before we leave Pam, I'm going to juxtapose two descriptions. Well, they were already juxtaposed since they occur in the statement together, but I want you, Dear Reader, to look at the difference in the way Pam describes Beth and the way she describes Vivienne.

'I have known Elizabeth Barnard since she has been working for the family which has been approximately two to three years. She was treated by all our family as a member of the family. She called Donald, Uncle Donald or Granpa, and my children treated her as a sister. I had formed a close friendship with her while treating her for a severe back injury, but she never mentioned or confided in me any close personal matters. Because of the close working environment of the farm, Beth formed a close friendship with Fergus but there were no overt signs of any sexual relationship and I was totally unaware of any serious affair going on between them. Over the 11 years that I have known Vivienne, whilst she has been married to Fergus, I am aware of problems existing with their marriage, which has resulted in arguments in front of family members. Although recently their relationship did appear to be better. Vivienne was also a very heavy smoker and very rarely went anywhere without her cigarettes.'

Of the two women, who do you think she liked best?

Not that it made any difference. She didn't leave work for either of them.

CHAPTER 14

THE PHONE CALL TO GLENDA

Glenda Frost was living on Phillip Island in September 1986 when Beth Barnard was murdered. She also worked with Vivienne Cameron at the local Community House. The women of the island had set up the house to support each other. It offered classes, counselling, craft and, most importantly, friendship. When they proposed adding daycare, one prominent wealthy local man publicly accused the women of wanting a 'dumping ground' for their children. I know, right. Doesn't he sound like a prince?

Glenda was dragged into this story when, at around 10 the morning after the murder, she received a phone call from a woman claiming to be Vivienne Cameron. The timing of the call conflicted sharply with the police's theory that Vivienne killed Beth, drove to the park near the bridge at 5 am, then jumped off. I know that sounds like a huge leap (physically and metaphorically) but that's where their thinking was at.

If that were the case, how could she possibly be calling Glenda five hours later?

*

When I began thinking about *The Vanishing of Vivienne Cameron* podcast back in 2020, it was fitting that my first interview was with Glenda. I'd first interviewed her back in 1992 and we'd kept in touch over the years after she moved interstate. We'd chat for hours on the phone, talking about what might have happened to her friend Vivienne. I hadn't heard from her for a while but then found out she'd moved into an aged care facility not far from my house. Glenda was happy to talk to me again.

She told me she'd been frightened in September 1986. There'd been a murder in her small community and she knew all the people connected to the case. It scared her that she lived among these people and that one of them was capable of such a horrific act and she didn't pick it. I asked her if it worried her that she could live among dangerous people now and not know it? She didn't think so. The Phillip Island case made her wary and gave her a way of sensing people with ill intent.

She said, 'You don't see what you don't watch for.' And now, she watches.

Glenda remembered meeting Fergus Cameron for the first time at a theatre somewhere. He was with Vivienne.

'I want you to meet my husband,' Vivienne said.

Glenda wondered with the wisdom of hindsight whether it was a bit of a test on Vivienne's part, considering her husband's proclivities – if I had a dollar for every woman who has called him an ogler, my pockets would be jingling. But Glenda would never have been drawn to Fergus because there was nothing about his looks or manner that she found attractive. Quite the opposite in fact.

'What was Vivienne like?' I asked her.

'She wouldn't have had an eye for the fellows,' Glenda said.

I wasn't surprised. Vivienne had more than enough on her plate. Two young children. A job at the Community House. A husband who worked days on the farm and nights at the Penguin Parade.

I got the feeling that if Glenda could step back in time, she might not have answered the phone that Tuesday morning, 23 September 1986. At first, she almost didn't. Her friend Pam – who sat by her side during our first interview – was visiting and had arrived the previous evening. When the phone rang, Pam was doing the dishes. She called out to Glenda to answer it, but Glenda protested. She was too busy to talk.

Pam called back, 'It won't be for me.'

Glenda had no idea that she would be the last person to acknowledge talking to Vivienne Cameron. Or someone who said they were Vivienne Cameron.

In the days of the old landlines before there were answering machines, phones could take several minutes to ring out. If no one answered, it would peal through the house for ages at full volume. Finally, Glenda lost the battle and picked up the receiver.

'It's Viv Cameron, Glenda,' said a voice. (Dear Reader, please note the use of the surname here. If you work with someone, do you say your surname when you call? Glenda certainly didn't need to use the surname when she whispered to Pam that it was Viv.)

'Hi Viv, you're lucky to catch me today, I'm normally at work by now but I'm hand-sewing at home for the fashion parade,' Glenda said. She was relieved it was just Viv. She'd known her for three years and Viv wasn't a talker. The call would be short.

'Have you found out where to buy the patchwork house gift for Isobel?' Vivienne asked.

At the post office the previous week, Glenda had run into Viv, who asked her where she could buy a patchwork house that she could sew as a retirement gift for their friend Isobel Addicoat. Glenda suggested that Viv call their friend Dianne.

'Do you want her number? I have it right here,' Glenda said. 'Have you got a pencil?'

When Vivienne went silent, Glenda assumed she was looking for something to write with. In the background Glenda could hear voices and assumed they were Vivienne's two young boys. Vivienne then asked Glenda to hold on for a sec. As the background noise stopped, Glenda covered the mouthpiece and said to Pam, 'It's Viv, I won't be long.' She turned her attention back to the phone as Vivienne came back on the line.

'Boys playing up?' Glenda asked.

'It's okay now,' Vivienne said.

Glenda knew that Vivienne was awkward on the telephone. They'd had plenty of phone conversations and Glenda always felt obliged to keep the chat flowing. But today she didn't have time. 'Is there anything else you want, Viv?'

'Why no . . . I don't think so.'

Just before hanging up, Glenda remembered the list of materials they needed for patterns they were working on. She asked if Viv wanted her to read out the items on the list.

'Oh, don't bother now,' Vivienne said. 'Bring the list with you to patchwork lessons next week and I'll get it then.'

There was another one of those awkward Vivienne silences that Glenda was accustomed to. 'Well I'd better get back to my sewing now, Viv. See you next week at class.'

And that was that.

*

Two hours after the phone call, Glenda and Pam went for coffee at a café in Cowes. It was there that they learned that Beth Barnard had been murdered. Like many islanders, Glenda and Pam were shocked. Neither of them was friends with Beth, but they knew her enough to say hello. While Pam no longer lived on the island and was going back to Dandenong that afternoon, Glenda had to go home to her house. As a single woman living on her own, she was understandably disturbed.

As shock slowly rippled through the community, few made any connection between Beth's murder and Vivienne Cameron. And why would they? When a brutal murder happens in a small community, you're unlikely to suspect a gentle, hardworking mother of two.

The police thought differently.

Glenda didn't make the link between Beth Barnard and her friend Vivienne Cameron until she turned on the television the following night. The murder was one of the lead stories. The reporter said that police were searching for a Mrs Vivienne Cameron in connection with the savage murder of a 23-year-old farm worker by the name of Elizabeth Catherine Barnard. Vivienne Cameron's car had been found on the Phillip Island side of the San Remo bridge and it was believed Vivienne had jumped from the bridge to her death.

The bridge theory must've been passed onto news reporters because this is what was reported. The reporter said the car had first been seen at 5 o'clock on the Tuesday morning although it wasn't positively identified by police until about 4 pm the same day.

Glenda froze.

She had spoken to Vivienne some *five hours after* the car was first seen parked near the bridge. She was still staring horrified at the news report when the phone rang.

'Glenda, it's Pam. Have you seen the news?'

Glenda could hardly speak. 'Yes . . .'

'Wasn't it Viv Cameron who you spoke to Tuesday morning on the phone? How could she be jumping off the bridge at 5 o'clock when you spoke to her at 10 o'clock? It just doesn't make sense!'

Glenda felt panicked. 'No. What am I going to do?'

'You've got to ring the police,' Pam told her firmly.

'No . . . I can't.'

'Glenda, you have to tell them *now*. They think Vivienne has got something to do with Beth's murder, but she can't have – not if she was talking to you on the phone about . . . what was it?'

'A patchwork gift,' said Glenda, lost in thought.

'Let's face it,' said Pam, 'nobody's going to discuss patchwork if they've just killed somebody, are they?'

'Oh my God, Pam, I can't believe this.'

'You have to call the police. Vivienne could be in danger or hurt.'

It was the thought that Vivienne might need her that spurred Glenda to agree to contact the police. Pam offered to make the call for her and dialled the Victoria Police emergency line.

She explained what she knew to a young constable, who said he'd pass on the information to the homicide squad.

Pam could tell how upset Glenda was to be caught in the middle of this horror. She rang her work and asked if she could take a few days off, then packed a bag, grabbed her car keys and drove directly to Phillip Island. Her friend needed her.

*

Detective Alan McFayden visited Glenda Frost at her home less than an hour after Pam's phone call to the police. He was still there when Pam arrived. She immediately corroborated Glenda's story: if Vivienne was talking to Glenda at 10 am, then she couldn't have jumped from the bridge at 5 o'clock that morning.

After carefully taking notes and going over their story, again and again, the detective left Glenda and Pam to discuss the shocking turn of events.

The following night, three detectives from the homicide squad stopped by Glenda Frost's house. They too listened to her story and Pam's corroboration. However, they were more sceptical than Alan McFayden. 'Are you sure it wasn't on Monday that Mrs Cameron called you?' asked Detective Rory O'Connor.

'I've told you, I'm positive,' Glenda said, 'because Pam wasn't even here on Monday morning, and I was at work most of the day. It couldn't have been Monday.'

'Are you sure it was her on the phone – not someone pretending to be her?' O'Connor pressed.

'I am absolutely certain,' said Glenda. 'It couldn't have been anyone else because of what she was talking about. Nobody else would have known about the patchwork house she wanted to buy – besides, I've spoken to Vivienne enough times on the phone to recognise her voice.'

The detectives were still sceptical. Glenda's story poked a hole in their neat scenario that Vivienne Cameron killed Beth Barnard, drove to the Phillip Island bridge and jumped to her death. There was no room in that scenario for phone calls about patchwork. It just didn't fit.

'She was normal – absolutely normal,' said Glenda, conviction in her voice. 'I don't believe she could have done it . . . not the way she spoke. I just can't believe it.'

'People can just snap,' said O'Connor.

Glenda had no doubt that people could snap, but what she couldn't believe was that the person with whom she had a completely normal conversation on Tuesday morning could have murdered a young woman only hours before.

'So you mean to say that you were talking to her on the phone . . . why have we had police divers searching for her body under the bridge then?' O'Connor said.

'I don't know,' said Glenda. 'All I know is that that's when she called me. I'm certain.'

Like a square peg in a round hole, Glenda's story still didn't fit. O'Connor believed that Vivienne would have been incapable of a 'normal' conversation after committing a vicious murder.

But after looking at this case for over 35 years, I want to take a very close look at this conversation. The more I think about it, the more a couple of things stand out about that phone call the morning of Tuesday 23 September 1986. Firstly, Glenda said she was sure it was Vivienne because only Vivienne knew about Isobel's patchwork gift. But what if Vivienne had written a note to herself, or even said in passing to someone, 'Remind me to ring Glenda about Isobel's patchwork retirement gift'? If she'd done either of those things, then someone else could have easily known about it.

Secondly, Glenda repeated to the detectives what she remembered Vivienne saying to her on the phone. *It's Viv Cameron, Glenda.* Vivienne worked with Glenda and they were good friends. Were there so many other women called Vivienne that she would include her surname? Not likely.

I do believe Glenda received a phone call that day. But I doubt it was Vivienne.

I don't think Vivienne Cameron was alive then.

*

Glenda Frost is one of the many on the periphery of this case who have never forgotten it and is still affected by it. She is forever 'the woman who received the phone call from Vivienne Cameron' – or someone claiming to be Vivienne. She is forever the one who had to pluck up the courage to go to the police. She is forever the one who the police and the coroner ignored and dismissed out of hand.

Gee, it's not like official men to ignore women! I hear you gasp. But then you laugh so I know you're joking, because of course, we all know that the words of women – especially when they contradict the stories of men – are ignored. White noise. *What's that? Did you say something? I thought not. Must've been the wind.* Note bitterness warning: when Wayne Hunt (a man) said he saw a car near the bridge, the official men and the coroner man absolutely took him at his man word. But when Glenda said she got a call from Vivienne Cameron, her story was ignored. If it was indeed Vivienne Cameron who rang Glenda, and there were voices in the background during the phone call, then someone was with Vivienne that Tuesday morning. Someone knew where she was. But because the police dismissed Glenda out of hand, they didn't ask those questions.

But if it *wasn't* Vivienne, then a different question needs to be asked: what woman was in the company of at least one child – or an adult – at 10 am on that Tuesday morning – might have a vested interest in a sleight of hand? Who might benefit from throwing the police off the scent? *Look! Vivienne is alive! She's ringing Glenda! Look over there, not over here.*

But enough for now. On with the show.

We know it can't have been the Cameron boys who Glenda heard in the background because one of them – Dugald – was at school. That left Hugh. We assume he was with Fergus, but Fergus was with Marnie. Glenda could never be specific about the voices. She heard them and that's all she remembers, but I always felt that if she said to Vivienne, 'Are the boys playing up?' then something must have suggested to her that at least one of the voices was a child.

Glenda told me about the voices she heard on the phone when I first interviewed her, but it's not in her statement to the police. In the re-telling, Pam remembered a break in the conversation. Remembered Glenda telling her it was Viv. Remembered Glenda asking about the voices in the background.

Let's backpedal a bit here because we enjoy doing that and it's good for the calves. When Detective Senior Constable Rory

O'Connor asked Glenda if the phone call could have been someone pretending to be Vivienne, what might have been behind that question? If it was someone pretending to be Vivienne, could it have been someone wanting to establish proof of life? But why would anyone need to do that? If O'Connor was in fact asking if someone might impersonate Vivienne, then the next natural question would be, 'Why?' Who would benefit from pretending Vivienne was alive? I wonder if the only answer to this question could be: someone who knew she wasn't. You would only make such a phone call if Vivienne was in fact *not* alive and you knew it, but wanted to make out that she was. You can only set someone up if you are absolutely certain that they can't reappear and refute the set-up.

And here's where men not believing women comes into it. Here we have two local women telling a total of four officials that there had been a phone call on the Tuesday morning at 10. Even if the police wanted to cling to their hastily formed belief that Vivienne dumped the Land Cruiser near the bridge and walked the half a kilometre to the centre and jumped to her death, why wouldn't they have looked into other possibilities? Was someone out there playing funny buggers with phone calls? And if so, why?

But it appears that the police only entertained one possibility: Glenda and Pam were mistaken. If only they had checked the phone records to see where that call came from.

Because that's where the answers lie. In the phone records. The ones that either didn't exist or were never checked.

*

While I was making the podcast, I contacted Pam again and we had a long talk about Phillip Island society. She described three tiers of people, kind of like upper, middle and working class, but it was more particular. People like the Camerons and their friends were on the top. They had an air about them; old families were the island's version of the landed gentry. Pam remembered one time she and Glenda were out at a restaurant and the Camerons walked in. She said all eyes turned to them, like they were royalty. But Vivienne, who came from the mainland and married into the family, was different.

'She was more like one of us,' Pam said. This feeling was reinforced when Vivienne took a job at the Community House. She hung out with the other local women and made friends outside of the Cameron clan.

The top tier on the island was also connected with those who made the rules: the police. For this reason, Sergeant Cliff Ashe was right up there, on par with the Camerons. Back in 1992, I didn't know that Cliff Ashe and the Camerons were friends. He certainly didn't offer that little peccadillo when Paul Daley and I interviewed him.

So maybe it was because of this division between people on the island, maybe it was because of power, maybe it was because of friendship – or maybe it was because they were women – but Cliff Ashe simply didn't believe Pam and Glenda when they came forward. The information they offered didn't fit the official narrative. Pam and Glenda told me that they'd even had an out-and-out argument with Cliff Ashe. He flatly told them they were mistaken.

'We aren't!' they cried in unison.

After the podcast came out, a man got in touch. Like many who were on Phillip Island back in 1986, he had since left and was no longer under the spell the place seemed to cast over so many locals. From a safe distance interstate, he said that soon after Glenda had come forward with her story about the phone call, he'd stopped by Glenda's sewing space and had seen Cliff Ashe talking to her alone.

'You'd better shut up about it,' the man heard Ashe say.

It looked like intimidation and the man described Glenda as 'a nervous wreck' after the incident. Everyone knew Cliff Ashe wasn't a man to be trifled with.

Glenda never told me about this and when I mentioned it to her 34 years later, she was vague. 'Yeah, that sounds about right,' she said. She then told me a few stories about Cliff Ashe that stopped me in my tracks. It reminded me that while the cops are watching people, people are watching them too. Whatever choices they make, people notice and talk. And they tell those stories to writers.

CHAPTER 15

THE CAMERONS' HOUSE

Crime scene examiner Senior Constable Brian Gamble's first task early on the morning of Wednesday 24 September 1986 was to head to the San Remo police station and inspect the Land Cruiser that had been found near the Phillip Island bridge the previous afternoon.

Brian and his team retrieved a towel from the passenger side footwell, and a large, black-handled kitchen carving knife that was lying next to it. From the dashboard they retrieved two packets of Claridge cigarettes and a box of matches. This meant that if Vivienne did leave the Land Cruiser and make the long walk to the bridge to take her own life, she didn't take her cigarettes with her. For a heavy smoker, you'd think she'd take a packet with her to steady her nerves. And from the passenger seat, they took a black handbag.

Spoiler alert!

The presence of the black handbag is going to be a spanner in the works. Remember Robyn Dixon telling Detective Alan McFayden that she saw Vivienne's handbag when she came to

107

collect the kids around 3.20 am. She recalled thinking that if Vivienne had left her handbag behind, they must have left for the hospital in a hurry. And remember the homicide detectives hearing from neighbour Margaret McFee that she'd heard a vehicle around 3.30 am in McFees Road. The clunking and grinding of the police drawing their conclusions put Vivienne Cameron in the Land Cruiser on the other side of the island at that time. Did she drive back to Ventnor to pick up her handbag only to drive across the island to the park near the bridge only to leave her handbag behind? Because now, it was here for the police to see on the front seat.

The police dusted the vehicle for fingerprints but none were found. This did not necessarily mean the Land Cruiser had been wiped clean. Fingerprints are made up of water, salt and fats. If they're exposed to heat, they can dry up faster than any alternative theories in this case. The weather had been quite warm that week and the Land Cruiser had been locked up for a day in the spring sunshine. That might have explained the lack of prints.

Another thing the police didn't find in the Land Cruiser were any traces of Beth's blood. Brian and his crime scene examiner colleagues had spent the best part of a day at Beth's house and it was hard to believe a killer could cause so much damage to her and not be covered in blood. Sure, they had washed their hands afterwards – police had the tap to prove it – but Vivienne Cameron was last seen wearing a mohair jumper. Surely there would have been evidence transferred onto her and then into the Land Cruiser. But there was nothing.

As for the outside of the Land Cruiser, the square hay bales sitting in the open tray meant little to me, but a couple of years back, I was contacted by a farm person familiar with farm vehicles who pointed out something important:

> Square bales are a thing of the past only used by farmers on a very small scale since the introduction of round bales in the early 80s . . . It was only when I saw the photo of the Land Cruiser ute with old square bales on the back that the penny dropped for me. This happened in late September. Farmers would rarely be feeding hay to cattle during the first flush of spring. It would have to have been a very wet winter to be still putting out hay and even then, large round bales would have been used.

My new farm pal also said that the sides of the Land Cruiser weren't secured so the vehicle couldn't have been driven very far, if at all, without the hay bales falling off. I didn't even know that you could secure the sides, but once my farmer friend pointed it out, it made sense that you'd want to. While we're on the subject of hay bales, I want to mention something that struck me at 4.56 one morning and woke me up. Yes, Dear Reader, middle-of-the-night revelations are the curse of the crime writer. McFees Road is one of those rough, corrugated roads that really rattle your car. If the Camerons' Land Cruiser, without the sides up, drove up and down McFees Road and then turned around, how were the hay bales still on it? And if it went up Beth's driveway so Beth would think Fergus was visiting, why wasn't there hay everywhere? And if the sides *were* up when it drove up McFees Road, and Vivienne *did* drive the Land Cruiser to Forrest Avenue, why would she let the sides down and move the hay so it hung over the edges? All before jumping to her death?

So many questions.

Once the examination of the Land Cruiser was complete, Brian Gamble and the crime scene team returned to Beth's farmhouse to finish up their work there. By lunchtime, they had moved on to their next stop: Fergus and Vivienne Cameron's home in Ventnor. As he had just done at Beth's, Brian made sketches of both the property and the house and walked from room to room, reading the scene and taking notes. A police photographer took pictures of yet another packet of Claridge cigarettes. This one was on the kitchen bench. When I first looked at this case, back in the bad old days when we were all smokers, I remembered thinking it's almost as if someone has scattered Claridge cigarette packets all over the place, because how many packets did smokers have on the go at any given time? By my count, there were three packets of cigarettes: two in the Land Cruiser and one in the kitchen. Then there were the butts at Beth's house.

Other photos of the Camerons' house captured the kitchen sink, a knife in the kitchen sink, bloodstains in the hallway and spare bedroom, a pink bloodstained tissue on the basin in the bathroom, a bloodstained blue shirt in the laundry, and blood on the bathroom floor. Outside, the photographer took pictures of the Camerons' Holden Kingswood and its bloodstained front passenger seat.

'I then entered the front spare bedroom,' Brian wrote in his notes. 'The doorway to this bedroom led from an area near the eastern end of the central hallway. The furniture consisted of a double bed with the head of the bed positioned up against the room's southern wall. Also against the southern wall was a wardrobe. In the northwestern corner of the room was a chest of drawers, a bookcase and a desk and a chair. Scattered over the bed were a number of papers. I observed a number of blood-stains in the room. On the floor between the western side of the bed and the western wall, were a number of blood droplets. On the bedspread and papers on the bed were a number of blood droplets. On the front of the chest of drawers was a blood smear.' The photographer captured all of this on film.

Brian continued his observations. 'On the outside part of the door was a blood smear. I collected the following blood samples from this room ...' He listed items such as two sheets of paper from the bed, and scrapings of blood from the chest of drawers, the doorway and the wall in the hallway.

After finishing with the front room, he collected the pink tissues from the Camerons' bathroom and some clothes from the laundry basket. He also took a scraping of blood from some droplets near the shower and toilet. In the kitchen, he collected a sponge and a knife from the sink.

*

Mid-afternoon, Fergus Cameron was photographed from the front, back and sides. From the front, he looked down and to the left, hair messed, lips pressed in a thin line. I remember when I first saw this photo. Such an ordinary-looking man to be at the centre of this horror story, to have created such obsession and jealousy that had ended the life of one, probably two women. The side shot shows the injuries to his left ear. His back shot shows a cluster of three wounds, stitched, but looking minor and small two days later. There are marks of band-aids around each of his back wounds, suggesting that band-aids rather than bandages had been removed in order to photograph them. And it's worth noting in these photos taken on the Wednesday that Fergus is dressed in a blue shirt and orange jumper. In other words, he's up and about. The following day when he gave his formal statement, he would be in his pyjamas in bed.

After photographing Fergus, it was time for the crime scene team to head off to the post-mortem examination of Beth Barnard at the Korumburra District Hospital. Brian Gamble would collect Beth's nightshirt and underwear, and all the samples removed from her body during the examination. Beth's final indignity was to be photographed for the record. Her injuries stood out in stark relief against her skin, pale in death.

*

When I first interviewed Brian Gamble, my big question for him was, 'Where was the broken wine glass?' Because in the examination of the items collected from the Camerons' house, the broken wine glass that Vivienne allegedly used to strike and stab her husband was pivotal to the story. Marnie Cairns said she'd cleaned it up when she arrived after Vivienne and Fergus left for the hospital.

'Did you check the bin?' I asked him.

Brian shrugged. 'We would have. If it's not in my notes, it wasn't there.'

'Because you would have been given the story of what had happened, wouldn't you?' I pressed.

Brian agreed. He would have been given an overview of the case before he examined both the Camerons' house and Beth's house.

That was the story. Fergus had been attacked with a wine glass. Only there was no glass. And there was something else that took me years to notice in the crime scene photos of the Camerons' kitchen. There was a wine goblet on the sink, but it wasn't glass; it was pewter. Anyone from the 1980s would remember the ads for Selangor pewter. It was surprisingly popular back then and I have a hazy memory of one of the famous comics – could have been Ugly Dave Gray or maybe Graham Kennedy – spruiking it on their TV show.

So, a pewter wine goblet and no broken wine glass.

Could this be the first crack in the story? Apparently not.

CHAPTER 16

THE PUB NIGHT THAT NEVER HAPPENED

It's easy to imagine the effects of a murder on the people closest to the crime. But murder has a ripple effect that sweeps out well beyond. A body is discovered, then family are notified, then friends find out, sometimes second- or third-hand. Decades after Beth Barnard was discovered dead on her bedroom floor, people who knew and loved her still remember where they were when they found out.

*

On Tuesday 23 September 1986, Beth's friend Mandy was looking forward to a night at the pub in Fitzroy with Jacquie and Beth. Since they'd finished their agricultural science degrees, the girls had gone their separate ways, but they remained close. Mandy had even done a couple of weeks' work experience on Beth's family farm and stayed with her at the house in McFees Road. The farm was a bit too isolated for Mandy and she wondered how Beth could live out there by herself. Mandy would have felt scared being there alone, but when she mentioned this to Beth, her friend just laughed and said she kept a gun under her bed. Mandy didn't know if she was joking or not. Every night, the girls made sure they locked up before they went to bed.

Mandy had offered to pick Beth up on the Tuesday night for their night out at the pub. When she pulled up at Beth's parents' house in Kew, she knocked on the door, expecting it to be flung open by Beth, but instead, she was swept into a house of grief. The story came tumbling out in voices jagged with crying and bewilderment.

Beth had been murdered. The police had come and told them. Not only that, the police said that Vivienne Cameron had killed Beth because she was having an affair with Fergus Cameron.

'Is it true?' asked Beth's mum, Margaret, in a voice that sounded distressed and hurt.

Mandy looked around at them. All eyes were on her. She didn't know what to say. It felt like Beth's secret – a secret Mandy hadn't wanted to know about – had tainted her too, as if she was guilty by association just because she knew. Mandy told them it was true that Beth was having an affair with Fergus Cameron. Everyone was crying at this point. Mandy had a cup of tea with them, then left. The Barnard family's grief and loss was tangled up in the news of Beth's affair, while Mandy's grief was perhaps more simple. She had lost one of her best friends in the most brutal way imaginable.

After leaving the Barnards', Mandy drove to Jacquie's sister's pub in Fitzroy. When she got there, she told the bunch of university friends what had happened. What was supposed to be a festive gathering soon turned into a wake of sorts. They all went upstairs to Jacquie's sister's residence to process the news and express their sorrow.

Beth had been murdered by Fergus Cameron's wife.

It was beyond belief.

Dear Reader, I have to point out something else here that was beyond belief. When Mandy arrived to pick Beth up that night, the family had already been told that Beth had been murdered by Vivienne because she'd been having an affair with Fergus. This was before the autopsy. Before any investigation had taken place. Before any statements – aside from Donald Cameron's and Robyn Dixon's – had been taken. Before any scientific examination of evidence. Probably before the Land Cruiser had been discovered near the bridge. And I suspect, before Beth's body had even been removed from the house. Before anything.

Beyond belief, indeed.

CHAPTER 17

THE POST-MORTEM EXAMINATION

When I started investigating the Phillip Island murder mystery back in 1991 – five years after the events took place – a respected forensic pathologist by the name of Dr David Ranson from the Victorian Institute of Forensic Medicine told me that by the early 1990s, the post-mortem examination of Beth Barnard would have been done in Melbourne. But it wasn't. It was done at the Korumburra District Hospital in South Gippsland. As such, many of the questions that watchers of TV dramas have about time of death, and rigor mortis, and stomach contents can't be answered.

Beth's body was examined by a regional pathologist by the name of Dr Anderson on the afternoon of Wednesday 24 September 1986. Also present were detectives Rory O'Connor and Alan McFayden, crime scene examiner Brian Gamble, and photographer Peter Gates.

The mortuary room was typical of a country hospital. There was a metal trolley, a set of shining instruments, a bench and a sink. The room was lit by fluorescent tubes and smelled of disinfectant. When the police team arrived, a mortuary assistant, who had been busy laying out the instruments, opened a fridge and removed Beth Barnard's naked, blood-smeared body.

When I interviewed Alan McFayden, he showed a very human side as he spoke of the sorrow of lost potential in these moments, looking down at a dead woman's body. He allowed himself a moment to feel bad for her, exposed and hideously abused. There was no room for modesty, no room for secrets.

Rory O'Connor would later tell me that Dr Anderson had little experience in this type of post-mortem examination. 'He hadn't done too many ... We had to tell him what to do from go to whoa. Unfortunately, we couldn't get the body back to Melbourne ... If it had've been done [in Melbourne], we'd probably find out a lot more ... but ... it's not going to alter anything, if you know what I mean.'

The time of death might have altered things, but determining that is an inexact science. If a woman's body was found at 9 am, would a skilled pathologist at the scene be able to tell if she'd been killed at 3.30 in the morning? We'll never know.

Once Peter Gates had taken his photographs, the assistant sprayed Beth with a fine mist of water and sponged away the dried blood. Dr Anderson then began his external examination. The assistant was on hand to pass him the necessary instruments.

'Young female, age about . . .' Dr Anderson began.

'Twenty-three,' said O'Connor, checking his notes.

'Yes, mid-twenties would be about right. Looks to have been a fit individual, well nourished.'

The detectives took more notes as the post-mortem proceeded.

Dr Anderson measured the wound to Beth's throat. 'The throat wound is 11 centimetres wide and 6.5 centimetres deep in the fold between the chin and the upper part of the neck.' He walked over to the bench near the sink and took a notebook and a pen from his pocket. He wrote down the measurements, inadvertently leaving traces of Beth's blood on the page. He walked back to the body and probed within the folds of the jagged neck wound. 'The pharynx has been completely severed just above the larynx,' he said, 'as has the right carotid artery, but not the left.'

Dr David Ranson later explained the significance of this to me. There is one carotid artery on either side of the neck. When one is severed and the other isn't, it might indicate the head was turned or held to the side as the throat was being cut. David Ranson sat patiently with me and the crime scene photos and the post-mortem report and explained what it all meant. 'See this line along the lower border of the neck wound?' He pointed to the graphic crime scene photo of Beth's neck. 'It's *intermittently* jagged. That suggests multiple cuts rather than a single slash. Cutting a throat isn't as easy as you might imagine.'

I tried not to imagine.

At the post-mortem examination back in 1986, Dr Anderson then measured the wound in Beth's face. The one that took out her tooth. 'The upper lip shows a thick slash wound which is ...' his gloved hands manipulated the tape measure, '... 3 centimetres long, extending from the mouth towards, but not reaching, the right nostril. The left corner of the mouth also has a 3-centimetre slash wound running towards the angle of the jaw and there's a further slash wound under the point of the chin. It is 2.5 centimetres long. The left front tooth has been completely knocked out.'

'By the knife blow?' asked O'Connor.

'Looks like it.'

McFayden and O'Connor exchanged glances. Seeing this kind of damage inflicted on anyone – let alone a young woman – was distressing.

Dr Anderson turned his attention to the chest. 'The upper chest showed a gaping stab wound 4.5 centimetres long in the midclavicular line, and there is a smaller gaping wound 2 centimetres by 1.5 centimetres near the third rib.' The doctor's gloved hands flicked the tape measure over the wounds.

The detectives readied their pens as the doctor went on to measure and describe the letter A that had been carved into Beth's chest. 'The right side of the A shape consists of a deep slash that measures 25 centimetres long. Two shorter and much more shallow slashes, which have not completely penetrated the skin, run parallel to the deep slash. The left side of the A consists of a slash that measures 29 centimetres long which has penetrated into subcutaneous fat. As you can see here, it's quite deep.' Dr Anderson indicated the exposed fat. 'Three shorter, much more shallow slashes run parallel and adjacent to it. The centre bar of the A consists of an 18-centimetre horizontal slash. I've never seen anything like this.'

Neither had the detectives.

Dr Anderson then examined the defence wounds. 'Looks like your victim put up a bit of a fight.' Beth's body had plenty of these wounds. Dr Anderson held up her left arm and measured the deep knife gash in her elbow. The police photographer snapped a photograph of the uplifted arm and captured on film the trickles of bloodied water running down the white surface of her skin.

Also captured on film were Beth's hands – the left hand had deep gash wounds in all the fingers and another deep wound in the web between the thumb and the index finger. The right hand had similar wounds. There was also a small slash near Beth's left ankle. Had she kicked at her killer in the struggle?

Once Dr Anderson had described the external wounds, and they had been photographed, it was time to open the body to assess the internal damage.

'The right lung, the pericardium – that's the sack around the heart – and the vena cava have all been pierced with the long knife blade, which has entered in a downwards thrust. Your victim has bled large volumes of blood into her chest cavity. The right pleural cavity here is completely filled with blood.' The detectives could clearly see the damage. 'Death by internal bleeding would have occurred some minutes after the upper chest wound was inflicted.'

McFayden murmured to O'Connor, 'I reckon the chest wounds would have been the first inflicted, from what we could tell from the crime scene. Looked like she'd been attacked while she was asleep. Murderer probably got the first strike in pretty cleanly.'

O'Connor agreed.

Dr Anderson examined the other major organs, which he found were all normal and free of disease. 'There's no sign of pregnancy,' he said.

The detectives noted this.

Dr Anderson then took specimens: fingernail scrapings, a lock of hair, vaginal and anal swabs, a piece of thigh muscle and 10 millilitres of blood. He carefully labelled the specimens and handed them to the detectives. Other samples, including the stomach contents and additional blood, were given to Brian Gamble to be taken for analysis at the Forensic Science Laboratory in Melbourne.

'I don't think there's much more I can do now. It's over to you.' Dr Anderson moved away from Beth's body to wash up.

Rory O'Connor used his fingerprint kit to take a set of Beth's prints, while McFayden walked over to the doctor, who was removing his bloodied gown. 'What's the verdict, doctor?' he asked.

'Well, I think she was alive when the chest wounds occurred because there is evidence of extensive internal bleeding around these wounds.'

'How about the "A" . . .?'

'I can't say for certain whether she was alive then, but I think not.'

'Anything else you can add?'

'Only that prior to the attack she was a healthy young woman with every chance of living till she was 80.' The doctor promised to pass on his written report as soon as it was ready. The cause of death would be: knife wounds in chest and throat.

The detectives left with their notes and their bottled specimens to continue their investigation.

CHAPTER 18

THE SEARCH FOR VIVIENNE CAMERON

We've seen it countless times on TV – distraught families appealing through the media: 'Please come home . . .' or 'If you've taken her, please return her to us . . .' or 'If anyone knows anything, please come forward'. But the Cameron clan did none of this. No appeals, no posters on bus stops, no teary interviews begging Vivienne to return.

What had she ever done to them to cause such indifference?

But even though the family didn't look for Vivienne, the police did. Sergeant Geoff Frost was a veteran of the police search and rescue squad when he was asked to coordinate efforts to find the body of Vivienne Cameron. Geoff was first alerted to the case on Phillip Island on Wednesday 24 September 1986 when he got a call from homicide squad detective Rory O'Connor. O'Connor briefed him on the brutal murder and told him that the prime suspect's vehicle had been found the previous afternoon near the bridge connecting the island to the mainland.

In all the interviews I conducted, I could never pinpoint why the police fixated on the bridge and suicide theory in their search

123

for Vivienne Cameron. Not all of them did, of course; Detective Alan McFayden had told me, 'That car was closer to a bus stop than the bridge.' McFayden never believed the bridge theory, mostly because it was his job to examine it. He would later say in a TV interview that he walked the length of the bridge, examining the railings for any breaks in the salt crust that would indicate someone had climbed over. He found none.

Every time I drive to the island and come along the coast and first spot the bridge, I think to myself, *It's just not high enough.* If you're going to suicide from a height, it has to be high enough to guarantee death. If you search YouTube, you can see clips of teenagers jumping off the Phillip Island bridge in summer for fun. It's only about 12 metres between the deck of the bridge and the water. Of course, the distance changes with the tides, but still. If Vivienne did jump, she might have found herself below the bridge in the water wondering, *What now?* The other thing was the Cameron farm backed onto cliffs on the other side of the island. If you were going to jump to your death somewhere really dangerous, that would have been a much better choice.

Nonetheless, the police – bar Alan McFayden – thought Vivienne jumped off the bridge. And that was Geoff Frost's domain.

Geoff explained to me the challenges in searching under the bridge. His squad could only search the water for 20 minutes at a time, for two periods a day, when the tide was at its lowest ebb. Despite the restrictions, he was confident that if Vivienne Cameron had jumped, there was a good possibility they'd find her. After an initial period of drifting where air is expelled from the body, a drowned person becomes a literal dead weight and sinks to the bottom. After it has been in the water for about four days, an enzyme reaction which is part of decomposition fills the body with gasses, and it floats to the surface.

Geoff and the divers from search and rescue arrived at the Newhaven boat ramp at 7.30 on the Thursday morning – about two days after Vivienne went missing. If she had gone into the water, it would be getting close to the time she might float to the surface, or, depending on the tides, be swept onto the mudflats surrounding the bridge. Other police combed those mudflats and nearby beaches for her body or any evidence she went in the water. None was found.

Two teams of divers searched under the bridge for the next two days. Metre by metre, in sweeping arcs, the divers covered the bottom of Western Port Bay under the bridge between Phillip Island and San Remo on the mainland. They kept a close watch on the surface, knowing that if Vivienne had jumped, she likely would have floated to the surface by the time their search was ending.

Geoff used a texta and a bit of paper to explain the way the divers went about their work. Two search and rescue boats were deployed, each containing a diver and a companion. Geoff said one diver from each boat entered the water and they were connected to their boats by long ropes. The divers then descended the 13 metres to the bottom of the bay, slowly swimming in arcs, sweeping the sand with their hands, ensuring that they covered every single centimetre. Once the arc was completed, the surface companion pulled their partner in a full body length to begin another arc. In this way, even though visibility was poor, Geoff could say with certainty if there was a body under the bridge, his men would have found it.

'It just wasn't there,' he told me. 'We searched every centimetre, according to the correct procedure, and it just wasn't there.'

He gave it four days and then he called a halt to the search. He remained unconvinced Vivienne Cameron had jumped. One of the reasons for his doubt was that none of the signs of a suicide ritual was present. In his experience, people tended to leave notes and tidy up their affairs before they killed themselves. Vivienne had done neither. Geoff also thought that if Vivienne had jumped, some of her clothing or possessions – her thick-rimmed glasses, a shoe, perhaps even the floral scarf she had been wearing – would have been found.

But it's not a definitive science. When I spoke to Dr David Ranson about drowning, he said there were always variables. Water temperature, depth of the water and clothing can affect whether a person will sink or float after they've drowned. While a body will generally sink to the bottom, it can also be swept along by a strong current. There have been cases of people drowning in Western Port Bay who were never recovered. And there are also sharks in the bay. Great whites, the biting ones. In 1987, just a year after this case, a shark hunter called Vic Hislop caught a huge great white off Seal Rocks on the western side of the island. A photo of the 2.4 tonne, 20-foot-long shark in the local paper made the man standing next to it look small.

*

Let's skip from sharks to nineteenth-century American fiction. Nathaniel Hawthorne's novel *The Scarlet Letter* is set in Puritan-era Boston in the 1640s. The protagonist Hester Prynne becomes

126

pregnant while her husband is in England. For her sin, she serves time in prison, then is sentenced to wear a scarlet letter A on her chest, branding her an adulteress. Hester is forever shamed, in other words. But in an act of defiance which today might be known as girl power, Hester sews each letter A in elaborate gold thread and wears them as an early 'screw you' to the community who condemned her. There's a whole bunch of other stuff in the story about the dude who did the deed, who doesn't come forward but feels guilty in private. Yada, yada. In short, the woman bears the brunt of the shame. It's a story as old as time itself.

And if truth be told, we're all a bit over it.

When I interviewed Rory O'Connor in the old Russell Street police headquarters back in 1991, he asked me if I knew what the A carved into Beth's chest meant.

'It reminded me of a book I read at uni, *The Scarlet Letter*,' I told him.

He looked a little crestfallen because I'd guessed.

I asked him if he'd noticed the book in Vivienne's house.

'No,' he said, pausing to call up a memory. He thought it might have been Vivienne's sister who'd said Vivienne studied the book at school.

I asked him if Fergus might have also studied it at school since he went to the prestigious Scotch College in Hawthorn.

'May have,' said Rory.

Because few Phillip Island locals had likely studied iconic Puritan literature, rumours quickly spread about the letter A that had been carved into Beth Barnard's chest. People wondered if it was an occult thing and whether the A stood for 'Antichrist'.

With one woman dead and another missing, could evil have somehow slunk onto the island? Or could it be someone's initial? Maybe it was a V instead; V for Vivienne. But no, it was definitely an A. A for 'Adulteress' has always been the most likely meaning even though by definition, adultery is when a married person has sex with someone else, making the *married* person the adulterer. Beth wasn't married so while she *was* the other person, she wasn't technically an adulteress. But I suppose the killer took a knife rather than a dictionary to McFees Road that night.

When rumours circulated that Vivienne Cameron was the chief and only suspect in the murder, locals had to come to terms with the fact that Vivienne had 'snapped' and committed this unspeakable crime. Because talk about the crime was not encouraged, speculation about Vivienne 'snapping' was whispered and repeated until it became the only explanation for something that otherwise defied explanation.

But is 'snapping' even a thing? Because if it is, why wouldn't we see it more often?

I contacted a criminologist friend to ask about this 'snapping' business. This was her response:

The official terminology would be a psychosis (it's not a clinical diagnosis, but a term used to describe someone who has lost perspective or connection with reality and might also be so confused that they behave in a completely irregular way). A psychotic break can be caused by sleep deprivation, drugs, severe mental stress, etc., but the thing is that people think it happens like a switch, but it doesn't. There's a build-up and a peak and then recovery. So it's unlikely that Vivienne had a psychosis.

And anyway, the idea of someone snapping is really a bit of a convenient narrative which essentially implies that we can't explain a behaviour, so informally we just have to rest on this idea that the person 'suddenly' became someone else. People who have sudden explosive behaviours are out there for sure, but they would typically have a few things that would be known underlying factors such as mental health conditions, personality disorder, neurological conditions, severe trauma history, and a history of the unpredictable volatile behaviour itself. Again, Vivienne doesn't fit the mould.

No one asked the obvious question: if Vivienne killed Beth and carved an A into her chest, wouldn't she have assumed Fergus would find Beth's body? And if so, why cover it with a doona? And why leave such an obvious sign of guilt? If Vivienne was alive the next morning, ringing Glenda Frost about patchwork patterns, then surely she meant to go on with things as if she was innocent.

If she was alive the next morning, that is . . . but I don't think she was.

In the quest to find Vivienne, police spoke to her friends. One was a woman called Sue Chadwick. Sue is one of the most courageous women I've ever met, because despite the pressure on the island to stay silent, she's never stopped talking about Vivienne Cameron and never stopped seeking the truth. The day before Vivienne disappeared, she'd been working, as usual, at the Community House. Sue, who also worked there, described Vivienne as acting normally. A week earlier, the pair had driven together to San Remo for a meeting. Vivienne told Sue she wished she could leave Fergus and take her two boys to live in Melbourne. This was not news to Sue, who had suspected trouble in the Cameron marriage for some time.

Vivienne's devotion to her sons should have made the police reconsider their 'snapping' theory. Detective Rory O'Connor was told by many people on the island about Vivienne's love of her children. In deciding to kill Beth then commit suicide, she was deciding to leave her precious sons. Was her motive that strong? Because it's a very high price to pay.

I'm not sure what the actual definition of 'snapping' is, but I would have thought it suggests something rash, or spur of the moment. But even if what Fergus said were true and Vivienne just found out about the affair at nine o'clock on the night it all happened, with the so-called wine glass attack, the hospital visit, hours of calm discussion, dropping Fergus at Marnie's, it's hardly 'snapping'. It's over six hours between Vivienne finding out about her husband's infidelity and the Land Cruiser driving up McFees Road.

So, not snapping.

Sue Chadwick spoke for many in the Phillip Island community when she said, 'I can't believe Vivienne killed Beth. I can't see her not leaving something for the boys.'

When I asked her what she meant, she said, 'Some kind of note or something to say goodbye. She thought the world of those boys.'

CHAPTER 19

TAKING STATEMENTS

When you're a crime writer and you're me, there will come a time in your life (or a couple of times) when you have to pass on information to the police. When that happens, you sit with a police officer and make a statement (or, when the police officer arrives at your house, slide your statement over to them and say, 'Here's one I prepared earlier.').

Until this happened in my life, I don't think I appreciated the difference between making a statement and being interviewed and then having that evidence tested in court. These three things are very different, but the lay person doesn't give the differences much thought. I know I didn't. Maybe if I hadn't been such a goody-two-shoes and waited for the actual detective to take my statement, I would have gotten the full 'statement experience'. I guess it would have gone something like this. 'Okay, Vikki, take me through what happened . . .' and as I spoke, the detective would have scribbled down my statement. Then at the end, he would have asked me to sign it, then at some stage, it's typed up and then I would sign it for real. Note: I would absolutely have corrected any punctuation or spelling errors because that is my nature, even if it would seem annoying to the detective. I can't help myself. I get it from my mum, and she can't help herself either. Second note: Fergus obviously wasn't like that because Vivienne's name is misspelled all through his statement and he signed it anyway.

So here's the thing about the Phillip Island case: all of the family members who were involved the night before and the morning after Beth's murder and Vivienne's disappearance gave statements, but none of them was actually interviewed at a police station and recorded with audio and video. Their encounters with police were more gentle and considered. The police took down their stories and that was it.

By the time Detective Alan McFayden got around to speaking with Fergus Cameron, it was Thursday 25 September. When I interviewed McFayden, he was still in the force, but I got the feeling he was already moving onto the finer things in life, like fishing. The reason McFayden is so important to this story is that he was the one who sat with Fergus Cameron for around ten hours taking down his statement. McFayden was every bit the professional copper, but I got the distinct impression that he felt there was something not quite right about the case. Later, after he'd retired, when dementia loosened his tongue, he had a *lot* more to say about all his cases – including the Phillip Island murder – to nurses and to his family and I guess to anyone else who would listen. He told others (but not me) that not once during the ten hours of interviewing Fergus Cameron did Fergus make eye contact. For a man of integrity like Alan McFayden, eye contact said something.

That Thursday in September 1986, Fergus was still at his sister Marnie's place. I suppose he wouldn't have been allowed back in his house until the crime scene examiners had finished their work, and that means they would have been there at least till the Wednesday. McFayden told me that when he arrived at Marnie's house, Fergus sat propped up in bed in his pyjamas, giving the impression he was too injured to get up. The photos of his injuries, taken the day before, make you wonder about this, because the day before, he was dressed and up and about. Marnie and Ian gave their statements in other rooms, and when she was done, Marnie brought in sandwiches and tea.

McFayden immediately noticed the wound just above Fergus's left ear lobe that had been stitched. Despite the injury and the pyjamas, Fergus appeared alert and composed. McFayden couldn't help but wonder what must have been going through his mind: how would you feel if your wife disappeared and your girlfriend was murdered on the same night? He expected a bit of emotion or regret, but he told me he'd never seen anybody so cool, calm and collected. McFayden had been told that Fergus was suffering from shock, which can last for hours, sometimes days. He took that into account and wondered if perhaps sedatives were responsible for the man's lack of emotion.

The language of the statement is kind of official, not really the way people speak in real life. So when I interviewed Alan, I asked him how it worked. Here's what he said.

'I write down these things and say well is it true that you're a farmer and reside at such and such? And he says yes. At the end of it, what I do, I get him to read it out, and then say, Well, are you happy with that? and he says, Yes, I'm happy with that. Prepared to sign it – yes/no, and put the duration at the bottom of it . . .

it's a long process . . . an eight-, ten-hour statement. I think from memory it went for over 25 pages.'

McFayden wrote in longhand while Fergus spoke. He prompted him with questions and noted his responses. Fergus seemed keener to talk about Beth than his wife, Vivienne. But he had to talk about Vivienne first because that was the chronology. So. He met her. He married her. They had kids together. Then he got a girlfriend. The way he spoke about his wife was very different to the way he spoke about Beth. No lovey-dovey first-meeting, first kiss, long walks along the beach. He gave their wedding date, 18 December 1976, the birthdays of their two sons, dropped a reference to his education at Scotch College (like they all do), then moved straight to 'the troubles'.

'During the first few years of our marriage,' Fergus said, 'we went through difficult times, asking ourselves, "Why did we get married?" But we weren't great ones for talking about it. This was because we come from different backgrounds. Vivienne was from Warrnambool and was living in the city when I married her and I was living in a town in country Victoria called Mortlake. At about the time of the birth of our two boys our relationship was at its closest.'

Clearly, their relationship had gone downhill since then. Not surprising, really. In September 1978, Vivienne gave birth to their first son, Dugald. Just two months later, Fergus was revving the engine in the driveway to speed off to his new night job at the Phillip Island Penguin Parade. When he became a park ranger at the Parade, he was in the prime position to interview and employ young Beth Barnard when she moved to the island some six years later after finishing uni.

The home on Phillip Island shared by Vivienne and Fergus Cameron.

Beth Barnard lived in her family's holiday house on McFees Road, Rhyll.

Beth Barnard was 23 when she was murdered. She was a young woman who should have had her whole life ahead of her.

The picture of Vivienne Cameron in the police files. Those close to her felt this picture did not look like her.

A picture of Vivienne at a community event.

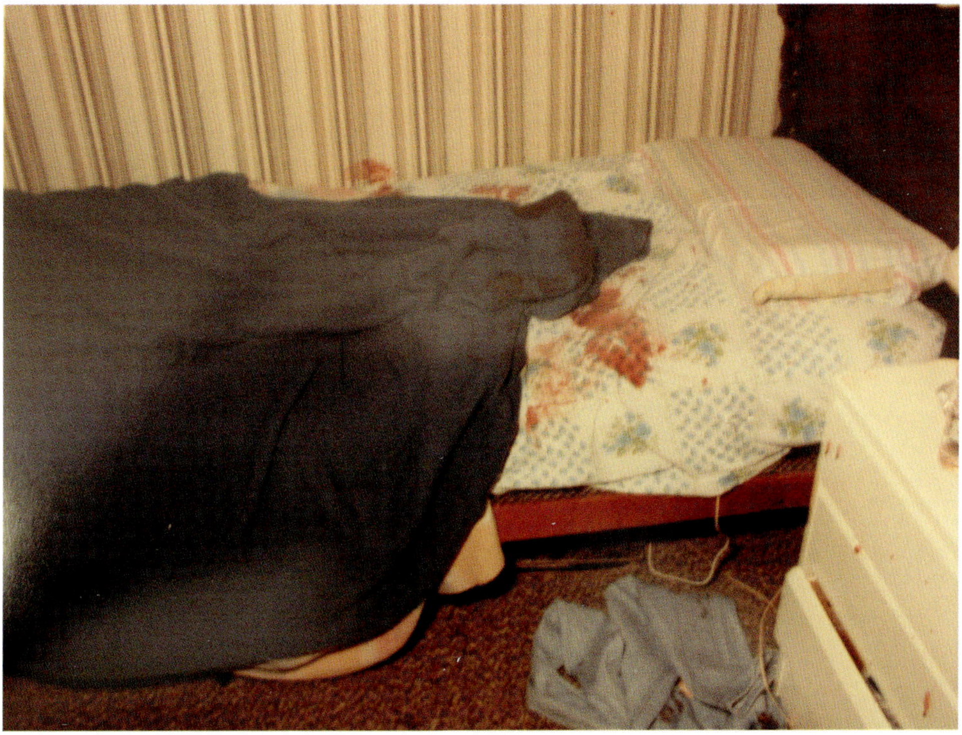

Beth was attacked while she was in bed. Note the bloodied handprint on the wallpaper. While she must have been dragged to the floor, the killer has pulled the blanket back up to cover much of the bloodied sheet beneath.

Beth's body is positioned on the floor of her room, covered by a doona so no injuries are visible. Nothing has been disturbed and the ornaments on her chest of drawers are still standing.

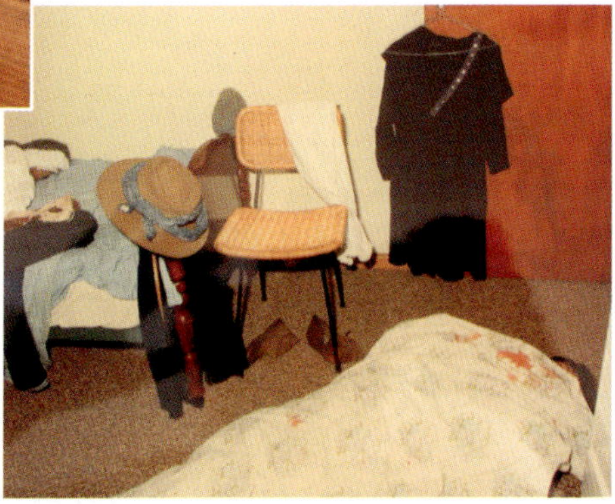

Small traces of blood were found on the tap in Beth's bathroom. It was human, but no other determination could be made.

The knife found next to Beth's body had three dots or rivets in the handle. The knife drawer at Beth's house had several knives with similar handles.

The knife drawer in the Camerons' kitchen does not appear to have any knives similar to the one found next to Beth's body. Note the two coffee cups and the pewter wine goblet on the sink.

A sketch of the kind of knife that might have made the 'double cuts' found in Beth's nightie.

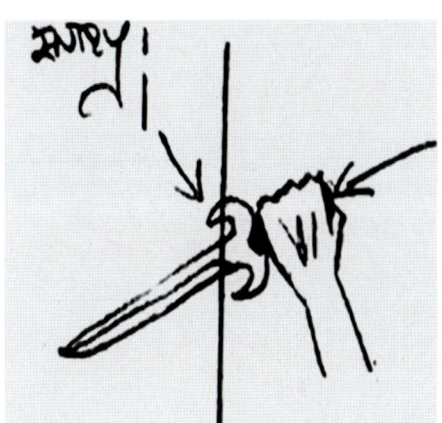

Outside Beth's back door, a crime scene examiner points to two smudges of blood. These tiny smudges – marked with chalk – made Vivienne guilty of Beth's murder. Note the rise in concrete right in this spot.

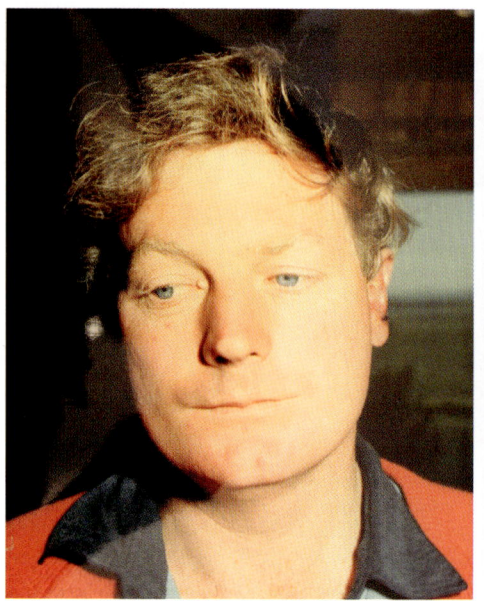

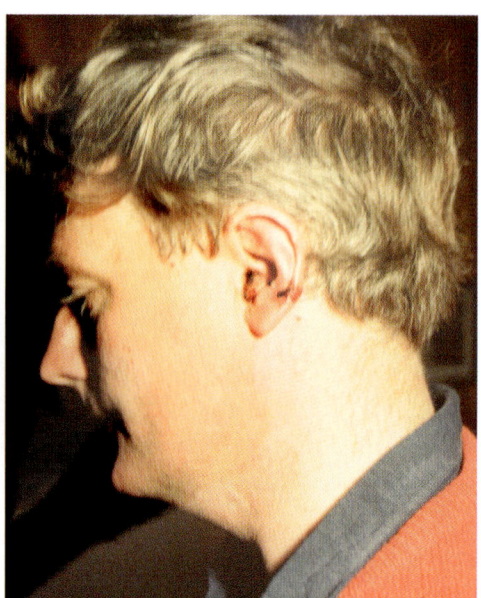

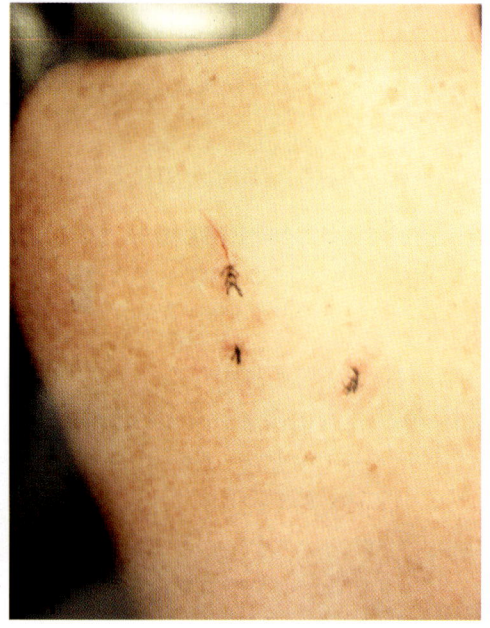

Pictures of Fergus Cameron taken two days after he received his injuries.

The Camerons' spare bedroom. Note the papers spread across the surface of the bed. Fergus said he sat on it, but it's hard to see where. The paper partially under the brown folder tested positive for Beth's blood. The straw matting on the floor is dotted with around 90 spots of blood.

A drag mark of Vivienne's blood was found on the bathroom floor at the Camerons' house. No explanation was ever given for how it came to be there.

A police officer points to the location where the Camerons' Land Cruiser was found on Forrest Avenue.

Looking from the air, you can see how far the Camerons' Land Cruiser was from the centre of the Phillip Island bridge.

The Camerons' Land Cruiser after it was removed from the corner of Forrest Avenue where it was found. Note that the sides are down, which makes you wonder how the hay bales didn't fall off on the bumpy road to Beth's house.

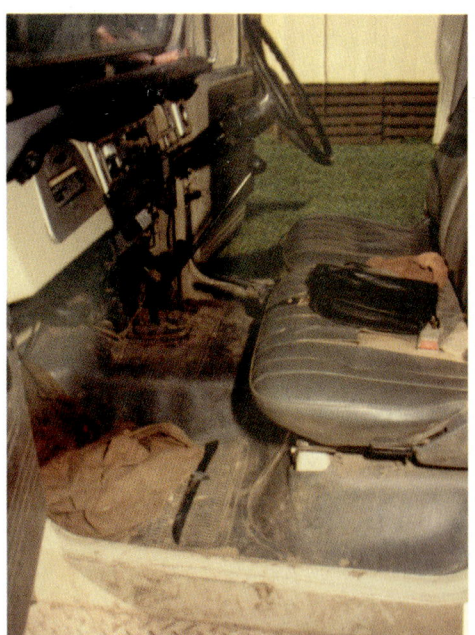

Vivienne's handbag was found on the seat of the Land Cruiser. On the passenger-side floor was a knife. Two packets of Claridge cigarettes were found on the dashboard.

'In December 1984 I was employed at the Penguin Parade when Elizabeth Barnard was interviewed . . .' Fergus said. 'She was successful in gaining employment and worked as a parade ranger. This entailed liaising with the general public and looking after the penguins. The hours she worked and mine coincided, but she worked more hours than I did. During this time, we got to know each other but nothing personally as she had her social life and I had mine.'

With his wife at home, with a three year old now and a six year old, Fergus spent his evenings at the Penguin Parade getting to know Beth. His memory for dates and times where Beth is concerned is a lot stronger than his memory for details in his own marriage. Just saying.

'In April 1985 I employed Elizabeth Barnard on my farm as a shed hand,' Fergus said. '. . . we needed assistance and it was at my suggestion as I knew of her rural background. She was on trial for a few days just to see how she handled the work which entailed general handling of wool and helping outside. At this time, I was bedridden with bronchitis and was unable to go to the shed . . . Elizabeth was employed over the shearing season which was from April 8th to the end of the month. She would work from 7.30 am to 5.30 pm weekdays.'

Not that I ever asked Alan McFayden about this, but I wonder if Fergus was consulting a diary as he sat propped up in bed in his jarmies, or whether the dates were burned into his memory.

'When I recovered from my illness I went back to work in and around the shed. My job was to run the sheep organising side of the shed and if I had time I would help inside.'

A month later, in May 1985, their affair started. And the rock was dropped in the pond that would send ripples wider and wider until they crashed violently against the outer edges.

'Sometime in mid-May just before the school holidays started,' Fergus said, 'I was due for holidays myself from work so the staff at the Penguin Parade decided to have a party. At the party Beth asked several members to go back to her place in McFees Road in Rhyll for a drink but subsequently I was the only one who did . . . At her place we sat and drank and talked, made love in her bedroom and I left after a couple of hours. I wasn't expecting to see Beth before we went on holidays but saw her three or four days later when I went to pick up my pay at the Penguin Parade. I can remember being delighted to see her and she was delighted to see me, and I didn't see her again until after my holidays being some three weeks later.'

McFayden dutifully recorded how *delighted* they both were in his notes.

But then Fergus told McFayden that he quickly got cold feet.

'When I finished holidays, I again returned to work at the Penguin Parade and determined that the relationship between Beth and myself should not continue because of my wife and two children and this was going totally against my values I did hold.'

Fergus then described how whatever values he held were quickly swept aside in his passion for the younger woman. 'Beth and myself continued to work side by side and we were both enrolled in a St John's Ambulance course. We started to use opportunities to see each other as much as possible as it was obvious that we had a loving relationship.'

And what did this loving relationship look like?

'. . . after work at the Penguin Parade we would go for a walk along the beach, sit in one of our cars or go back to her place . . . Beth and I knew that we were on the wrong track and should finish the relationship, but this wasn't a reality, and we would make love on a regular basis, approximately twice weekly. This took place mostly at her place although occasionally on the beach or in one of our cars.'

So in a nutshell, Fergus employed Beth on his farm in April, they first had sex in mid-May 1985. He didn't see her for three weeks. They resumed their affair in early June. Their relationship was by then two months old and it was clear to people who knew the lovebirds what was going on. Fergus skated around that in his statement though. He'd employed his girlfriend on the farm right under his wife's nose. And Vivienne smelled a rat – whether Fergus wanted to believe it or not.

'. . . at this time my wife Vivienne expressed resentment towards Beth. She said that Beth was receiving favoured treatment in the day-to-day work, but I don't think she suspected the relationship between Beth and myself at this point.'

Yeah, right.

One can only imagine the strain Vivienne was under, watching her husband flirting with the young farmhand while she bore the brunt of the child raising and no doubt the physical and mental labour of the family.

'Even before my relationship with Beth, our marriage was under strain partly because I was working a 90-hour week plus the fact I was hardly ever home having very little social life. Through July and August Beth was working on a regular basis at our farm and the relationship between the two of us continued in the manner in which I have previously described.'

And where did Vivienne fit in with all of this?

'My sexual life with Vivienne was extremely quiet. I am sure that she had feelings towards me, but I found it difficult to have feelings towards her. This was the situation before I met Beth, but things deteriorated between us since I met her.'

Three and a half months after the affair began, Fergus said he and Beth 'made a concerted effort to end it, and Beth moved to a town somewhere in northern New South Wales to work with a cousin dealing in sheep'. This was the first time Beth tried to leave him. But Fergus wouldn't let his young girlfriend go. 'She was away for about six weeks and during this time I was ringing her on a regular basis. From memory I would ring her about once a week.'

Perhaps Beth moving interstate wasn't a loud enough message for Fergus. When she returned in October 1985 for a ten-day stay at her family's farm in McFees Road, Fergus was around there day and night. '. . . we saw each other as often as we could. I would go and see her . . . around the farm early in the morning or after I finished work at the Penguin Parade.'

And then Beth left for a second time. On this occasion, she put an ocean between herself and Fergus. The Indian Ocean. She took a trip to the Maldives off the coast of India with two friends. They broke up again when she left but the on-again, off-again was soon on again. After about three weeks, she returned from her trip; the relationship continued and Beth once again started work on the farm.

Things were about to come to a head. Not surprisingly. Beth

was working almost full time during the day at the Cameron farm. And soon enough, Vivienne caught Fergus red-handed.

'In mid-December 1985,' Fergus said, 'Vivienne walked into the shearing shed when I had my arm around Beth. I can't remember why I had my arm around her, but I guess that it was an affectionate hug, the sort of hug you could give to anyone to whom you are close.'

I wonder if Fergus hugged his male co-workers like that.

Vivienne asked Fergus to go back to the house with her. He refused and instead spoke with her in the garden. She asked him if he was having an affair with Beth.

Fergus lied. 'No, we are very good mates.'

Side note to Fergus: She doesn't believe you.

'I can't remember but there was a long one-sided conversation with Vivienne very distraught and I was answering her questions with a yes or no, denying any affair with Beth,' he went on. 'During this conversation she said that she had tried to talk to me about our relationship but had given up because I wouldn't talk. At this stage I still wanted to keep our marriage intact, mainly for the boys' sake.'

I know, right. What a prince.

Not surprisingly, Vivienne wanted Fergus to quit the Penguin Parade and spend more time with her and the children.

'Immediately after Vivienne caught me with my arm around Beth, she started applying for work elsewhere and got work at the Werribee Board of Works farm.'

This was the third time Beth had tried to leave. Is anyone else here screaming, 'Let her go! Let her go, for God's sake!' Because we all know if she stays, she will die.

But of course, he didn't let her go. He convinced her to stay so she could continue to be his plaything on the side while he stayed with his wife.

In the next part of his statement, Fergus began to portray Vivienne as violent. He does this three times. Just flagging it for you so you'll pay particular attention. It's also timely to note that no one else painted Vivienne as violent. *She's not the one with the temper in that marriage*, people whispered. But in Fergus's account, it all started with the Christmas party. 'Two days before Christmas,' he said, 'the Penguin Parade staff had a party at Beth's place which went into the early hours of the morning and I was by no means the last to leave and at about 5 o'clock. I might have kissed Beth but nothing else happened.

'I arrived home shortly after 5 o'clock, hopped into bed and thought Vivienne was asleep. She wasn't and immediately began attacking me. She punched me in the face to begin with, and I rolled over on my stomach and she punched me on my back and she was crying, extremely distraught, wanting to know why I was so late. I said that it was a good party and after about five minutes she quietened down and I held her as tight as I could and she cried some more and I went to sleep.'

Here's my sarcastic response: Boy, Vivienne must've been comforted by that. Her husband is out all night, but gee, it was a good party. There, there.

Here's my realistic response: *WTF?* Because I'm trying to picture a man being punched in the face and simply rolling over and getting punched in the back. (Reminds me of when he describes the later attack with the wine glass, now that I think about it.) If this were a movie scene, how would it look? And when he says, *it was a good party*, is he still on his stomach being punched in the back? Has he got a face full of pillow when he talks? Or does he roll over? I ask these questions because I'm a writer and when you write a scene, it has to be realistic, and this seems off. If actors were playing the part, can you go from anger and violence to tears to calm in five minutes? I don't think that's how it works.

*

When Beth accepted the job in Werribee, she resigned from the Penguin Parade and was set to leave Fergus. From Fergus's statement, she'd kicked him to the curb. Again.

'Through the month of January I didn't see much of Beth but she was still working at the Penguins as her resignation had yet to take effect.' They did meet late one night at the pub. 'I can recall going out one night with her to the Isle of Wight Hotel in Cowes. I drove in my vehicle and she drove in hers. We spent about an hour and a half together getting there about 10 pm and leaving about 11.30 pm. This occurred in mid-January. I came straight home and nothing happened between Beth and myself.'

Not even a kiss it seems, because Fergus told the detective when those occurred.

Now we come to the bit that makes me feel most sad. It's that sliding-doors moment where if he had've kept his mouth shut and allowed Beth to follow the course of action she had decided on, two lives would have been saved.

'Early February 1986,' Fergus said, 'Beth was due to start work in Werribee and a couple of days before, I sat with her in the commentary box at the Penguin Parade and I told her that there

141

was no way I wanted her to go and she told me that there was no way she wanted to go and she immediately spoke to the senior staff and she was immediately reinstated.'

And there it is. The moment lost forever in time. She stayed and she died.

'She recommenced work on our farm in February 1986 on a weekly basis until the Friday before she died. She was employed in a responsible position making day-to-day decisions as to what happened to the livestock. At the time of Beth deciding to stay and not going to Werribee we could see that she would probably not last there.'

Why wouldn't Beth last at a job for which she was qualified? Perhaps Fergus was trying to say the pull of their love was too strong. And here comes the bit where the married man says he will leave his wife and then doesn't. I know, right. So surprising.

'I was thinking that the only course open to Vivienne and myself was for us to separate but I don't think she saw it that way at all,' he said. 'I thought that with me and Vivienne separated, the relationship between Beth and myself could be more open. Up to this stage Vivienne didn't say anything to me about my relation-ship with Beth but on a number of occasions she questioned the wisdom of having Beth working around the place.'

I'm in agony with this bit. I feel for the two women entangled with the man who shafts them both. But while making promises to Beth, Fergus was also making promises to Vivienne.

Just before we get to this bit, let's have a date refresher. In mid-December 1985, Vivienne catches Fergus in the shed with Beth and she applies for a job in Werribee. She gets it and just before she leaves, Fergus convinces her not to go and tells her he will leave his wife. In early February, Beth is back working on the farm with a pocketful of promises. There, you're all caught up. But wait! The next thing Fergus described was attempting to reconcile things with Vivienne. *Huh?* I hear you murmur indignantly.

'Over a weekend in February 1986, Vivienne and I went away to Lorne to try to reconcile our marriage but didn't talk about anything and later on we had a couple of weekends in autumn or early winter [when] we went away to Melbourne for the same purpose but again we didn't talk about anything. During the May school holidays we had a week with relations at Warrnambool and relations in the western district but things didn't really improve.'

So *at the same time* Beth gives in and decides to stay, Fergus takes Vivienne away for several marriage-saving holidays. Why would he do that just when he convinced Beth to stay on the island with him? Talk about playing with the emotions of the women who love you. Today, we have a new set of words – love-bombing, gaslighting, coercive control, abuse – to describe men who do this to women.

So while Fergus was pretending to patch things up with Vivienne, he was also ramping things up with Beth.

'At no stage did the relationship with Beth decrease, in fact we became closer,' he said. 'If her family were around, we would go for a walk along the beach and if they weren't we would go to her place and if there was no one at home she would come home to my place. She would have lunch at my place whenever she could . . . I wasn't concerned who knew about the association between Beth and me, but I didn't want to hurt my family. Beth felt the same and was getting to the point of letting her family know. This was how the situation was about the beginning of May 1986.'

And Dear Reader, just when you think things can't get any more awkward. They can.

'I forgot to say that during the month of April being the shearing season Beth and Vivienne were . . . working close together under my direction. It culminated at the end of shearing when everyone including Beth had gone home . . .' Here's the second reference to Vivienne being violent. Watch closely. Picture the scene. 'We had all been drinking . . . and when we had gone up to the house Vivienne became violent with me over Beth. She said that Beth was a scheming little bitch and in general criticising her to the point of hatred. She was very disparaging as to my admiration for Beth but did not to my knowledge accuse me of having an affair with her, but I think she assumed I was. Vivienne also said she was annoyed that Beth didn't leave and go to Werribee four months before. During this argument she punched me half a dozen to a dozen times around the face, arms and chest and at the time I was sitting on a stool in the back porch.'

Okay, am I the only one picturing Fergus perched on a stool like a gargoyle, arms raised, warding off up to a dozen blows? Coz I reckon if anyone did that to me, I'd have either jumped off the stool or fallen off the side. Or is this simply a case of good balance? Is it just me, or does this seem off too? At any rate, Fergus is oddly passive in these two scenes of violence . . . as he will be in the third. He paints himself as a picture of understanding.

'I feel that she had every right to do what she was doing, not because of my association with Beth but because she deserved some answers, and I wasn't giving her any. Although Vivienne was drinking on this occasion, she wasn't drunk but probably had enough drink to say what she had wanted to say for a long while.'

144

Rather than learn a lesson from this, Fergus told Alan McFayden how he decided to throw caution to the wind. 'From May 1986 on I was concerned less about protecting the interest of my family ... At times we would discuss our marriage and Vivienne would say things like, "Let's engage [the] services of a marriage guidance counsellor," and my reply would be, "I don't see what good that would do but give me a few weeks to think about it." In other words, I was delaying talking about it.'

Is anyone else's heart going out to Vivienne here ... if what Fergus says is true, then it's hard to believe her so-called surprise on the night of the murder that he was having an affair. Vivienne was clearly trying to keep her marriage together.

'Another approach she made during this time was that she received a $5000 inheritance and asked that I give up the penguins. She suggested that we use the money rather than invest it. She said she wanted me away from the penguins as this was furthering any relationship with Beth. Although I didn't actually tell her, I knew she was right, but I was totally opposed to giving up the penguins if it meant seeing less of Beth who at this time I was in love with.'

Yep, that affair was not a surprise to Vivienne.

If statement taking had a soundtrack, the next bit might be violins playing into a crescendo of romance, because Fergus started talking about the first time he told Beth he loved her. This must have been around the time Vivienne caught them in the shed and Beth wanted to leave. 'I first told her I loved her in December [1985] and she was immediately reciprocal. Beth was prepared to wait until the end of the year to see what happened to our marriage and I thought I would be leaving the matrimonial home and live somewhere else on Phillip Island but there was no way I was going to move in with Beth because I felt it was not a fair thing on their family.'

You can't hear me over the violins, but I'm making vomity noises.

Then Fergus admits that Vivienne knew. 'Quite often Vivienne would say to me how nice it is that you and Beth work together and get on so well and things like that. These things would be said at home in a sarcastic manner. I would have thought it was obvious to Vivienne that I was having an affair with Beth . . .'

What Fergus says next is interesting because on the night Vivienne vanished, he said she told him what an excellent father he was. Hard to see how he could fit in all that excellence when he was never there.

'I could see that even more strain was building on our marriage and all sexual relations between Vivienne and myself had been non-existent for the last two or three months before Beth's death and prior to that was very rare . . . I was working 90 hours a week which was not helping. It had got to the point that if I had any sexual relations with Vivienne, it would have been an enormous feeling of guilt towards Beth. Although Vivienne didn't say anything, I could tell that she felt rejected and I tried to compensate by doing all the things a loving husband should do such as making her comfortable and making her wanted and needed in other ways and I used to confer with her in everything but our own personal relationship.'

Weird, right? As if that would fool her.

It also seems the 'excellent' father sometimes forgot to pick up his children.

'Each morning I used to go down to the shearing shed at 7.30 am to commence the day's activities and quite often I would have to be home by 9 am to pick up one of the children and, as Vivienne works at the Community House in Cowes, I would take my son Hugh to kindergarten on some occasions but most of the time I would have him with me.

'Approximately seven weeks ago on a Monday morning, I was late picking him up at the house as I was helping Beth loading some hay. I caught up with Vivienne . . . and she was furious with me, and she abused me for spending my time with Beth loading the hay and [said] that she had had enough. I can't remember what else she said but it was along the lines of us getting help immediately to save our marriage, but I said something like, "Don't be stupid," and then drove to the racetrack. Vivienne was right behind me at this stage and stopped at the front gate at the racetrack . . . Vivienne and I had a talk but I have no idea of the conversation, but it was the last we had of a personal nature prior to the events of last Monday night.'

Here's that selective memory again. Fergus forgot what Vivienne said in their last big fight when he neglected his duty as a father because he was with Beth. But things were coming to a head, that much was obvious. Bringing the narrative closer to the murder of Beth and the disappearance of his wife, he described the recent weeks, saying, 'The intervening last seven weeks were polite and cooperative and included Vivienne's birthday and Dugald's birthday on the 5th of September and a trip to Wonthaggi last Friday week, a trip to Winton to the bike races, dinner last Saturday night.'

On the final Saturday night, Fergus and Vivienne had dinner with another couple on the island to discuss a business venture. I suppose Vivienne went because while you can cheat on your wife and flaunt a girlfriend under her nose, you can't really bring your girlfriend along to a business dinner. In a rare moment of reflection, Fergus told McFayden how, at the dinner, the other husband had mentioned a friend of his who 'virtually started off with nothing and worked his way up; in doing so, [he] lost his loved ones on the way. This statement Vivienne drew on later.' As well she might.

It's not long now. We are getting closer to the end. Beth left the Penguin Parade and the Cameron farm the Friday before. She intended to head to Melbourne and, according to her friends Mandy and Jacquie, they were going to do everything they could to ensure she didn't return; it would be an intervention of sorts. But Fergus wouldn't have known about this.

Fergus told McFayden how he had gone around to visit Beth on the Sunday night. 'On Sunday evening I left the Penguin Parade at about ten minutes to eight after work and got to Beth's place at about 8 pm. Beth wasn't working at the Penguin Parade this night and wasn't to work for a fortnight and she wasn't to work on my farm as she was taking leave from both jobs.

'When I got there Beth was despondent as she had been having trouble with her sinus infection and Dr Paul Flood had put her on antibiotics. She said also that she couldn't see any change in our relationship. By this she meant between Vivienne and [me] and I assured her that it was. I told Beth that Vivienne and I had discussed the question of separating but I was hung up on the question of timing. I left at about 9 pm and promised to return between 7 am and 7.30 am the following morning.'

Is it just me, or is Fergus staking his claim on her before she leaves for Melbourne?

'I arrived home a little bit after 9 pm which Vivienne had always assumed was the normal finishing time for the penguins. I was met by a barrage of telephone calls which is normal but on this night they continued until 12.30 am, and because of early morning phone calls I didn't get back to Beth until about 8.30 am. Beth was still very despondent but she was most anxious that I ring her at lunchtime and she was a lot more cheerful and was keen for me to see her after the penguins on Monday night which I did.'

While researching the original book, Paul Daley and I were told that Beth spent several hours with a friend called Maree. It seems she poured out her heart to Maree and decided to give Fergus an ultimatum that night, but whether she did or whether she didn't, Fergus doesn't mention it.

'After I finished work at the penguins about 8 pm or shortly afterwards, I went to Beth's place in my 1978 Holden sedan,' Fergus said. 'I drove up the driveway with my headlights on and parked in the backyard on an angle between a big gum tree off to one side in the yard and where Beth parks her car in a garage immediately behind her house.' Even though others said she was security conscious, Fergus told a different story. 'Beth came to the back door to meet me and to my knowledge this security type door was not always locked and on a number of occasions I told her to be more security conscious and keep the door locked. I went in and we sat down in the bean bag in front of the heater in the lounge room and talked about a lot of things. We were both more optimistic than we had been for a while about Vivienne and myself separating.'

This next part of Fergus's statement must've been hard for Alan McFayden since he'd been at the autopsy the day before and had seen the pathologist scrape intimate evidence samples from Beth's brutalised body. I wonder if he thought about this as Fergus volunteered details of his last sexual encounter with Beth.

'I left Beth's place at about five minutes past nine that night and we did not make love at all but we did kiss and cuddle and exchanged affectionate words and I departed . . . I said that we didn't make love that night which is true but we did the previous evening being Sunday when I visited her. This took place in her bed in her bedroom.'

This would explain traces of his sperm identified in the samples taken by Dr Anderson, but didn't explain how his sperm from the Sunday night could still be present in the external sample. We assume Beth would have showered on the Monday before she went out with her friend Maree. It also meant that sex on Sunday night occurred on the same day she had been to the doctor's, sick enough with a cold to warrant antibiotics and cold and flu tablets and a box of tissues by her bed. It's a wonder she would have been in the mood for an intimate encounter or that Fergus didn't read the signs and leave her alone.

Then came another sliding-doors moment. 'Before I left Beth's that night she said that she might go back to Melbourne that night and stay with her parents for a week at least. If not that night the following morning. I thought that she would stay overnight and go the following morning as I told her I would come around then and we never missed a chance to see each other.'

McFayden asked what Beth was wearing when Fergus left her on the Monday night.

'. . . she was wearing a woollen jumper but I don't remember the colour, and shirt, bra and light blue tracksuit trousers,' Fergus said. 'She used to wear a light blue night shirt to bed . . . On her right wrist she was wearing a silver band bracelet and chain bracelet which was a gift from me.'

And their final moments together.

'When I left Beth on the Monday night this was the last time I saw her alive . . . she walked with me to the car and kissed me goodbye so I am unable to say if she locked the door or not but I think she would have.'

The rest of Fergus Cameron's statement details the events after he got home.

Before he finished his statement, Fergus wanted to clarify something. 'When I have said I made love to Beth I am referring to sexual intercourse but I don't like using that term.'

I'm sure we're all glad he cleared that up.

*

Before we leave this statement taking, let's talk about the word 'bitch', because it comes up three times in Fergus's statement. First, he says, 'We had all been drinking including myself and when we had gone up to the house Vivienne became violent with me over Beth. She said that Beth was *a scheming little bitch* . . .' Next he says, 'She then raced at me with the glass of wine and screamed, *I knew you were with the little bitch.*' And finally, 'When we arrived at the hospital Vivienne parked outside and she was turning off the ignition she turned to me and said, *I'm just going to get the little bitch.*'

Fergus repeats the word and creates the impression that Vivienne's anger was directed at Beth . . . and not at him. But that wasn't what Vivienne's friends said, and it wasn't what Marnie Cairns would tell the police. According to Marnie, Vivienne told her, '. . . if it wasn't Beth, it probably would have been someone else'. Another of Vivienne's friends told me she wanted to leave Fergus and the island and take her two boys to Melbourne. And before we leave this point, think about who used the word 'bitch' back in the 1980s; was it a word women used about each other? Or was it a word men used when they hated women?

I was curious about Alan McFayden's impressions of Fergus Cameron. He struggled to describe the man until he settled on a single word – 'unemotional'. Yikes. Two days after his girlfriend is killed and his wife goes missing, unemotional was the best Fergus could do.

*

When I first interviewed Detective Senior Constable Rory O'Connor from the homicide squad back in 1991, I was 26 years old. The recording of our conversation demonstrates my ageist revulsion.

'God, he's 36 and she's a kid,' I said. At the time I wasn't much older than Beth had been. Any man of 36 was old and gross.

Back then, Rory agreed. 'Yeah, look, it's a real wimpy statement, believe me. And we thought that from the moment we read it.'

I also referred to Fergus and Beth's relationship as 'a midlife crisis'. Apologies Dear Reader. I now know that you don't have a midlife crisis at 36. That's ridiculous. But there was one thing that I said all those years ago that has never wavered. Fergus's statement, with all of its one-true-love, meant-to-be, couldn't-keep-away-from-each-other stuff, struck me as sickening.

'I think it struck everyone the same way,' Rory O'Connor said. And then he added something that didn't mean anything at the time. 'That's probably why they didn't want it read out – not that that mattered.'

Novice 26-year-old me didn't ask what Rory O'Connor meant, nor did I ask any follow-up questions. But what he was referring to reminded me of something crucial that Glenda Frost had told me. Not all of Fergus Cameron's statement to the police was read out at Beth's coronial inquest.

But more about that later.

CHAPTER 20

MARNIE AND IAN

On Thursday 25 September 1986, while Alan McFayden was taking down Fergus's statement in the Cairns's spare bedroom, Fergus's sister Marnie and her husband Ian were giving their statements. The detectives separated the pair and Garry Hunter interviewed Marnie while Rory O'Connor interviewed Ian.

We'll examine Marnie's statement first because new information has come to my attention that calls her account of events into question. She began with the basics by stating her full name, address and occupation as a nurse at the Warley Hospital in Cowes – the same hospital Vivienne had taken Fergus to after their argument. Marnie said she lived on a farm with her husband Ian but that the various family members were all connected. She explained that she and Ian, and Pamela, Donald, Vivienne and Fergus all operated a family business but lived in separate houses close to one another along the same road. All of the men – Ian, Donald and Fergus – worked on the farm and Beth Barnard had been their full-time farmhand.

According to Marnie, her relationship with her sister-in-law, Vivienne, had started to strengthen in the year before her disappearance. 'I would normally only see Vivienne and Pamela at family functions or when they would drop in from time to time,' she said. 'We all had part-time jobs during the week. In about May this year, Vivienne and I decided to go out for lunch on a weekday that we both had off and also decided to see more of each other . . . Vivienne confided in me about different matters.'

One of the 'matters' Vivienne spoke to Marnie about was her concern over the long hours Fergus was working. Marnie then said that in early June that year, Vivienne had also raised concerns about a relationship between her husband and Beth Barnard.

'I said, "What, her adulation for him?" and she replied, "I think it's mutual." I told her not to be concerned because it was probably only the long hours that they worked together on the property and at the Penguin Parade. She said that she had noticed the way that they looked at each other and that it was more than just their working together . . . it had caused her so much anxiety at one stage in desperation she had rung Lifeline. She . . . felt that he had fallen out of love with her. I then strongly suggested that they seek some counselling and she doubted that Fergus would agree.'

Marnie told Garry Hunter that the family all liked Beth. But because Vivienne suspected that her husband was having an affair with her, she could no longer feel the same way. While Marnie sounded matter-of-fact in this next bit, it must have gotten up Vivienne's goat because it felt like the family had already chosen sides. Marnie told Hunter she thought that Vivienne was bitter about the affair but realistic about her husband's proclivities. She'd said, '. . . if it wasn't Beth, it probably would have been someone else.'

After Vivienne told her that, Marnie began watching out for signs of the affair, but she could see no difference between the looks Beth gave Fergus and anybody else on the farm.

The next part of Marnie's statement details the night of Monday 22 September. In a nutshell, she'd called the Penguin Parade because she wanted to talk to Fergus. They said he'd left so she went to his house, but he didn't come home. Awkward visit with Vivienne. Fergus came home. She left. She got called back. Saw blood. Left it where it was. Waited up for Vivienne to drop Fergus off. Gave her Mogadon. Waved goodbye.

The following morning, she went in to see Fergus about 7 am – before leaving for work – and suggested he ring Vivienne and the local doctor to arrange an appointment. Marnie said she left for work a little after 7.30 am – *before* Robyn Dixon's call.

'At about 9.30 am, I received a phone call at work from Fergus telling me that Vivienne had phoned Robyn Dixon at about 3.15 am and asked her to look after the children as they were by themselves in the house, and that he was concerned about Beth. He then asked me to ring her number and let her know. I phoned Beth but there was no answer, so I then rang Fergus back and told him.'

I know I mentioned it earlier, but this is the bit that doesn't make sense in a sea of things that don't make sense. Again, we can only wonder why on earth Fergus would ring his sister in the middle of her nursing shift to ask her to ring his girlfriend, then ring him back.

In her statement, Marnie said, 'He was obviously very concerned and worried, and asked me to come home. I then arranged this with the matron . . . I drove straight home and found Fergus sitting at the kitchen table looking out the window. He said, "I know something terrible's happened" or words to that effect. We waited, and I kept trying the Barnards' number but there was no answer. Fergus told me that he had asked Donald and Ian to go over and see if Beth was all right.'

Nurse Lisa Price said it would have been 8.30 am, no later than 9 am. But that begs the question: what was the emergency at 8.30 that morning? The family knew that the Dixons had collected the children in the middle of the night. They hadn't expressed concern that Vivienne was missing, and certainly weren't concerned enough to check her house. They hadn't gone to Beth's yet to discover her body. Pam wasn't concerned enough to stay home from work. So why did Fergus summon Marnie home? Lisa Price remembers it was Donald who rang, not Fergus. She was the one who answered the phone. Donald ringing makes more sense because Fergus ringing Marnie at work during a busy shift to ask her to make phone calls to Beth then to ring him back makes no sense at all. But why would she say that in her statement if it wasn't true?

Marnie didn't know that nearly 40 years later we'd be asking these very questions and so she pressed on. She said she continued ringing the Barnards' house but got no reply. By this time, CIB would have arrived and the police would have been all over the property. No one mentioned hearing the phone ringing. Marnie said she then called Dr Paul Flood at the Newhaven doctors' surgery. That was when he told her that he was waiting to be picked up by the police to come over to her place.

'They arrived a short time later and Dr Flood told us that Beth was dead. Dr Flood took Fergus aside and spent some time with him.'

Towards the end of Marnie's statement, Garry Hunter asked her if she had anything else she wanted to add. Marnie did. 'Just prior to leaving Viv and Fergus after they had arrived home from the hospital, I saw the broken, jagged base of a glass under a chair in the corner of the family room. I then picked it up and put it in the bin.'

This was the last time the wine glass was seen. Like her sister-in-law, it too vanished. And as this is the only description we have, let's take a moment to consider that if Vivienne smashed the glass against Fergus's head – and the only bit left was a broken jagged base – then what did she stab Fergus in the back with?

Marnie Cairns signed her statement at 4.20 pm.

*

I wanted to wait and do a later reveal, but it turns out, I can't. I'm not good at keeping secrets. So before we go on to what Ian Cairns had to say, I want to time travel to 2023, so hold onto your flux capacitors. It was Monday 17 August 2023 when an email arrived from a man who said *he* was with Vivienne that evening in September 1986, not Marnie. But more about that bombshell later. Back to the DeLorean and power the flux capacitor to 1.21 gigawatts and punch 25 September 1986 into the keypad. If we're quiet, no one will ever know we were gone.

Ian Cairns began by explaining how Beth had come to work on the family farm. 'Elizabeth, who we all call Beth, started working for us approximately 18 months ago and helped us in all farm duties and, in particular, the handling of the stock. My brother-in-law, Fergus Cameron, and Beth had known each other for some years prior . . . as they had both worked as rangers and were still employed in that capacity. These were evening duties at the Phillip Island Penguin Parade.

'Beth worked with all members of the family [on the farm] but worked closer with Fergus as he was responsible for management of the stock. This didn't mean that they worked continuously together all day. It usually involved Fergus taking Beth to the hay storage and loading the truck. Beth would then continue around the farm whilst Fergus would continue with some other aspect.'

Unlike other members of the family, Ian had noticed signs of an affair between Beth and Fergus. 'In January this year, I did mention to my wife that I had noticed Beth and Fergus just looking at one another over the stockyard fence and I had felt that there was some feeling which had concerned me. There was another incident in March whilst Fergus and Vivienne were at our house which involved a picture from the Penguin Parade Christmas party . . . of Beth and Fergus sitting together along with other members of the family and when it was shown to Vivienne, I noticed she obviously took offence.'

Ian says he spoke to Marnie of his suspicions in January, but when Marnie heard these same suspicions from Vivienne after they started their weekly lunches in May, she told her 'not to be concerned'.

How this all must've played with Vivienne's head.

Ian then described the events of Monday night. He said he hadn't waited at Vivienne and Fergus's house till they got home from the hospital and instead left around 11.15 pm after he'd been there for an hour and a half. He only went to bed after Marnie got home and assured him they'd all had a 'calm and objective talk' and everything was all right.

The next morning, Ian was up early. While Marnie said she checked on Fergus at 7 am and had a conversation with him, Ian told a different story. 'I was up the next morning at approximately 7 am. I checked on Fergus and found him to be heavily asleep. I attended to some farm duties and gave [Marnie] a cup of tea at 7.20 am. I continued on with other duties and took a phone call from my sister-in-law Pamela at approximately 7.45 or 7.50. She asked, "What's going on?" and I told her that Fergus and Vivienne had had a difference of opinion last night and that Fergus was at my place and Vivienne [was] at home with the children. I then told her that I would talk to her when I saw her.

'I then proceeded to Fergus's shearing shed in my car to collect the Toyota Land Cruiser tray for the hay feed out. When I arrived, the Land Cruiser wasn't there and I presumed Vivienne had used it to take their eldest child to the school bus which comes about 8.10 am.'

This is odd since Pam just had called to say the Dixons had the two boys.

'Marnie had told me previously that Vivienne was travelling to Melbourne that morning to stay with her brother . . . I wondered if anything was wrong with her own car as it was not normal practice to take the Land Cruiser. I went to their Holden which was parked in the garage and turned the ignition key. I noticed that the petrol gauge was on empty and decided to fill it with petrol and service the car in preparation for her trip to

Melbourne. The farm has its own petrol tank. I then returned to my house to see if anything was wrong.'

Ian said that after he got back to his house, he received a phone call from Pamela and Donald. Donald said he would come over. When he arrived, Fergus urged both men to go to Beth's house and tell her about the argument he'd had with Vivienne the previous night. According to Ian, Fergus said, 'I am concerned for Beth.'

'Donald and I then proceeded to Rhyll in the Toyota Hilux ute,' Ian said. 'I feared the worst had happened and suggested to Donald that we should go to the police first, however we proceeded straight to Beth's house.' Ian doesn't mention calling in to Fergus and Vivienne's place along the way.

Why did Ian fear 'the worst had happened'? Why would he jump to such a conclusion this early?

'We arrived at Beth's at approximately 9.10 am and drove down the drive and parked in the backyard. We observed that Beth's Toyota ute was in a shed on our right and her white car [was] in a carport on our left, and we believed Beth was at home.

'Donald proceeded from the car to the back door whilst I waited nearby. He opened the flywire door and knocked on the back door which opened as he did so. He then called out, "Anyone there?" or something like that and getting no response, he took a couple of paces inside. I then heard him say something like, "Oh God, the worst has happened, you'd better look."

'I then entered the back door and Donald indicated the first room on the left. I looked down and saw Beth, apparently in a sleeping bag, and she appeared to be dead. I glanced quickly around the room and it showed signs of a struggle, in particular blood on the bed and blood on the wall. Donald and I left the house and drove to Cowes police station where we spoke to Sergeant Ashe . . . and reported what we had seen.'

When asked about Vivienne, Ian said, 'I have known Vivienne for approximately nine years and always found her to be a quiet and organised person. I had not seen her display any physical violence in my presence.'

Ian Cairns signed his statement within five minutes of his wife, at 4.25 pm.

CHAPTER 21

MICHAEL, MAREE AND DENISE

It was Detective Alan McFayden's job to interview a friend of Beth's called Michael. Michael ran a sporting goods store in Cowes but he'd met Beth when they'd previously worked at the Penguin Parade together. By the time McFayden got around to speaking with Michael, a week had passed since Beth's murder.

While writing the original book, Michael kept saying he wanted to talk to me, and while we had a number of cryptic conversations on the phone during which he suggested he knew more about the case, we never got around to meeting. I heard rumours that he'd been threatened. I don't know by whom. I do know that, at the time, he was living with his mother and she did not want her son talking to me.

When Alan McFayden took Michael's statement, he saw a young man's naïveté. He and Beth were close friends, but it seemed Michael wanted more from the relationship, so Beth created a narrative he could live with. With the wisdom of age, I think we can all see that now.

'She seemed to get on well with everyone,' Michael told McFayden. 'About two weeks after I started work at the Penguin Parade, I formed a friendship with Beth and over the last six months, we would be together almost every weekend as well as seeing each other almost every weekday.' They also saw each other at the Cameron farm. Michael had offered to help with the lamb marking so that he could spend more time with Beth. He explained to McFayden, 'I would have been there helping for about six days and the main reason I was there was to be with Beth – as well as liking the work.'

Michael also spent a lot of time at Beth's family farm. 'Since knowing Beth, I have been to her place in McFees Road in Rhyll many times and I believe we developed a very special relationship.' When McFayden asked him to elaborate, Michael was specific: their 'very special' relationship did not include sex. 'We never went to bed together or had sexual intercourse, and I didn't press this point as she said that she didn't want to have sex until she was married . . . she was so definite about this.'

It's a story as old as time. One person wants a friendship; the other wants a relationship.

'About a month ago, Beth and I were in my car when she said to me that she wanted to tell me something. She said that there was a little bit more between her and Fergus Cameron than being just good friends and she wanted me to know because I was so honest, and she was feeling dishonest in not letting me know.

'This matter wasn't discussed again until last Friday night when we were at the Isle of Wight Hotel in Cowes . . . she said she wanted to have a talk and told me that she was still worried about her relationship with Fergus, and me knowing about it, and she told me she decided to take three weeks off work from the Penguin Parade and Cameron farm.'

Beth brought it up again the following night when they, along with Beth's friend Maree, went out for dinner. 'Have you thought anything more about what we were discussing about Fergus?' Beth asked Michael. He replied that he hadn't.

Beth was feeling sick that weekend. She had plans to see the local doctor, Paul Flood, on the Sunday. Michael took this into account. 'I didn't say anything else as I knew it was pointless – about what was happening between her and Fergus – and she was sick anyway and I didn't want to take the matter any further.'

When McFayden pressed Michael on his thoughts about the nature of Beth and Fergus's relationship, he said, 'Although she never said, I assumed that the relationship was one not of a sexual nature because of what she told me of her beliefs of sex before marriage – strongly disapproving.'

Michael may have chosen to ignore the obvious, but McFayden had a different insight, having interviewed Fergus Cameron the previous Thursday. Fergus had freely admitted the sexual nature of his relationship with Beth Barnard.

Michael then spoke of the last time he saw Beth. 'Last Sunday morning at about 11 am, on 21 September 1986, was the last time I saw Beth alive. She came into my sports shop in Cowes and appeared to be in good spirits, and said she was looking forward to Tuesday night as we were going out somewhere in Melbourne to [see] a band. When I say we, I mean Beth and her brother Doug and another girlfriend, Jacquie . . . Beth was in the shop for about 15 to 20 minutes and left.'

Michael added he'd spoken to Beth again that Sunday afternoon and had said to her that the break from work would be good for her '. . . and that was the last contact I had with her.'

On Thursday 25 September 1986, two days after Beth's body was found, Michael placed a short notice in *The Sun* newspaper:

BARNARD Beth: My life has been enriched by your love & kindness which you shared with everyone. Friendships like ours come once in a lifetime. Thank you for being part of mine. The memories we have will keep us strong until we meet again. You will always have a place in my heart.

– Michael

The day after Michael gave his statement to the police, Beth's friend Maree spoke to Detective Senior Constable Graeme Inch at the Phillip Island Penguin Parade. It had been a week since Beth's body had been found but everyone was still reeling. Inch asked Maree about her friendship with Beth. Maree told him they'd met two years earlier, when Beth started working at the Penguin Parade.

Because Michael had just been interviewed, Maree was asked about their friendship too. Maree said that, on Saturday night, Michael and Beth had called over to Maree's house and they'd all gone out to dinner at a local hotel. When Michael went to the bar to get some drinks, the two women spoke.

'Beth told me that she had told Michael all about Fergus,' Maree said, 'but she said that she didn't think he really heard what she was saying, and she didn't get any sort of reaction or reply from him. Beth told me that she was going to bring it up again on their trip home and ask him if he had understood what she had told him the night before.' The two women quickly changed the subject when Michael returned from the bar with their drinks.

Maree said she'd worked for Michael at his sporting goods store in Cowes before he came to work at the Penguin Parade. 'After he had been working at the Parade for a couple of months, I was having a conversation with him about a couple of young girls . . . having a bit of a crush on him. When I told him this, he said that he was not really interested, but thought Beth was really great.'

Michael's interest in Beth didn't surprise Maree because a lot of young men on the island were attracted to her. Like Michael, another young man got work on the Cameron farm just so he could be close to her. He would come around when Beth wasn't home and mow her lawns and leave flowers for her. 'At times she would have a house full of flowers from admirers,' Maree said. 'Beth was a very popular girl with all people, as she had a bright and kind personality along with good looks.'

Maree said that during the previous eight months, a group including Beth, Maree, Maree's boyfriend, Robert, and Michael would meet often for dinner at various places on the island or in nearby mainland towns. 'The group,' she told Inch, 'would not always be the same, but Michael always seemed to be there with Beth and it was obvious that he was taken with her.' According to Maree, Beth often spoke about Michael, saying that he was a good, kind friend, but that she wasn't interested in him in the same way he was interested in her. 'Beth thought that Michael was infatuated with her and couldn't really be in love with her as she was just so different to him.'

Maree was aware of Beth's relationship with Fergus and the two friends spent a lot of time talking about it. 'Approximately 12 months after Beth had been working at the Penguin Parade, I noticed that she had formed a close relationship with another parade ranger, Fergus Cameron. This was apparent as when they were at work, they would always be together and the way that they would look at one another gave me the opinion that they had a special relationship.'

Maree confirmed that she, Beth and another friend, Denise, had taken a holiday to the Maldives. 'After that trip,' she said, 'Beth started to confide in me in more personal matters, although she never spoke to me about any relationship with Fergus other than that they were really good friends and shared the same interests.'

Asked when she realised the relationship between Beth and Fergus was more than just good friends, Maree said, 'Approximately two months ago, I went over to Beth's one Friday night and Fergus was there also. This was the first time that I had seen the two of them together other than in the work environment. The two appeared to be in love with each other as they were sitting together and holding hands and cuddling.

'After this night, Beth became closer to me and confided in me more about her relationship with Fergus. She used to say things like it was really difficult, because they couldn't be together and that his little boys were really important to him and that she wouldn't be able to have a normal relationship for a while. Although Beth never spelt it out, I knew she was having a sexual relationship with Fergus by different things she'd say to me, and while we were overseas, she started to take the pill.'

*

In the early 1990s, five years after Beth's murder, Paul Daley and I spoke with her friend Denise. Denise had left the island by that stage and was living in the Melbourne suburb of Hawthorn. Denise had a lot of stories about Beth she wanted to share. She also had stories about their friendship with Maree who, unlike Denise, still lived on the island and didn't want to talk to us. This was a theme I'd see repeated often over the years. Those on the island didn't want to talk, but those who crossed the bridge were happy to break the code of silence.

I remember Denise asking in a small and shaking voice how long it would have taken for Beth to die. Having interviewed forensic pathologist Dr David Ranson, I repeated what he told me: that the injuries Beth suffered would have proven fatal within minutes. Denise got teary at this point and said that in the years since Beth died, she had imagined her friend lying on the floor all night, suffering, injured, and dying a slow and painful death. It was a huge relief to know that it was quick. In that moment, I understood that the truth really does set people free.

Denise told us how she, Maree and Beth all had parents who had holiday houses on Phillip Island and that's how they all came to be living there. They were all in their early twenties and very close and spoke on the phone most days. Beth and Maree met working at the Penguin Parade and Denise met them through her then husband, who also worked there.

'We told each other everything,' said Denise.

Paul and I were keen to know what Beth was like as a person. In death, she had become 'the mistress', marked with a scarlet letter, but your final moments aren't who you are.

Although Fergus told the police that Beth wasn't very security conscious, Denise said the opposite was true. 'She always kept the doors locked.' Denise then told us about the holiday in the Maldives she took with Beth and Maree in October 1985. The time away had given Denise and Beth space to think seriously about their respective relationships: Denise's marriage was rocky, and Beth was having an affair with a married man who so far had not left his wife. In among the usual touristy things like shopping and sunbaking on the beach, Beth explained that she was deeply in love with Fergus, but that she didn't want to break up his family. She loved Fergus's two boys and at the end of the day, they needed to come first. Beth had never had a serious boyfriend before Fergus; she said he was her first true love – and the first man she had slept with. But things couldn't go on like that indefinitely. After hours of talking, Denise decided to end her unhappy marriage and that Beth was considering ending her affair with Fergus.

Something haunting happened on that trip to the Maldives. Denise told us that they had gone to dinner one night, and a palm reader approached them and offered to predict their futures. They thought it would be fun and showed their hands to the elderly mystic. Denise and Maree went first. They weren't too surprised when he promised them the usual love, longevity and children. But when it was Beth's turn, the man examined her hand and refused to read her future. Despite their light-hearted begging, he wouldn't budge and said he was too tired.

The girls laughed it off and didn't give it another thought.

When they got back to Australia, Denise stuck to her resolve and ended her marriage. Early the following year, she flew to London for an extended stay. It may be hard to believe now, but back then, overseas landline phone calls were expensive. Communication was typically by letter or telegram, or in some cases you'd make a tape recording and post that. Back on Phillip Island, Beth and Maree would record themselves on a little tape recorder chatting about island gossip – sort of like an 80s version of a podcast – before posting the tape to London.

During one of the tape recordings, Beth and Maree were having dinner with Maree's fiancé, Robert. At a certain point, Fergus appeared and can be heard talking in the background. With the tape recorder on the dinner table, Beth and Maree chatted to Denise about the most recent developments in their lives. Denise gave me this tape, and while I no longer have it, I still have the transcript. One of the things Beth spoke about was the trouble her relationship with Fergus was causing her at the Penguin Parade.

'Work hasn't been too good for me,' Beth said. 'I've been pulled up into Peter's office the other night and given the run around and we found out what happened. How I got into trouble – he seemed to know everything I was doing – all about my personal life, and we found out that [Beth names a female co-worker] dobbed on me. She found out that I had a phone call from Fergus and she told Peter, and I got into trouble because I was seeing too much of Fergus.'

The feminist in me wondered if Fergus also 'got into trouble' for spending too much time with Beth. I suspect not, because why pick on someone your own size?

A lot of the conversation was about the young man who lived on the island and mowed Beth's lawns. The women spoke about how he would sit outside her house in his Land Cruiser at night and leave bunches of flowers on her doorstep every couple of days. He'd been doing this for months. Before she left for England, Beth used to give some of the flowers to Denise.

While we understand so much more about this kind of behaviour now – along with its dangers – that wasn't the tone Beth and Maree used when they were discussing it some 40 years ago. It was more amused annoyance. Fergus was there for that part of the conversation and joked with Beth that he was surprised that she 'hasn't put up the sign'. Beth laughed before explaining to Denise, 'The sign that Fergus is talking about is a "No Right Turn After 5 pm" sign. They were going to put it up outside my house so that [the young admirer] won't keep coming around.'

Laughing, Maree said, 'He spends days and nights here, Bethals.'

'I've got this problem how he keeps mowing my lawns,' Beth said, 'and I don't want him to, coz I feel as if I owe him something when he does it. And he mowed them again on Monday and I get home and yelled at him and he got really pissed off . . . so anyway he just took off . . . I thought, *Oh beauty, I've got rid of him now*. And he came back Monday night and got mad at me and, fair dinkum, I just feel like telling him where to go now, and then he came to work at Camerons' on Tuesday coz we were lamb marking all day. I was in a real shit and I kept trying to find other jobs to do and he just comes and takes over my jobs and tells me what to do. Fergus thought I was being really good trying to do all these other things and I was just trying to get away, and so I'm just sick of him. I wish they'd do something to stop him coming around. We gave him all these hints not to come around tonight, so if he comes, I think I'll just knock him out!'

Maree then said to Denise, 'I don't know why she complains. I love having the flowers at my place. They're better off at my place than at the tip.'

Denise told us that listening to the tape in London, she could imagine she was back on Phillip Island with her best friends.

While the young lawn-mowing, flower-giving admirer certainly annoyed Beth, she never indicated that she was afraid of him. According to those who knew him, he was devastated by Beth's murder. Two days after she died, like Michael, he too put a death notice in the newspaper:

Beth, you filled a very special place in my heart. I will always hold our special friendship close. You made my life complete.

But it seems that wasn't the young man's only response to Beth's death.

According to Denise, the day after Beth's murder, he called Maree and allegedly asked her if she'd spoken to the police. When she said she hadn't, but expected to, he told her not to talk to them. Maybe he was worried that his visits to Beth's farm would look bad. Maree didn't take his advice. She told him she would do anything to help find Beth's killer.

Decades later, I was sitting in the living room of a lovely couple who knew Beth Barnard's young admirer, who by this stage was a middle-aged man. They told me he used to boast about 'the writer' who was chasing him for his story, but he valiantly refused to speak to me.

'That's not true,' I said. 'I never approached him.'

*

173

Back in 1992, there was one thing Denise told Paul Daley and me that I've never forgotten – but have never shared. The reason I never shared it was because Maree was the source of the information and she wouldn't speak with us. But the time has come. Denise said that Maree had gone over to Fergus's farm one day to offer to help with the two boys. But something happened on that visit that made Maree question whether Vivienne's disappearance and Beth's murder meant anything to Fergus Cameron at all.

CHAPTER 22

BETH'S FUNERAL

The Holy Trinity Anglican Church on High Street in Kew is a bluestone glory built in 1863. With a castle-like turret, stained-glass windows and a dark wood–panelled ceiling, it has everything you want in an old church.

Back in 1986, it was the church the Barnard family chose for their daughter Beth's funeral. Its only deficit was that it wasn't big enough for the enormous crowd that came to pay their respects. Beth's friends Mandy and Jacquie reckoned the numbers were partly due to Beth's large family. Her dad was a lawyer with lots of connections and her mum was active in the local tennis community. And Beth had two sisters and two brothers. Add the family connections to Beth's own friends and colleagues, and that meant hundreds of people turned up to mourn her loss.

Mandy thought that Mr and Mrs Barnard looked both in shock and broken. They'd had no idea their daughter was having an affair with Fergus Cameron. To lose her in such a way was a tragedy with many layers. Mandy couldn't forget the blunt message the police had given the family: Beth was killed by Vivienne because she was having an affair with Fergus.

Jacquie had never been to such a large funeral. So many people. So many memories. So many lost opportunities to intervene, to stop the tragedy from happening. Jacquie kept thinking about how stressed Beth was in her relationship with Fergus. Vivienne had caught Fergus with his arm around Beth in the shed and Beth felt really guilty about it. It was one thing to conduct a clandestine relationship, but quite another to be confronted by an angry and upset wife while her husband had his arm around you. Beth felt bad about that horrible reminder of the consequences of what she and Fergus were doing. All Jacquie wanted was to get her friend off the island and away from Fergus Cameron.

But now it was too late.

As a crime writer, I know when you lose someone you love to murder, it is unlike a normal death. When my uncle had a stroke and didn't survive, I could go to work and say, 'My uncle had a stroke and passed away.' My colleagues would respond with, 'Oh, I'm so sorry, I know what that's like. My nana had a stroke too.' But when your daughter is murdered, there are very few people who know what that's like. People react differently; some are in shock, some react with horror, and some react like it was somehow her fault. We now see this as victim blaming, but back in 1986, victims were blamed all the time and we didn't know it was wrong; it was just the way it was. Few really challenged it. And when you think about it, until #MeToo in 2017, we happily blamed victims because if you blamed victims, nothing had to change.

For Beth's family to lose their daughter with the bright eyes and infectious laugh and inherent toughness and independence, to lose her to a story that makes her death her own fault because we didn't know back then how wrong that was, must have been horrific. But now we've had time to think about it, Beth Barnard's death was the fault of the person who took her life and nobody else.

After the funeral was over and Beth's coffin had been carried out and placed in the hearse, a few close friends and family followed the procession to the Springvale Cemetery. While Beth's body was being lowered into the grave, Mandy saw a man watching from a distance, standing under a tree. She could have sworn it was Fergus Cameron. She hadn't seen him at the funeral but then again, there were hundreds of people there, so he may well have been.

*

The following day, Jacquie and Mandy visited Beth's family. The Barnards gave Jacquie a present for the wedding Beth was supposed to have been a bridesmaid at. Everyone was so sad but the murder wasn't really spoken of. They took the police at their word. Vivienne killed Beth and then killed herself. End of story.

And because it was so brutal and so unthinkable, Mandy and Jacquie didn't speak about what happened to Beth either. They thought they might have to if the police checked Beth's phone records and discovered they had both spoken to her on the night she died, but no one ever contacted them, so they figured those calls weren't important. For many years, they tried to focus on memories of how their friend lived, not how she died.

Because that was just too painful.

CHAPTER 23

ALL THOSE WOMEN . . .

I remember talking to a detective about the Phillip Island case many, many years ago. I won't name him but I think his attitude was typical of the time. I said that I'd spoken to some of Vivienne Cameron's friends and they had a hard time reconciling the kind woman they knew with the vicious killing of Beth Barnard. The detective said something like, 'Oh, you know what women are like. They all get together and gossip.'

Um, we call it talking, but anyway, go ahead.

'Yeah, they tried to tell us all that stuff but it doesn't mean anything. She just snapped.'

You may think that times have changed but they haven't.

I was recently on a true crime panel with a couple of retired detectives. I got the feeling that when women spoke, all they heard was blah, blah, blah. One of the men who was working around the same time as the detectives who investigated the Phillip Island murder told me he was certain Vivienne suicided.

'How can you be certain when her body was never found and there's no evidence that she jumped from the bridge?' I said.

To which this gentleman replied, 'Well, Vikki, her husband had just left her, what else did she have left?'

I kid you not.

'Well, for starters,' I began slowly, 'she'd have a bottle of wine with a bunch of girlfriends, and they would all toast good riddance to bad rubbish and then she'd have the rest of her glorious life to live!'

The second was another retired man detective. I had offered for the organisers to pass on my number to him beforehand if he wanted to get up to scratch with the case, which is rather complex.

Yes, Dear Reader, I can hear you laughing because you know he didn't call.

I'm going to approximate the next bits of conversation. The retired man detective declared that Vivienne was a liar and therefore guilty. The panel's rather startled host asked why he would say that.

'She lied when she made that phone call in the middle of the night,' the man said. 'She said they were at the hospital and they weren't!'

'Well, Fergus lied too,' the host said. 'Do you really believe him when he said Vivienne agreed to leave him with the children?'

To which the detective replied, 'When men talk like that, it's just white noise.'

WTF?

To think these people were actually in charge of investigating crime.

I'm going to digress a bit here to address the woman-as-liar trope. I'm always attuned to this because it's a highly effective accusation levelled at women that seems to work as a trump card.

Once a woman is labelled a liar, the world turns ferociously against her. Think about examples in recent years: Hillary's a liar, Amber's a liar, Meghan's a liar . . . These words are whispered on the winds and they take hold. But here's my advice: whenever you hear a woman labelled a liar, look in the opposite direction and see what a man is trying to hide. When women are branded 'liars', the patriarchy breathes a little easier, because no one has to act on the accusations they make. Nothing has to change.

If we accepted they were telling the truth, *everything* has to change.

And let's not forget what homicide detective Rory O'Connor said: 'A frenzied killing like that is what we would expect of a woman who just had her whole life cave in on her. Where the husband was having an affair, and he's thrown his hands up in the air and he went out of the house for the night – the only thing she could do was to try and seek revenge. And that's why I believe it . . . I've heard the stories about Vivienne . . . Nobody said a bad word about her, but it happens.'

The only thing she could do?

Seek revenge?

And *had* she just had her whole life cave in on her? Or would she be feeling such relief to escape the constant undermining that comes when your husband is having an affair right under your nose and gaslights you every time you mention it?

If the detectives had investigated who Vivienne Cameron was – beyond asking her husband, who painted her as ill-tempered and violent, and her in-laws, who suggested she was unhappily married, argumentative and in need of help – what might they have found?

We know Vivienne began working at the Community House in Cowes in September 1984 – two years before she vanished. Her job was to coordinate courses that were offered to women who used the facility. By all reports, she was good at her job and seemed to find her power away from the Cameron family. A woman who knew Vivienne messaged me and shared her observations:

> I was introduced to Vivienne at a Toastmasters' meeting in 1984 . . . My first impressions were – and not knowing anything about her at all – that Vivienne was a person who quietly assessed situations before opening herself up to let other people into her life. When l found out that she had been appointed Community House Coordinator . . . I immediately thought that she was a good choice because she would not offend anyone and would always 'play safe' having cleverly thought through her strategies to deal with the locals.

Vivienne had always enjoyed helping people, but she didn't seek acknowledgement. Her brother, Keith, said that before she got married, Vivienne volunteered to teach English to migrants at night classes. Vivienne never told anyone about this. She just did it.

Once she and Fergus wed, she quickly adapted to married life on the Cameron farm. She embraced the hard work, even after the birth of her two children. Friends remembered her driving the family Land Cruiser around the property and unloading hay bales while her two youngsters rode along with her. One friend recalled seeing the youngest boy in a pusher while she gave the sheep their immunisation needles. Vivienne also took riding lessons on the quiet with a local woman so that she could upskill for life on the farm.

Many friends recalled Vivienne's dry sense of humour. One colleague from the Community House was handing out pro-choice abortion pamphlets at a political meeting one day, and remembered seeing Vivienne. Vivienne's reaction was immediate – she roared with laughter, quickly explaining that she found it extremely funny to see the woman handing out such materials to a bunch of staunchly conservative locals. By all reports, Vivienne enjoyed seeing the establishment – to which she belonged by way of marriage – challenged.

Vivienne told the same friend that she loved her job at the Community House in Cowes because it gave her the opportunity to meet people outside the Cameron family's tight social circle. Other friends testified to her great sympathy for those less fortunate than herself.

One young mother on the island spent a lot of time with Vivienne as their children were the same age. The friend recalls visiting Vivienne often at the Cameron farm and described her as 'very quietly spoken, yet quietly confident'. This friend also said that Vivienne was very much a part of the farm business and management.

All of Vivienne's friends bore witness to her great love for her two sons and many shared memories of the enjoyable birthday parties she'd throw for them. Vivienne's boys were relatively unrestricted. They lived on a large farm and they had free run, but their mother was never far away.

One friend was driving to school to give her son his lunch when she heard the news on the radio. She'd heard about

Beth's murder, but had no idea that Vivienne was in any way connected. 'I burst into tears and had to drive straight home again,' she said. Another friend recalled that Vivienne was supposed to have been on 'milk and fruit' duty at her son's kindergarten on the day she vanished.

Vivienne's colleagues at the Community House couldn't believe she had anything to do with Beth's murder either. Isobel, the woman who was nearing retirement, first heard of it while out shopping. 'I went down to our little shop down at Smith's Beach and the man in charge there said, "Have you heard about the murder?" and I said, "What murder?" and he said, "Oh there's been a murder, a girl from the Penguin Parade." And I never thought anything more about it. And then it was the next day and I still hadn't managed to get in touch with Vivienne and I was rung to be told the terrible news that it was believed that Vivienne had killed this girl and also had jumped off the bridge at San Remo. Well, I could not believe this.'

Hearing people's accounts of how they found out about the tragedy is a good reminder that regular folk got caught up in what happened and were stunned by it. Beth Barnard's murder shocked Vivienne's friends. Her possible involvement perplexed them. Vivienne Cameron was, as one islander put it, 'the last person you'd expect to kill someone'.

*

I'm going to move away from the women who *want* to speak about Vivienne, and address the ones who shut down any mention of her. When *The Phillip Island Murder* book I wrote with Paul Daley was released back in 1993, Paul was working for *The Sunday Age*. The newspaper ran a long extract from the book under the headline 'Phillip Island's Murder Mystery'. Perhaps unsurprisingly, the paper wasn't available for sale on the island that particular Sunday. We don't believe gremlins took it, but rather it was stopped by certain locals committed to keeping the story off the island. Not all locals, but a small band who have been aggressively pushing for silence since the day Beth Barnard was found dead on her bedroom floor.

I met one of these locals the very first day I went to the island to begin my research. I stopped by the local newspaper offices, walked in the door and asked the woman in charge if I might access the archives on the Cameron–Barnard case. The woman asked what I wanted with them and I told her I was writing a book. She told me to wait right there and disappeared into the office. A while later, she came out and said she'd just rung 'the family' and they didn't want me to write the book. In other words, 'Bugger off.'

I went away empty-handed that day but if life has taught me nothing else, it's this: when one door slams in your face, you go through another that's open.

*

Years ago, an academic researcher called Noel Turner from Monash University got in touch. Noel was looking into the Phillip Island case for an article he was writing and we met up for coffee. I helped him where I could because I felt that any research into the case was good. Noel had had more luck with the local newspapers than me and painstakingly examined the coverage of the murder back when it happened. His research supported what I found. For such a sensational case, very little of it made it into the press. In his research, Noel wrote, '. . . there were clearly local elements quite content to literally bury any search for truth. Those within the Cameron family and the extended Cameron family of Phillip Island residents saw discussion of the case as an intrusion into their affairs, in both senses of the word.'

The day after Beth's murder, on page three of *The Age*, there was an article titled 'Woman Found Murdered in Phillip Island Farmhouse'. It was a graphic piece, saying the victim had been found 'with her throat cut'. The last sentence said, 'Police wish to interview a 35-year-old woman from the island'. For an article to appear in the paper on Wednesday 24 September, it would have to have been written on the night Beth's body was discovered. This suggests where police attention was at the time.

There was no mention of the murder on the Thursday, but by Friday 26 September 1986 both *The Age* and *The Sun* were squarely focused on Vivienne Cameron. The first sentence in *The Sun*'s page three article read: 'A woman police believe could help solve a murder on Phillip Island is missing, presumed dead'. *The Age* was graphic in its short article on page four: 'The killer of a woman found dead at Phillip Island this week had stabbed her in the heart, almost severed her head by cutting her throat, and carved a letter of the alphabet on her chest, police said yesterday.' It ended with, 'Police fear for the safety of Mrs Vivienne Janice Cameron.'

In the various articles, Beth's body had been found by 'an island sheep farmer', 'an employer' and 'a friend'. In a grab at sensationalism, *The Sun* on Friday 26 September printed the same article in both editions of the paper but changed the headline for the second edition. 'Woman May Be Key to Murder' became 'Letter Carved on Victim's Chest'. There was no doubt that police were only looking at one suspect in the days following the murder.

Vivienne Cameron.

On Saturday 27 September on page eight, *The Sun* detailed the failure to find Vivienne's body. The article said that police believed Vivienne 'committed suicide after visiting the murder victim'.

The case then virtually disappeared from the metropolitan print media.

The Phillip Island newspapers weren't any better. The local papers were weekly and were always behind the eight ball. In its first issue after the crime, the *South Gippsland Sentinel-Times* ran a full front-page story on a proposed quarry development at Grantville and relegated the Phillip Island murder to page 36, despite claiming that the crime had 'rocked the island'. The article ran under the headline 'Island Murder Search Continues' and suggested that the search was for Vivienne Cameron's body, not for truth, let alone other suspects. The following week's paper declared 'Missing Woman Presumed Dead' on page two. Oddly, the front page of this edition centred on a local man who had attacked another man with a machete. No one died in that incident and it's unclear why an assault would have bumped a murder off the front page, or indeed why a story about a quarry development had done exactly the same thing the week before.

The Phillip Island Sun's first coverage of the murder was on Monday 29 September 1986. The headline read 'Island Murder Devastating' and the ensuing article took up almost the whole of the front page. The article described 'shock waves' running through the community and 'rumours surrounding the murder last week were rife on Phillip Island'. Like the other articles, there was no doubt that Vivienne Cameron was the only suspect and she had committed suicide.

On page three of the next week's edition of the paper, local readers were told Vivienne Cameron's body had not yet been found, but it was assumed that she had drowned. Some stories referenced the sighting of the Camerons' Land Cruiser near the Phillip Island bridge early on the Tuesday morning. Bakery delivery driver Wayne Hunt's vague 'all I can say is that there was a car parked there' statement planted a seed. If the car was near the bridge, Vivienne must have jumped, surely. And if locals who knew about such things muttered that she would have been swept onto the mudflats and her body would have been found, they didn't say it loud enough for anyone to hear. So despite its obvious flaws, the story of the vehicle and the bridge and the suicide quickly took root. Any islanders devouring those papers for news would have cast the story in stone. Vivienne Cameron was dead before dawn and Glenda Frost's claim that she'd had a phone call from Vivienne five hours *after* dawn – despite her having an independent witness with her at the time – was summarily dismissed.

Because what would they know, those gossipy women?

CHAPTER 24

MEMORIAL SERVICES, PLURAL

Real homicide investigations are nothing like TV. They do not move quickly, and all the loose ends are rarely tied up. It would be a number of weeks before several key pieces of evidence were handed over to scientist Dr Bentley Atchison at Victoria Police's State Forensic Science Laboratory.

On 16 October 1986 – 23 days after the murder – Dr Atchison took delivery of two bags of crime scene items. His job was to analyse the evidence from Beth's house, the Camerons' house, and the Camerons' Land Cruiser. Dr Atchison would take delivery of the rest of the evidence the following week.

The next day, 17 October, just 24 days after Beth's body was found and Vivienne Cameron vanished, a family memorial was held for Vivienne. It was invitation only and took place on the Cameron farm. While it might have been intended to bring closure to Vivienne's family and children, many felt that it was too soon for such a ceremony. Especially when a lot of Vivienne's friends still half-expected her to turn up. So it was a memorial for a woman that no one was certain was dead.

There was plenty of speculation swirling about, but to this day I've never met anyone who truly believed that she jumped off the Phillip Island bridge.

One friend, Anne Davie, told me, 'People had mixed feelings about it because I think we were still in shock, but still wanting to think that Vivienne could be found, that she might still be somewhere. I couldn't go that day but I know some people found it just too hard and didn't attend.'

Dr Paul Flood, among others, spoke to the gathering about the friend they had lost. Vivienne's boys planted roses to remember their mother. Those who attended recalled many cars lined up on the surrounding paddocks – it was clearly a big turn-out.

A co-worker from the Community House, Isobel, did attend the memorial that day. It was Isobel's retirement gift that the phone call to Glenda Frost was about. Isobel said, 'It was very odd. We were invited. You only could go if you were invited and we were checked at the gate of the farm when we arrived. I went along with Marie who is now 98 years old and in care, but Marie has still got quite a lot of her marbles and she has always been terribly upset about this because she would not believe that Vivienne could do such a terrible thing.

'The children were there and they planted a rose in the garden in memory of Vivienne. And we sat there and looked out towards the sea. The house was behind us. And then we had scones, jam and cream ... everyone who was invited obviously had something to do with Vivienne – there was no mention of Beth ... But it was strange because this lady arrived, and it was very creepy because it happened to be Vivienne's sister and she looked just like Vivienne and she wore a big black hat.'

*

On the very same day, Vivienne's family announced in *The Age* that they would hold their own memorial service for her the following Wednesday 22 October at 2 pm at the Toorak Uniting Church. This was the church used by St Catherine's, where Vivienne had gone to school. A friend didn't believe the family's decision to hold the memorial was connected to the Camerons holding theirs. She said Vivienne's mother, Marjorie Candy, was very religious and would have wanted to mark her daughter's passing.

The friend remembers Fergus attending the Toorak church service, but not the boys. She's never forgotten the awkwardness. 'We were all staring at him and I think Deirdre and her mother, Marj, were trying to be civil because of the boys and wanting to keep up contact with them. It was an awful service because it was presumed that Vivienne had killed herself and the minister made reference that we shouldn't judge.'

Thank heaven for small mercies.

CHAPTER 25

THE SCIENTIFIC ANALYSIS

The investigation into Beth's murder and Vivienne's disappearance continued and detectives spoke to as many people as they could. With each lead and each new piece of evidence, the police went back to Fergus Cameron. From where they stood, the detectives began to notice a growing impatience with their visits. I was surprised when Detective Rory O'Connor told me this back when I first interviewed him.

'I think he was sick to death of us at the end of the inquiry. I think that you'll find that he's er—'

'Why would he be sick to death of you?' I interrupted.

'Well, I suppose he had it in his mind that Beth's dead, Vivienne's jumped, it's all over. I mean, let's get the coppers out of this and just get on with this as soon as possible. Every time we called at the house, the children would run and hide from us. Whether anything was said to them or not, I don't know, but I think someone must have said that we were looking for their mother and we were going to lock her up, or something like that, because the kids were petrified of us every time we called at

191

the house. You don't know what's been said of course, what the other family members have said, because they're all living in a little community there.'

While we don't know what was said, the fact the two boys were 'petrified' means that whatever *was* said scared them.

When I caught up with Rory O'Connor again to interview him for the podcast, he could still recall how the Cameron children ran from him. I asked him why the police didn't talk to them.

He said, 'They were far too young. They ran from us as soon as they saw us. Given the circumstances and given what they'd probably heard about us, and Mum wasn't there, or anything like that. We didn't blame them. We're not about to interrogate kids.'

But there's a lot of space between 'interrogating' kids and 'talking to' them. I wonder if the detectives back then stopped to think about *why* the Cameron kids ran away from them? That's not a natural reaction because kids are normally drawn to cops, even if it's only to ask if they've shot anyone. Most law-abiding parents teach their kids that cops are there to help and protect them. In my experience, the kids who would be reticent or fearful around cops are the ones whose parents pass these attitudes on to them.

I had other questions for Rory O'Connor and wanted to clarify some points that had come up over the years. 'If that Land Cruiser was missing,' I said, 'and they knew that it was missing right from the start, how could everyone have driven past it all day?'

'It seems difficult to believe,' Rory said.

'Would you have expected to have found more transference of evidence if Vivienne had committed this murder? If Beth is saturated in blood, then Vivienne has to be saturated in blood too. Not just on her hands, but on her mohair jumper. Wouldn't you have expected to find traces of Beth in the car?'

'Yes.'

'And you didn't?'

'No.'

You know by now that the scientific results in this case don't add up. While visually, the crime scene fit the story, when the analysis came back, it didn't. But that wasn't immediately obvious because scientific analysis is never fast. TV shows make us believe in instant answers. In the Phillip Island case, the results would take months.

*

On 16 October 1986, Dr Bentley Atchison at the State Forensic Science Laboratory received the first two bags of evidence. Then, on 24 October – a week after Vivienne Cameron's memorial service and four weeks after Beth Barnard's murder – he received the two final bags.

When Paul and I interviewed Dr Atchison in 1992, he explained that if a piece of evidence was labelled 'brown matter' and tested positive as blood, they would analyse an enzyme in the blood called phosphoglucomutase (PGM). By doing so, the scientists could sub-group the different blood types. In this case, Fergus and Beth were both type O blood, but they had different PGM sub-groupings: Fergus was type O, PGM 2-1, while Beth was type O, PGM 1. According to the hospital records from when she'd had her children, Vivienne was type A.

All up, Dr Atchison examined 53 items relating to the case. I have spent years going through these items, making tables about what was found and where. In my chart, I colour-coded each item to show whose blood it carried. Vivienne was labelled red, Fergus was blue, and Beth was green. There were a lot more red items than any other colour.

Except for the piece of paper found on the bed in Vivienne and Fergus Cameron's spare room, Beth's blood was found only at her house in McFees Road. Dr Atchison found traces of her blood – type O, PGM 1 – on her doona cover and other bedclothes, a pair of jeans on the floor by the bed, on her chest of drawers, and on her blue and white underpants she had been wearing when she was murdered.

Curiously, although Dr Atchison was able to determine that both Beth's pink nightie and the knife found near her body had type O blood on them, he was unable to determine the PGM sub-grouping. Looking at crime scene photos of Beth lying on the floor, you can see a small fold of fabric in her pink nightie that doesn't have blood on it. While the rest of the nightie is saturated in deep red, the small fold of pink really stands out. This fold lies on the floor on her right side – directly underneath where she would have bled from the A carved into her chest. The lack of blood suggests she wasn't alive when it happened.

Traces of Vivienne's type A blood were found on the maroon Myer Heritage brand towel taken from Beth's bathroom; on the concrete path outside Beth's back door; and on a cigarette packet, match box and face washer, all found in the Camerons' Land Cruiser. Dr Atchison also found type A blood in the scrapings taken from the spare bedroom at the Camerons' house and from their laundry and bathroom. Clothing taken from the Camerons' house also tested positive for type A blood, including a La Chic pullover, a blue skivvy, a yellow pullover, a green pullover, and a blue Cherrylane pullover. It was obvious that if this blood did indeed belong to Vivienne Cameron, she too had bled a great deal. Vivienne wasn't wearing any of these clothes when she took Fergus to the hospital. She had been wearing a pink mohair jumper, blue jeans and a floral scarf.

Dr Atchison found Fergus Cameron's type O, PGM 2-1 blood on only three items: some pink tissues found in his bathroom, the blue shirt he had been wearing when Vivienne allegedly attacked him with the wine glass and, curiously, on the blue Cherrylane pullover which also had Vivienne's blood on it. Of the six bloodstains on the pullover, two were type A and four were type O, PGM 2-1. With the blue shirt Fergus was wearing when he received the injuries to his back and ear, Dr Atchison could sub-group the blood on the back of the shirt, however only the collar had PGM 2-1 to indicate the blood was definitely Fergus's. Heavy type O blood staining on both front panels of the shirt could not be sub-grouped. Dr Atchison also measured, recorded and sketched the three jagged cuts in the back of the blue shirt, which were consistent with Fergus's injuries.

One thing that was really interesting when we spoke to Dr Atchison was his impression of the kind of knife that was used in Beth's murder. Of course, there was one found lying right next to her body, and it was his job to see if it was consistent with the damage it had made to Beth's nightie. Examining the fabric, Dr Atchison found three double cuts in the front and one in the back. They were unusual, he told us, because normally, a knife penetrating fabric would make a single cut. Longer cuts with a small gap, then a shorter cut, were odd. He asked the experts but the best they could come up with was that a fishing knife may have been used.

Dr Atchison also found two cuts in 'Item 8' – the blanket on Beth's bed – but he didn't indicate if they were double cuts as well. On the sketch diagram in his notes, he marked the blood stains at the end of the blanket that would have been over Beth's upper body.

Testing revealed no blood group substances on the cigarette butts that were found in Beth's house. The butt in the bathroom wasn't the brand smoked by Vivienne Cameron. The ones in the kitchen on the counter near the phone *were*, but again, no trace evidence was found that could point to who had smoked them.

In her statement, Marnie Cairns mentions blood on a face washer and a towel in the Camerons' bathroom, but the only face washer to be collected in evidence was the one found in the Land Cruiser. It had blood on it in a couple of spots, but the blood was Vivienne's type A. The only towel to be collected into evidence was taken from Beth's bathroom and again, it had spots of type A blood on it. According to Dr Atchison's sketch, there wasn't a lot of blood on the towel and it was maroon. If this was the towel Marnie saw earlier, one would imagine the blood would have been difficult to spot given the similarities in colour. If these were the same towel and face washer later found in Beth's bathroom and the Land Cruiser respectively, did that mean Vivienne took a towel and face washer when she set off on her murderous encounter?

Dr Atchison examined the scrapings from beneath Beth's fingernails but there was insufficient blood for him to determine its type. He also analysed the vaginal and anal swabs by putting the specimens under his microscope. He found sperm to be present on both the internal and external vaginal swabs. His notes indicate that the sperm was 'rare'. This could mean either a low sperm count or that sexual intercourse hadn't been recent. 'Vaginal external – which I take to mean vulval – is normally washed off in the shower or in the normal course of the day. I'd be surprised if you still found it there after two days,' Dr Atchison told us. Fergus Cameron admitted to having sex with Beth on the Sunday night before her death. We know Beth was out with her friend Maree on the Monday so we assumed she would have showered.

The blood found on the tap in Beth's bathroom was tested. It was human but couldn't be typed.

Dr Atchinson's report is dated 10 February 1987. It lists all of the items numerically and states what blood type he found on each of them. It took me ages to sit with that report and cross-match it to the report with his sketches, and then match each item to its location to create a table that made it all seem clear.

I wonder if the detectives ever did that. And if they did, what did they do about it when the story didn't add up?

*

When you try to fit the evidence around the story, you can't. The presence of Vivienne's blood type on so many items has never been explained. Many of these items were purported to be seen as early as 10.15 pm on Monday 22 September 1986 by Marnie and Ian when Vivienne and Fergus went to the hospital, but none of the hospital staff saw any injuries on Vivienne. Which begs the question: *Was Vivienne's blood there that early?* Because if you've bled enough for there to be more than 90 drops on the floor in the spare room, blood on the bathroom floor, and more on a sponge in the sink, then you're probably in trouble. How do you hide that from a medical team? And *why* would you hide it?

And if the blood wasn't there as early as Marnie and Ian said it was, then at what point did Vivienne bleed? Did she hurt herself before going to Beth's to kill her? And if she hurt herself enough to bleed that much, how come there are only two smudges on the concrete path outside Beth's back door and none anywhere else? And if Vivienne did kill Beth and end up covered in blood, how did she wash up so thoroughly and leave no trace of Beth's blood in the bathroom nor in the Land Cruiser? Vivienne was last seen wearing a mohair jumper. How could there be no mohair fibres found at Beth's house? She would need to completely strip down, shower and change into different clothes in order to leave no trace of Beth in the Land Cruiser. She would have had to bag her blood-soaked clothes and destroy them since they were never found. Did she bring a change of clothes with her to Beth's house?

And if Marnie and Ian's account was wrong and the blood wasn't at the house that early and Vivienne wasn't injured and bleeding when she went to Beth's, did she come home and inflict sufficient injuries to herself to bleed so much around the house, get her handbag, then drive back across the island in the Land Cruiser, park it near the bridge, and walk to the centre to jump off? All without leaving any traces of her blood in the car or on the half-kilometre walk to her death?

Yes, Vivienne's blood is very inconvenient to the story.

But there's another scenario the police didn't consider. If Vivienne bled so much at her house, could someone there have trodden in her blood, then walked it onto Beth's path? Because there's one thing I noticed recently in the crime scene photo of a man pointing to the droplet on Beth's concrete path. There's a rise in the concrete as it angles up to the step, and maybe if half your foot hit the rise, it would press your heel down. If there was blood in the tread of your shoe, it might work like a stamp.

Blood at the Camerons' house was mostly Vivienne's, not Fergus's, like his story suggested. The blood on the piece of paper in the Camerons' spare room was Beth's. If the police ever noticed this, it was dismissed. They would conclude that two drops of Vivienne's blood at Beth's house meant Vivienne was guilty of her murder, while two drops of Beth's blood at Vivienne's house meant nothing.

*

A couple of months after *The Phillip Island Murder* came out in 1993, the Victoria Police did some follow-up work. An officer by the name of Detective Sergeant Kevin Casey took statements from people who came forward, and he requested DNA testing.

In writing this chapter, I highlighted the items on the list that Kevin Casey wanted tested and found it was all the items that had already tested positive for Vivienne's type A blood. *Bloody hell*, I thought, *what a wasted opportunity*. There was already a good chance all these items had Vivienne's blood on them. The thing about the Phillip Island case is that most of the blood found at

Beth's house and at the Cameron farm was typed back in 1986–87 so we know who bled where. Naturally, the DNA results were consistent with what we already knew.

What would have been really interesting is if Kevin Casey had sent off items that *didn't* yield results under the earlier blood testing system; items that still held secrets. One of these was the shirt Fergus was wearing when he was bleeding. There are cuts in the back of it consistent with the three injuries to his back and the blood-flow pattern radiating downwards on the scientific sketches is what you would expect to see. The sketch shows heavy bloodstaining on the collar of the shirt on the left side, consistent with the injury to Fergus's ear bleeding onto his collar. There is blood down the left-hand front panel of the shirt like you might expect if your left ear is bleeding, but what seems out of place is the blood down the right-hand front panel of the shirt. All of this blood is type O, but only the sample on the back can be sub-grouped into Fergus's PGM 2-1. The blood on the right-hand front panel is type O and that's the blood I would have had DNA tested.

And let's not forget 'Item 34' – Beth's pink nightie. It was saturated with type O blood that, for some reason, couldn't be sub-grouped. I would have tested the hell out of that one.

In a volley of calls to the forensic lab the morning of 9 March 1994, Kevin Casey spoke to someone who made notes on the file. 'Unable to obtain blood sample from children of suspect (missing person). Asked if mother and sister of suspect ok to provide blood. Told him will be able to get useful information if blood sample from both these persons is provided.' So we gather that Fergus wouldn't permit his children to give samples for forensic testing.

Vivienne's oldest boy was around 15 at that time, the younger one was 12.

But Kevin Casey was undaunted. By lunchtime, he called back. Here's the note: 'Able to obtain blood sample from brother and sister. May not obtain blood sample from mother until results of brother and sister complete. Also may want further stains retested or further tested along with husband's blood sample.' I imagine Vivienne's siblings, Keith and Deirdre, were only too happy to provide blood samples if it helped the police find answers in the case. By this time, I had met with them and we had discussed the case at length. Deirdre was unwilling to create waves because, above everything else, she valued her relationship with her sister's two sons. I can also imagine Deirdre and Keith shielding their mother from having to give a blood sample unless it was absolutely necessary.

In the message notes on the file, taken that afternoon at 2.20, was another exchange between the lab and Sergeant Casey. 'Told him hair samples from children and mother would be sufficient for PCR if he was able to obtain them.' This would have presented an interesting question for Fergus Cameron. If he had refused to allow his two sons to give a blood sample, perhaps not wanting to subject them to a needle, it would have been harder to refuse the request for a hair sample on the same grounds. But we don't know what happened behind the scenes. What we do know is that the DNA testing was ultimately based on samples from Vivienne's mother, Marjorie, and sister, Deirdre, so it doesn't look like even hair samples were collected from the two boys at all.

*

When the DNA results came back that the two smudges of blood on the path outside Beth's back door belonged to Vivienne, a notation in the forensic science lab's file was made on 10 October 1995. By then Kevin Casey must've moved on from the case because the information was passed on to homicide detective Jeff Maher. The note read: 'Summarised statement for him over the phone and explained it. Findings released to media same day.'

The police had set out to check what they already knew and prove what they'd already found, and their first response was to call the media.

I wish they had set out to discover, not prove.

Well before the DNA results which told us nothing we didn't already know, when the original findings of the scientific evidence came back in February of 1987, the homicide detectives completed their brief for the inquests.

Once the evidence was presented, the case would be in the coroner's hands.

CHAPTER 26

THE INQUESTS

On 20 August 1987 a coronial inquest into Beth Barnard's murder was held at the court house in the South Gippsland town of Korumburra. I don't know how long it went for because I have been unable to obtain any records of it. You'd think records of a public court hearing into a reportable death would be available to the public, but alas, you'd be wrong. Anything after 1985 in Victoria is locked. A lawyer I spoke to, who appeared at the inquest, suggested there would be a transcript of it, but when I inquired at the Coroners Court, I was told there wasn't. So what I'll write here will be what I've heard from others over the years.

Glenda Frost was a witness that day and remembered seeing Vivienne's sister, Deirdre. Glenda got the impression that certain parts of Fergus Cameron's testimony were not heard in the open court.

'Even at the court case,' Glenda told me, 'everything didn't come out. It was the most played down on Fergus's behalf. I told all I could, there wasn't much to tell. Viv's sister was there with her husband because I looked at her and thought, *Gosh, she's the image of Viv.* I think the same sister and the husband were at the inquest of Beth that I was called up to. I could see the Camerons – you couldn't mistake them – they would have been aware.

'Fergie didn't want to be interviewed in public and the judge said, "Well, the others have been; you will be". The little they asked him wasn't the whole case ... They were outside for ages and when Fergie came in there definitely wasn't the whole questioning. It was done outside.'

Whatever was going on that day, it was perceived by those watching as some kind of special treatment. Irrespective of whatever was or wasn't said, the coroner delivered his findings at the end of the inquest. He found that 'the deceased was located at her residence in McFees Road, Rhyll with extensive injuries to her body; such injuries were caused by knife wounds and were inflicted by another person. And I further find that Vivienne Cameron contributed to the cause of death.'

'Contributed to the cause of death' is as close as a coronial finding will go to laying blame, but the inference is crystal clear. Vivienne Cameron did it.

Case closed.

*

The Cameron family was keen to have Vivienne declared officially dead. I've always wondered why; it's not a fast process – it can take years to get someone who's missing declared dead. But at the time of Beth's murder, the family was in the process of getting the racetrack and the Grand Prix up and running.

Detective Rory O'Connor wondered if that might have had something to do with the urgency.

'It's just my opinion,' he told me. 'That's just one reason I could think of ... At the time, they had around 12 months before the Australian Grand Prix was held at Phillip Island. Now, the actual track was in Vivienne's name too, and documents being signed had to be signed by Vivienne. How they overcame all that, I don't know.'

And Rory O'Connor is correct. The Grand Prix racetrack on Phillip Island was reopened on 4 December 1988 for the final round of the Swann Insurance International Series for motorbikes.

*

On 23 September 1987 – the first anniversary of Beth's murder and the day Vivienne vanished – Fergus Cameron signed an affidavit with his solicitor in Melbourne to commence Vivienne's probate process. We have no way of knowing whether this was pure coincidence, or whether Fergus had to wait precisely 12 months before starting probate proceedings. Whatever the case, on the front page of his affidavit he wrote, 'I believe that the Deceased died on 23rd September 1986.' To settle probate, Vivienne had to be declared dead, so Fergus's solicitor appealed to the coroner for an inquest.

*

Around 2003, Vivienne Cameron's two second cousins got in touch with me. Lesley Avery and Pat Hammond were researching their family tree and had found Vivienne on one of its branches. Then, just a couple of years ago, they contacted other cousins, who I also met with. They were all keen for Vivienne's case to be looked at again, especially after her mother, Marjorie, and siblings Keith and Deirdre, had died. When Pat and Lesley first contacted me, I gave them copies of my research and they in turn passed on anything they'd found. At the Public Record Office Victoria they made a copy of Vivienne's last will and testament. The handwritten document was dated 10 June 1984.

> I give to my husband Fergus A S Cameron my estate. If my husband pre-deceases me, I wish my estate to be divided equally between my children. If my husband and children pre-decease me, I wish my share of the Cameron Agribiz [the family company] to be divided equally between LAD [Donald] Cameron, PG [Pamela] Cameron, ME [Marnie] Cairns, and ID [Ian] Cairns and the remainder of my estate to be divided equally between my brother EKC [Keith] Candy and my sister DJ [Deirdre] Candy.

I felt sad when I read Vivienne's will. I bet she never imagined just two years later, she would be gone.

*

Around 1991, when I first contacted the Coroners Court to get a copy of the Cameron–Barnard file, I spoke to a helpful young man called David. He retrieved the file for me and asked if I was ringing from South Australia. I told him I wasn't and then asked nervously if maybe another writer was working on the case. 'I want to write a book about it,' I told him. 'Do I have competition?'

'No,' he said, 'the call from South Australia was from an insurance company.'

I didn't want to be nosy so didn't ask any further questions, but I wondered if an insurance company had called to find out if Vivienne had been declared dead because she had life insurance. Why else would they call and a notation be added to the file?

When I first interviewed Rory O'Connor, that was one of the first questions I put to him. 'Did Vivienne have life insurance?'

'No, we couldn't find any. We looked into it,' Rory told me.

I mentioned my conversation with David from the Coroners Court and the reference to a South Australian insurance company.

'I don't think we found any life insurance,' Rory repeated. 'We asked about it, but it's physically impossible to check every insurance company. None of the other family members thought that she had insurance.'

This might be a fanciful memory, twisted and coloured by decades of experience, but I also recall Rory saying something like, 'We checked and she was worth nothing'. If he did say these words, it was in the context of money, not her worth as a person. But women are conditioned to read into things. So here's the rub. Vivienne was *not* worth nothing. Years later, when her second cousins Pat and Lesley gave me a copy of her will, Vivienne's assets were listed as being worth $190,224.07. Part of this was money that went to Fergus after Vivienne's stepmother passed away. She'd had a life interest in Vivienne's deceased father's house, and when she died, money from the sale of the house was split three ways between Vivienne's sister and brother and Fergus, as Vivienne's heir.

While $190,000 doesn't sound like a lot these days, to give you a context for this, I bought my first house in 1986, that same year Vivienne died. It cost $64,000 – so Vivienne's monetary worth was the equivalent of three houses in the suburbs.

So, not nothing.

Is it too much of a leap to wonder if Vivienne's share of her estate was worth $190,000, is that what Fergus would have had to pay her if they divorced – less the money from the sale of Vivienne's father's house?

But none of this mattered because the homicide squad detectives thought she was worth nothing and the family claimed she had no life insurance and it was too hard to check all the insurance companies . . . so that means money was never considered as a motive.

Speaking of money, in 2004, when the Cameron family offloaded their racetrack on Phillip Island, there was an article in *The Age* in which Fergus spoke about selling it to the trucking magnate Lindsay Fox. The sum quoted in the newspaper was between $10 and $20 million. Friends and relatives of Vivienne were saddened by the fact that while Vivienne was present for the struggling years on the farm as a young wife and mother, she missed out on the more lucrative years when the Cameron family business profits skyrocketed.

*

A few days after Fergus Cameron lodged his affidavit on the first anniversary of Beth's murder and Vivienne's disappearance, Donald and Pam Cameron and Marnie and Ian Cairns signed their affidavits too. Each ended their document with a version of: 'I believe Vivienne took her own life in the early hours of the morning on Tuesday 23 September 1986'.

But why the hurry to push for probate and for Vivienne to be declared dead? According to another affidavit that Fergus filed in the Supreme Court on 19 November 1987, the surviving family members wanted to sell off some land. The document read:

> That the remaining partners desire to sell approximately 10 acres of partnership land to an adjoining party. The price of 10,000 per acre has been negotiated, which represents a very advantageous price for the land as compared with its value regarding it simply as farming land. I and other partners desire to proceed with such sale, but until a grant of representation to the Deceased's estate is made, it will not be possible to obtain a registration of an application by surviving proprietor by the Registrar of Titles to enable the sale to proceed . . .

Item 5 of the same affidavit is especially poignant. It reads, 'That the Deceased left a Will, a true copy of which is now produced and shown to me marked with the letter "A"'.

Did you all just get the chills?

*

A notice was sent out from the coroner advising that Vivienne Cameron's inquest would be held on 21 July 1988, also at the court house in Korumburra. Vivienne's sister, Deirdre, and brother, Keith, had briefed a Queen's Counsel. They wanted their sister represented in court and they wanted to hear the evidence against her. The QC travelled with Keith and Deirdre to the Korumburra court house on the appointed day. Vivienne's mother, Marjorie, was by that stage in her late sixties and had decided not to attend. Deirdre, Keith and the QC got to court before the scheduled start time of 10 am – only to find that the inquest was already over and the coroner had made his finding.

When I spoke to Deirdre years later, she told me that the family had made a formal complaint to the state coroner, who had agreed with them that they had a right to be represented and present at their sister's inquest. He offered them a new inquest, but when the family weighed it up, they decided not to go ahead with it. Deirdre was worried about their mother. She told me, 'Mum had been through enough already and we thought, *What would it achieve?*'

What was decided in the inquest? Here are the coroner's findings:

I, Mr B J Maher, Coroner, having investigated the death of Vivienne Janice Cameron, with inquest held at Korumburra on the 21st day of July 1988, find that the identity of the deceased was Vivienne Janice Cameron and that the death occurred on the 23rd of September 1986 near the bridge which separates Phillip Island from the mainland in the following circumstances.

During the night of the 22nd or the 23rd of September 1986, Elizabeth Barnard died from knife wounds in her chest and Vivienne Janice Cameron has not been seen since 1:00 AM on the 23rd day of September 1986.

On the night in question it is believed that Vivienne Janice Cameron was driving [a] Toyota Land Cruiser registered number CIL-809. This vehicle was found abandoned near the said bridge on the Phillip Island side of the bridge.

Despite an intensive police search, no trace has been found of the said Vivienne Janice Cameron with whom they wish to speak concerning the death of Elizabeth Barnard. Although her body has not been found, I am satisfied that she is dead and that she leapt from the bridge into the water and I further find that the deceased contributed towards the cause of death.

The finding that Vivienne hadn't been seen since 1 am made it clear that the coroner accepted Fergus Cameron's story that he and Vivienne had arrived at Marnie's at that time even though Fergus was mistaken. In his statement to the police, he talked about getting home from the hospital after midnight, talking to Marnie about his marriage, then talking for a further hour and a half with Vivienne. Anyone could do the maths on that one. It would have been at least 2 am. But the coroner didn't do the maths. Nor did he wonder about any of the anomalies. His finding made it very clear that Vivienne did it all. But many questions remained unanswered.

And is it just me, or did that coroner make a bigger leap than he said Vivienne did when he found she jumped from the bridge?

What evidence did he draw on to determine that Vivienne had suicided? Did he wonder about her blood in the Camerons' house? Or the moving handbag? Or the lack of transference between the murder scene and the Land Cruiser? Or the lack of a suicide note, or even a lack of a motive? Did he wonder how Vivienne got into Beth's house in the first place when the back door would have been locked? Most of all, did he understand that, with his precise findings of Vivienne's guilt, he was effectively shielding the case from further scrutiny?

For five years, the case lay dormant and was not talked about on the island except perhaps by people in the privacy of their own homes. That is until Paul Daley and I came along and began working on a book. I thought it was the perfect story to write about, and that the family would welcome it because a book would help spread their message.

The first hint I got of how wrong I was, was when I rang the Catholic Education Office to speak with the woman who'd given the talk at the teacher professional development day. She weirdly clammed up. I thought it was strange but I pressed on undeterred. I got the copy of the file from the Coroners Court and then began contacting various people to talk to them about the case. Quite early on in my investigations, I was threatened. One day I got home from work and there was a message on my answering machine from Fergus Cameron's solicitor asking me to call him. I phoned him back and will never forget what he said. 'The last person to cross the Camerons is poorer by $150,000.' The joke was on him though. I was a lowly paid teacher, and mortgage interest rates were running at 12 per cent. Talk about a woman who was worth nothing.

Not surprisingly, none of the Cameron family contributed to the book. They asked for a copy before publication but the publisher refused. After the book came out, Paul Daley and I didn't hear anything further from Fergus Cameron's solicitor. It was just like after the murder; word on the street was that nobody spoke about it. The book wasn't available on the island. The newspaper extract in *The Sunday Age* wasn't available on the island. And the cocoon of silence was barely ruffled.

But despite the strict prohibition, people still talked. Or rather, whispered.

CHAPTER 27

SENSING MURDER

Rhonda Byrne is now world famous for her TV show and book, *The Secret*. Millions of people put things 'out to the universe' because of her work. But back in 2005, Rhonda was a TV producer. She made a one-off episode of *Sensing Murder* on the 1977 Easey Street murders of Suzanne Armstrong and Susan Bartlett in Collingwood. The show proved so popular, Channel 10 commissioned six more episodes – and one of them was on the Barnard–Cameron case. To this day, I don't know how Rhonda got my number, but she called me to see if I had any copies of the book I'd written with Paul Daley. *The Phillip Island Murder* was no longer in print but I sent her a printout. I warned her it would get under her skin. She said she'd read it when she got back from a holiday but she ended up taking it away with her – read it – and had a million questions when she got back.

It was nice finding someone who shared my enthusiasm for uncovering the truth. In the long lead-up to filming the episode, Rhonda's team did their research. One day she rang me with some incredible news. She too had matched items through complicated documents and scientific findings and found out about 'Item 23', the piece of paper from the bed in the Camerons' spare room which had Beth's blood on it. This was before I'd done my elaborate grid matching all these items. It was so weird that it had been under my nose the whole time. What struck us both was that Beth's blood had been in the Camerons' house while Vivienne had taken Fergus to hospital. Marnie had described blood in the spare room and on papers on the bed in her statement.

For the episode called 'The Scarlet Letter', I was interviewed about the case, as were detectives Rory O'Connor and Alan McFayden, and several locals who wanted to speak up for Beth and Vivienne. Part of the story was reenacted. When the episode finally went to air, the thing that absolutely floored me was the reconstruction of Donald and Ian's trip that Tuesday morning, 23 September 1986. To illustrate how the timing simply didn't work, the producers overlaid a sped-up version of the trip – complete with clown music.

Remember, this was back before Google Earth and whereis.com, and so it really brought home just how impossible their timing was. Donald and Ian simply didn't have time to drive from their farms in Ventnor, check on Vivienne and Fergus's farm, drive to Beth's, discover her body, and then get to the police station ten minutes later. It would have taken at least 45 minutes. If you look at the map, all they had time to do was drive from their farms to the police station. The question that then begged to be asked was: if that wasn't what really happened that morning, what else about what the family said hadn't really happened?

'The Scarlet Letter' was all about giving the case a national airing almost two decades after it occurred. The first half of the show set out the known facts of the case. The second half brought in three psychics to see if they could provide any insights. After pondering the case for so many years, I was curious to see what the psychics would say. I'm only human. The main thing that stood out to me was that all three psychics sensed the murder scene had been staged. I always had that feeling.

The episode thrust the case back into the public conscious-ness, and while most of the 500-odd emails that flooded in after the show aired simply called for the case to be reopened and looked at again, some of the emails contained genuine leads. The producers passed on the emails to me and I got in touch with the homicide squad. Detective Senior Sergeant Jeff Maher agreed to visit so I could hand over the correspondence. I had sorted the emails and only gave him the ones that contained potential information, rather than just calling for the case to be looked at again. We discussed everything over tea and cake but at that stage, he didn't believe there was anything strong enough to warrant another look.

I contacted Rhonda Byrne a year or so after the episode went to air and asked her what she was working on. 'Can you tell me,' I wrote, 'or is it a secret?' Rhonda was highly amused with my phrasing because, of course, it was *The Secret*!

CHAPTER 28

TRUE CRIME PODCASTS

When I began making *The Vanishing of Vivienne Cameron* podcast I went back to the island and had lunch with Vivienne Cameron's friends Anne Davie and Sue Chadwick at a café in Cowes. Both women had been interviewed for the *Sensing Murder* episode nearly 20 years earlier and the decades had not quietened their quest for the truth. I admired their tenacity – and their bravery.

When Anne walked into the café, I recognised her instinctively. She was warm and friendly. Sue arrived soon after and we spent a lovely couple of hours talking about Vivienne and the island and justice, and who else might be willing to talk. I was very grateful for their participation.

After lunch that day, I went around to the local bookstore and introduced myself to the proprietor. She said in a low voice, 'Have a look at this.' I watched as she moved aside a jigsaw puzzle box on a shelf behind the counter to reveal a stack of copies of *The Phillip Island Murder*. Then she moved the jigsaw puzzle back so the books were hidden again. 'If we display them, some people get angry,' she told me. 'One woman comes in and asks to buy all the copies and I tell her that I know she just wants to buy them and burn them, and I refuse.'

She named a name that I was familiar with and it didn't surprise me.

'She always says, "Think of the grandchildren!"'

This didn't surprise me either, because there is a band of islanders, mostly women close to the Cameron family, who many years ago used the 'think of the children' cry to try and stop any talk of the crime. They then used the same cry to stop any talk of the book. When the podcast came out, and when I posted about writing this book, their cry changed to 'think of the grand-children'. These cries are ironic. Very early on, I heard that photos of Vivienne had been removed from the Camerons' house. This made me sad, because whatever Vivienne was accused of, her two little boys were precious to her, and she to them.

I was also told that the events of 22–23 September 1986 weren't really spoken of within the Cameron family, so I guessed that Vivienne wasn't spoken of either. I wanted the book I wrote with Paul Daley to be a fair and frank record of the events that her two sons might be able to access one day, should they ever wish to. The podcast would add another dimension to the story. If Vivienne's sons wished to listen, they would hear people speak fondly of their mother. And no doubt, they would hear stories about her kindness and her wit that they might not have heard before.

One of the first people I spoke to for the podcast was Vivienne's sister-in-law, who had been married to Vivienne's brother, Keith. She had been overseas at the time of Beth Barnard's murder, so felt a little removed from the events. In the end, she chose not to do a formal interview, but she did tell me lots of stories.

'What was she like?' I asked her.

'Vivienne was an earth mother,' she said with a note of nostalgia in her voice. 'I used to be jealous of her. She was so good with the kids and she seemed so happy with Fergus.'

That must have been in the early days, I thought, because in all the stories in the lead-up to the murder, Vivienne didn't sound happy at all. She sounded like a woman doing anything to save her marriage only to see it crumbling before her eyes. Was the crumbling marriage made worse because she'd known such happiness in the beginning? When a marriage turned sour, did only one partner lament the loss?

'If you ever met Fergus, you would think he was the nicest person on the face of this earth,' she went on. 'He was one of those men that women would fall in love with. He was charismatic. They were in love. But one Christmas, there was clearly something wrong. Fergus went and had a nap during Christmas dinner. You would never have thought it would happen.'

I cringed at the awkwardness for Vivienne with her family visiting for Christmas dinner and Fergus not even bothering to sit and eat with them. Afterwards, I wondered if this was the final Christmas when he'd been at Beth's for the Penguin Parade Christmas party and had come home at five in the morning.

She then told me that Vivienne's brother, Keith, had died more than a decade earlier. By then, she and Keith had separated, but they remained close. 'He died because of Vivienne,' she said, sadly. 'He never forgave himself. Vivienne called him three days before this all happened. They were going out on the Friday night to a B&S ball. Vivienne asked to come early. She wanted to leave the island and stay with him. Keith was busy and told her to come on Friday as planned.' She paused. 'He told her, "Don't come, I'll see you on Friday."'

We both knew Vivienne didn't make it to Friday.

'He felt really guilty. He felt if he had've let her come, it wouldn't have happened. Even a couple of days before he died, he talked about it. She had never asked before and when she did, he said, "I'll see you on Friday."'

*

While I was making the podcast, someone told me to interview Jane Maber. Jane was a shire councillor on Phillip Island and had been viciously attacked at the Camerons' racetrack around the time of Beth's murder. After bunny-hopping through various contacts – Jane doesn't live on the island anymore – I finally got an email address for her. I sent off a note with my contact number and within minutes, my phone was ringing.

Jane explained what happened on that dark and rainy night over 30 years ago. She had been on her way to a council meeting from her home next to the Lukey Museum at the racetrack where she worked. The gates to the racetrack had to be locked at night and as she climbed out of her car, she shone her heavy-duty torch at the padlock. Out of nowhere, a man appeared and punched her in the head. Jane went sprawling onto the ground as the man rained blows upon her.

Jane's voice was husky with age and possibly smoking. 'I'm a country kid,' she said, 'so I bloody fought back. Thank God I kept the torch in my hand. I thought he was going to rape me and kill me.'

'Did you see who it was?' I asked.

'Because it was pitch black, I couldn't see anything. And that's always frustrated me, that there wasn't something where I could have said, "Well, it was this person, I think." The weight of that torch, he would have had to have gone somewhere to get medical assistance because I could see the blood pouring out of his head. I don't think I knocked him out because he was virtually curled up in a ball but I could see him moving. He had one hand on his head and I could see the blood.'

Did the police at the time issue an alert for anyone injured? Jane didn't know. She drove to the council chambers and Councillor Steve Fullerton took her aside. No doubt her cuts, abrasions and torn dress would have raised concerns. Fullerton drove her to the police station where she reported the attack, then to the hospital where she was treated for shock as well as her injuries.

I interviewed Jane despite one of the men who was with her on the council at the time telling her not to trust me and that my book was full of lies and I'd just made the whole story up. I guess this is the stock standard response from people who want to shut down any discussion and maintain the silence.

'It doesn't work that way, Jane,' I told her. 'You can't just make stuff up and put it in a book. Everything was either verified or came straight from the statements of the Camerons and the police and everyone else involved.' I gave her a copy of the book and she became a convert to the cause.

Jane Maber never found out who assaulted her at the racetrack gates that night. But off the record, she had her suspicions. She would call me at least once a week after the podcast came out. Her message was always the same. 'Vikki, we need to get justice for Viv.' After a while, she stopped calling and I got a message that she had passed away. I hope she found the truth at the pearly gates.

*

Another person I interviewed for the podcast was Graeme Burgan who worked at the Penguin Parade with Beth and Fergus. I first visited him at his house on the island a quarter of a century ago. He still lives there. We were both older when I returned to talk to him; 34 years had passed since the events of September 1986. It's a long time to remember back, but when run-of-the-mill workplace parties that would normally have been forgotten are hitched to the memory of a murder, they become burned into consciousness.

On the drive down to see Graeme, I had the same thought I always do about the Phillip Island bridge not being high enough for someone to commit suicide. It became even more obvious as my car swept up the slight incline. From the top of the bridge, it looked even less of a drop. I also noticed something that I hadn't considered before. At 11.30 on a Sunday morning, the tide was so far out that the sandbanks encroached into the water. There was even a clumpish island where, if a person did go over the edge, they might quickly find themselves sitting on a sandbank, feeling a little foolish. Of course, the tides might have been quite different at the time Vivienne was said to have jumped. But still.

When I put this observation to Graeme, he disagreed. Having spent nights on patrol near the bridge, he's seen the worst the swirling waters could do. Once, he told me, a dingy capsized under the bridge with four men onboard. One swam to shore. One drowned. Two vanished, never to be seen again.

We quickly got down to it. Graeme told me that for most islanders, Beth Barnard's murder had been relegated to history, but it resurfaced when new people moved to the island and came across the book Paul Daley and I wrote, or the old episode of *Sensing Murder* on YouTube. They asked him in particular because he was filmed for the episode. He said the memories were fading now, but what stayed with him were the feelings.

'I remember back to those days when just about everyone knew everyone else,' he told me. 'And half the time everyone knows your business as well, because the walls talk.'

I asked him if the walls talked when Beth and Fergus began their relationship. Weirdly, the walls were quiet on that particular subject. Graeme thought it may have been because a lot of people wanted to spend time with her. 'Beth was such an outgoing person and she was new to the island and she was a bubbly young 20 year old.' It was a sharp reminder of just how young she was. Graeme said the reason that Beth attracted people was that she was a great communicator. And she needed to be because as a park ranger at the Penguin Parade, it was a key part of her job.

'A lot of the men down here were attracted to her. You gotta remember way back then, we had a nickname for Phillip Island. We used to call it "Bloke's Island". It's not so much like that now but [back in the 1980s] there weren't any women down here, especially young single women. If they came here, nine times out of ten, they would get frightened away coz a lot of the blokes were either builders labourers or surfers. A lot of the other people had grown up here and were involved in businesses or the farming community. It was isolating for most people. If you got married and had a family, well, you were lucky.'

'What else do you remember about Beth?' I asked.

'She was very social. You could always have a chat to her. Again, like I say, her getting that job at the Penguin Parade would have been partly because of that nature that she had; she could easily have a conversation with you, and she could speak with some authority.'

Graeme pinpointed something about Beth's personality that I'd heard before. 'If the boys gave her a hard time, joking about stuff, she'd give it back to them and so the guys sort of liked that because it made her one of the guys. A lot of other women would just not say anything and walk away.'

'So with all the blokes on "Bloke's Island", why did she choose Fergus Cameron?' I asked.

Graeme considered his response. 'It might have been easier to hide if she was doing it that way. She mightn't have wanted people to know that she was having a relationship with anyone. So doing that with a married man might have been an easy way to hide that she was having a relationship. It might have been just for the pure convenience. Being with someone day-in day-out, working with them, you start to feel comfortable with them. The normal barriers that you have up because you're not interested in having a relationship because you're only seeing the people for an hour or two here or there, well, you're not going to go there. Someone you're seeing all the time, you start to get comfortable in the space . . . that barrier drops away.'

Beth's friends whom I'd spoken to said she had avoided relationships because she wanted to be young and free and mates with everyone. I suppose having a married boyfriend with limited availability was like having a foot in both camps. She was mostly free to socialise, but still had someone to care about.

*

Another person I interviewed for the podcast was Wendy Orchard. Wendy had been a neighbour of Beth's on McFees Road in Rhyll and knew Vivienne too. Wendy told me that a while before Beth's murder, Vivienne would come to her riding school for lessons. Vivienne wanted to learn how to ride a horse because she was living on a farm and this was a useful skill that many others seemed to have. Wendy remembered Vivienne would drop her younger son off at kindergarten, then stop by for her riding lesson. It was a lovely memory, but it also spoke of something within Vivienne: a desire to fit in and not be looked down upon. Wendy also spent a lot of time with Beth, never dreaming that the two women she knew would be lost on the same night.

*

Released in November 2020, *The Vanishing of Vivienne Cameron* podcast resulted in an avalanche of messages, emails and new contacts. It was like a line of ants, each carrying a crumb, marching forever towards me. It was my job to position the crumbs back into a recognisable piece of cake.

One of the first messages was from an islander who didn't wish to be named. 'I listened to your podcast. Why didn't you mention that my dad saw Vivienne Cameron the day after the murder? He made two statements to the police about it.'

There were no notes about this in the file I had. I asked him how certain his dad was. The man messaged back, 'My only reservation about his report was that he didn't know Vivienne very well and had probably only met her two or three times. Nevertheless, he seemed certain enough of his identification of her to feel compelled to report the sighting to the police.'

Then came the email from the woman whose family were on their way home from Melbourne and had seen the Camerons' Land Cruiser leaving the island in the small hours of the morning. The woman's father had done the right thing by going to the police station in Cowes and reporting what they'd seen to Cliff Ashe. I asked Rory O'Connor if he remembered being told of this report. He didn't. That's not to say he wasn't told, but he certainly didn't remember it. And nowhere in Fergus's statement is he asked about it, which he surely would have been if that knowledge had been shared with the detectives. It's also something the family could have been questioned about, yet it appears in none of their statements. This information might also have increased the parameters of the search and rescue brief. The homicide squad might have wondered where the Land Cruiser was headed and directed searches for Vivienne off the island.

The sighting of the Land Cruiser, allegedly reported to the police the day Vivienne Cameron went missing, is significant because between 1 and 1.30 am, Fergus said in his statement to the police that he and Vivienne were standing in the family kitchen in their farmhouse in Ventnor. Fergus claimed that Vivienne was telling him about how she was going to go to Melbourne and was going to leave the boys with him because he was such a great father and that he could move his girlfriend in to replace her. You'll recall this part of Fergus's statement is usually met with incredulous laughter from the women in the audience whenever I mention it at author talks.

Of course, even though Fergus told Alan McFayden that only he and Beth drove the Land Cruiser, we know Ian Cairns did too because he had gone to get it the morning Vivienne vanished. We also know that Vivienne drove it, because when it went missing, Ian assumed Vivienne was driving it. It begs the question: could one of the other family members have been driving off the island between 1 and 1.30 that morning?

When I spoke with the woman who'd seen the Land Cruiser with her family on their way back from Melbourne, she said it was odd for another reason, which was why her father had noticed it in the first place. She said farm vehicles – trucks and utes and so forth – were typically for driving on the farm. 'Going-out' vehicles – like the Camerons' Kingswood – on the other hand were for when you left the farm. In other words, it was highly unusual to see the Camerons' Land Cruiser driving around the island. The woman said her dad wouldn't talk to me – and I totally understood – but he would give a statement to the police if need be. And that forced me to solve a problem that was perhaps inevitable. How could I hook him up with a detective and facilitate the interview process?

Dear Reader, I don't want to burden you with the problems of contacting the police. But it is harder for an author to squeeze through the eye of a needle than enter the gates of police officialdom. How was I to do it? Then I remembered Detective Pete, a fine and noble police officer whom I'd written about in other stories. Maybe he could help. He could. And sure enough, he pointed out something really important when I told him that the homicide squad weren't interested in looking into this case. He said, 'It's an open case. It's a murder where no one has been charged. If someone comes forward with new information, the police are bound to investigate. They *have* to take his statement.'

Pete connected me with two lovely female detectives who paid me a visit and listened carefully while I walked them through the case. They agreed it was important to get this man's statement. The statement was critical, because if it was accurate, it posed a big question: who was driving the Camerons' Land Cruiser off the island at 1.30 am?

And an even bigger question: Why?

*

Much of my discussion around this case has always been about the capability of women to commit this kind of extremely violent crime. At one stage, Rory O'Connor made the comment, 'What would you expect from a woman who's lost everything?'

I don't want to be disrespectful, but in my mind, my response was something like, 'I'd maybe expect her to go round to a friend's place or go out with the girls and drink too much wine.' That's what I'd expect because that's what I've seen many times when marriages end. The wife left with the kids while the husband found a new younger replacement. It's not an uncommon story. And yet, I've never heard of a woman arming herself with a knife and going round to murder the girlfriend. Never. I know

228

of one who confronted the 'other woman' but she did so when her husband had gone to the other woman's house. The wife knocked on the door so the confrontation was with both of them. It was the husband she was . . . I hesitate to even say angry at. She was broken by it.

And then I talked to another man who also wanted to remain nameless, and he echoed the sentiment. 'Of course Vivienne did it. What do you expect?'

It struck me the lengths men think women will go to in order to exact revenge. And I don't know why. Where in history do we have bunches of women going out with knives to exact revenge on their husbands' girlfriends? Or anyone else, for that matter? So without a shred of evidence, statistically speaking, there are plenty of men connected to the case who are happy to believe that Vivienne Cameron would have thrown caution – and her children – to the wind to seek revenge by murdering Beth Barnard. It makes me wonder why these same men – particularly homicide squad detectives who constantly see the damage that men do to women and almost never the other way around – are so quick to believe Vivienne was the culprit.

When I asked an islander who knew the Camerons well whether the family was fond of Vivienne or not, he felt they were. But when I asked why none of them seemed to look for her the day she disappeared, this man became angry. 'Why would they look for *her*?' he said. 'She'd just hurt their brother.' He said it like family loyalty would trump concern. 'Would *you* look for a sister-in-law that hurt *your* brother?'

'Sure,' I said. 'I'd be worried about her.'

'Why?'

'Um, because I'd be worried that she might have hurt herself.'

'Bah!'

He rang me back the next morning for Round 2. 'And don't forget,' he said triumphantly, 'it's women who attack with knives.'

I am instantly weary of assertions that aren't evidenced based. Men who throw random pieces of information at me contending they're facts and then baulk when I return with the truth. Thankfully the phone connection faltered and our call cut out. Just as well. Neither of us was getting any younger.

It's astonishing but sadly unsurprising that bullies who browbeat women, trying to shout them down and catch them out on 'gotcha' points, are the very ones who imagine women rising up against them with knives.

Maybe if women actually did that, these men would be more polite.

CHAPTER 29

'WHAT'S A PARADE OF PENGUINS?'

Among the flood of people who got in touch following the podcast's release was Lauren McCarthy from the North Carolina Criminal Justice System in the United States. Lauren had heard about the podcast from her friend and defence attorney, Stephanie Williams. Lauren told me she and Stephanie were sitting in Lauren's office when Stephanie first mentioned *The Vanishing of Vivienne Cameron*.

'Stephanie was like, "Girl, you have got to listen to this podcast. It's Australian. There's penguins. There's a murder." When she said it was Australian, I immediately envisioned kangaroos and all these tan people relaxing on a beach, having a drink. I've never been to Australia, so I've no idea what it's like. I basically assumed it was all beaches. So to have a story about farmers on an island was a totally foreign concept to me, and I was interested right away.

'I remember being really confused in the beginning, mostly because of the Penguin Parade. I seriously could not wrap my head around it. I was driving since I usually listen [to podcasts]

231

during my commute, and there was no question that I could google it at that time. I like to think I consume more Aussie TV than the average American. I have a basic understanding of some of the differences in the way we speak, but this "parade of penguins" . . . I thought for a minute that they called their police officers penguins and paraded them around the town each evening, but that's a bit weird, even for Australia.

'When I got home, I found out that the Penguin Parade in gorgeous Phillip Island was actually real penguins that come out of the sea every night, and so after clearing that up, I settled in to hear the story.'

Like so many others around the world, Lauren McCarthy quickly became hooked and she began spending every spare minute discussing the case with Stephanie. Then they contacted me, never imagining I would answer, but of course I did. And so, from across the world, these two women offered their expertise. It was obvious right from the start that they had a drive and determination and, of course, the professional backgrounds to bring some real insight to bear. We met over a Zoom call and mapped out ways of furthering the investigation. In due course, Lauren and Stephanie reached out to witnesses and police involved in the case.

With her background in law enforcement, Lauren saw the same anomalies as I did. She didn't believe Vivienne made the middle-of-the-night phone call to the Cameron family friends Robyn and John Dixon. Another thing Lauren found perplexing was the exchange of phone calls that appeared in all the Camerons' police statements. In particular, she noted what Donald Cameron said in his statement: 'My brother seemed very distressed and handed the phone to Ian, who said something had happened and he would speak to us later.' Lauren couldn't believe Donald didn't insist on knowing what was going on right then and there. And when Pam Cameron said, 'I informed Ian of my conversation with Robyn, and Don was going to pick up Hugh. I was very cross with the response I got from Fergus and Ian,' Lauren felt she was cross because Ian and Fergus were uncommunicative after hearing that the Dixons had the children.

'At no point do the two men say the things that every other person would say, "Oh my God! Why would Viv call them at 3 am? What did the Dixons say specifically to you, Pam? Where is Viv?"'

Lauren found it curious that the Camerons' Land Cruiser was woven into the statements of all the family members. She spent a lot of time thinking about what that might mean. Her interest was piqued when she discovered something in the files that I hadn't seen the significance of. It was 'Item 52', listed simply as 'a jacket'. Cross-checking the analysis of the jacket through several documents, it seems that this jacket was collected by Rory O'Connor on Monday 29 September 1986 from the Camerons' property.

We know that the homicide detectives took a number of items from inside the Camerons' house that day. But here comes the kicker. Rory O'Connor's statement also states: 'We then accompanied Fergus Cameron to a shearing shed on the property where he handed me a blue zip-front jacket.' The statement yields no clues as to *why* Fergus and the detectives made the trip to the shearing shed for this particular item of clothing, but it was the *analysis* of the jacket that intrigued Lauren: 'heavy soil stains inside flaps – torn on right side appears to be in pattern of deep treaded tyre, outside front-left flap heavy stained'. The sketch of the 'deep treaded tyre' found on the jacket and included in the scientific report was very similar to the photos of the Land Cruiser's tyres.

Did that mean the Land Cruiser ran over the jacket?

Or could there be a more sinister explanation – could someone have been wearing the jacket at the time?

Several other items were collected that day from behind the door in Vivienne and Fergus's bedroom and there was dirt and blood on some of them. There was 'Item 48', a blue Cherrylane pullover with both Vivienne's type A blood and Fergus's type O, PGM 2-1 blood on it. There was 'Item 45', a pair of blue jeans with a small amount of plant debris on the outside and the entire left leg stained brown. The jeans returned a weak positive for blood on the right leg and the waist. 'Item 49' was a blue skivvy that tested positive for type A blood on the back inside and front outside. Then 'Item 46', a pair of socks, was found to be soiled with plant debris under the feet.

Lauren sent me a message:

The top clothing items based on stain location indicate to me that they were actively worn while blood was being spattered/ dispersed because it is on the back and front as well as some articles on the inside and outside. The soiled pants that were positive for blood as well as the socks with plant debris under the feet. Typically, you would not have plant debris under the feet unless your shoes were off and walking outside.

The feeling I am getting is that Rory asked Fergus, 'Where is Vivienne's clothing?' It seems that the jacket was

Vivienne's. The articles found near the blood smear on the dresser were most likely lying on the floor when the blood was dispersed because of the random spatter and only on one side.

The tyre track on Vivienne's jacket, plus bloody jeans and soiled socks with plant debris, especially on the right-side leg of the jeans and right inside flap of the jacket makes me think they are all connected as being worn at the same time while she was bleeding.

You also have the location of the jacket at the shearing shed which is where the Land Cruiser was stored which is the vehicle with tyres that match the tyre [tread] on the jacket.

With so many items of Vivienne's clothing stained with blood and soil and plant debris, as well as the jacket with its tyre tread impressions, Lauren wondered if the police ever looked into the possibility of the Camerons' own Land Cruiser being used as a weapon.

Like so many aspects of this case, we might never know the answer to this question, but the questions still need to be asked.

*

The DNA report that was done back in 1994–95 is complex and I have no experience in interpreting these kinds of scientific results. Lauren offered to do it for me. 'The other thing that still really bothers me is the control testing for the DNA showing a blood group A result for the blue skivvy,' she messaged. 'It should not have had a result as a control. This could have contaminated everything else tested as well as the blood scraping [the only thing

235

putting Viv at the scene] showing both A and B activity.' I'll take her word for it because it's incredibly hard to interpret.

Another thing Lauren did was smash wine glasses against things to try and approximate the alleged wine-glass attack on Fergus. She sent me a photo of one of her experimental wine glasses with the note: 'There is no way she [Vivienne] could have hit him in the ear then three more times with the glass if it had already broken against his ear. It would've shattered and cut her hand if she continued to try to use it.'

While Lauren looked at the case from a law enforcement perspective, Stephanie looked at it from a legal perspective. She found it hard to believe Vivienne had a motive to kill Beth. She knew her husband was unfaithful. Fergus said she told him she would leave the marriage. Whether his account is credible, we don't know, but Vivienne had hinted to others that she wanted to take the boys and move to Melbourne. She had even called her brother, wanting to come and stay with him earlier than the planned visit on the Friday.

'Fergus was fine maintaining the marriage as it was,' Stephanie said, 'which was the point of contention with Beth. Vivienne would have no reason to kill Beth because Beth was not a threat to her lifestyle, kids or finances.' Stephanie also queried the so-called rage described by Fergus when Vivienne had told others she had either suspected or known about the affair for a year or more.

I asked Stephanie if, in the 18 years she'd been a lawyer, she'd ever had a client who learned information then acted on it many months later.

The answer was no. 'That's simply not how emotions work,' she said.

If Vivienne had've left like Fergus said she intended to, she would have been entitled to half of their assets of the farm and her share of the racetrack, which was just about to get the Grand Prix. When she vanished, there was no messy divorce or custody battle, and Fergus got to keep everything – the house, the farm, the kids, and Vivienne's share of the racetrack. And because the blame fell squarely on his missing wife, Fergus maintained his reputation and not only got sympathy from the community, but its staunch support. He also got its silence. So from a legal perspective, there were no gains for Vivienne in killing Beth. Quite the opposite in fact. She lost everything, and everything she lost went to Fergus.

What followed with the North Carolina women was months of back-and-forth emails, Zoom calls and messages. I also spoke with Nikki, who was a homicide detective friend of theirs. Nikki felt the crime scene in Beth Barnard's bedroom showed rage, but it was clear to her that the person who did it had control over Beth almost instantly because very little around her was disturbed. Nikki felt the covering of the body with the doona was a sign of remorse and attachment. And with regard to the fact the police settled so quickly on Vivienne as the only suspect, Nikki said, 'Men can't see past a jealous bitter woman.'

And that really summed up how this case was perceived. Vivienne Cameron was jealous and bitter and she just 'snapped'. According to the men who investigated it at least.

So why did this case capture the attention of these two women from the other side of the world? Lauren tried to encapsulate what it meant to her.

I think what was so striking to me was the further I got into the details of the case, the more questions I had. The brutality of Beth's murder and the attack on both women's character really angered me, especially this idea that Vivienne would leave her young boys.

The conflict of interest and narratives in the investigation just did not make practical sense to me. As a woman, a mother and as someone working in this field of investigations, I believe the individual capable of such blatant disregard of human life should be held accountable.

Maybe it's the advocate in me that believes these women deserve dignity and justice in the lives they lead as well as in their deaths.

With all the help and guidance that Lauren and Stephanie provided, the most important moment came when Lauren drew my attention to the Camerons' bathroom floor. I'd sent them all the photos and statements, and I knew the bathroom floor had tested positive for type A blood. But I hadn't blown up that particular photo. That's what Lauren did. She enlarged it and pointed out the blood. What was revealed was upsetting. I knew it was Vivienne's blood, but when you looked closely, it came into focus.

There was a huge drag mark in Vivienne's blood. Right across the bathroom floor.

I'd missed it, but most importantly, so had the police back in 1986.

CHAPTER 30

UNDER INVESTIGATION

In early 2021, the Channel 9 show *Under Investigation* expressed interest in the story. The format of the show had the host, journalist Liz Hayes of *60 Minutes* fame, sitting at a conference table discussing cases with a handful of experts.

I met with producer Danielle Collis and we discussed the importance of getting female voices into the story. I thought it was fitting because most of the people who spoke up on the podcast were women. The friends of Vivienne's and Beth's who had lived over three decades with the feeling that justice had never been done, that their stories hadn't been told, and that the women had just been lost in time; they should be the ones to speak. Women could more easily step into the shoes of Vivienne or Beth and feel for them. They could imagine how they became ensnared by the charismatic charms of Fergus Cameron; charms that ultimately led to their demise. Women felt Vivienne's plight as a mother. And they felt for her two little boys.

I told Danielle about Lauren and Stephanie in North Carolina, and she was fascinated that two women on the other side of the world had become so interested in the case that they started their own casefile on it. She made immediate plans to include an interview with them on the show.

Danielle and I then did a day trip to Phillip Island. Driving along the sweep of road approaching the bridge – the one that gives you your first view of the island – I took in the bridge and said what I always say, 'It's just not high enough.'

Danielle could see what I meant. She got out her camera and took pictures of the bridge from that vantage point.

Having spent so much time investigating, writing and talking about the case, I can no longer visit Phillip Island as an innocent. The beauty in the rocky outcrops looks treacherous and dangerous to me. The splendour of the sea is diminished because its choppy waters once held boats with police divers looking for Vivienne's body. But sometimes, the pull of the place and its undeniable majesty makes me forget. Looking out over the Nobbies on the western side, you see a rugged beauty that draws the eye and doesn't let it go. It's wild out there. Waves crash over dark rocks, and the water turns turquoise and luminous at the point of impact, before spraying into the air. The vista is hypnotising.

On our visit, Danielle and I had lunch with Sue Chadwick. Sue had always been Vivienne's champion. Even when Paul Daley and I were researching the original book back in the early 1990s – when the case was fresh and the atmosphere on the island was especially charged – Sue was willing to speak to us because she wanted justice. For people like Sue, the truth was much more important than any repercussions that might come from the telling of it. On a cold winter's day, Sue made us spicy pumpkin soup. I could see Danielle was charmed by her. Loved her forth-rightness. We made plans to meet again that would be thwarted by a re-emergence of COVID-19.

After we left the warmth of Sue's house, Danielle and I drove down McFees Road in Rhyll. She had never been there before. We went right to the end of the road and turned around, just as the car Margaret McFee said she heard the night Beth was murdered had done. We then pulled up outside the Barnards' old holiday house, Pleasant Point, and talked about how different things looked.

*

I was booked to fly to Sydney to film the episode of *Under Investigation* but like so much in 2021, it was cancelled and then cancelled again. Sydney locked down, then Victoria locked down, and travel became impossible. Filming, however, wasn't, because the media had exemptions during the pandemic, and so it was arranged that Rory O'Connor and I would film at a studio in Port Melbourne along with the investigator Valentine Smith whom the show had used on a number of other cases. Val is a retired cop, perhaps of a similar vintage to Rory, who by that stage was long retired from the Victoria Police.

Because I'd hardly left the house during lockdown, it was exciting to get in my car and drive to the studio. The deserted roads made heavy traffic a distant memory. It was good seeing Rory and his wife again. Even though we held quite different views about the case, it didn't make us adversaries.

Anyone who's been on a film set knows it takes ages for the cameras to finally roll. But roll they did, eventually. We could see Liz Hayes through the monitor. She was sitting with police forensic psychologist, Dr Sarah Yule, and retired homicide detective and author, Gary Jubelin. When Danielle had told me that the panel would have Gary, Rory and Val on it, my first thought was, *My panel of women is mostly men.* But these things were out of my hands.

Once the filming started, Liz Hayes skilfully guided us all through the case, starting at the beginning. It soon became pretty clear that the three male panellists were convinced that the case was exactly as the coroner found it. Vivienne Cameron killed Beth Barnard, then jumped off the bridge to her death. Any part of the narrative that didn't make sense was brushed over. Glenda Frost must have been mistaken about the phone call. It didn't matter that Vivienne's friends claimed she was a calm and devoted mother, because all the retired cops had seen cases where murderers were people their friends thought unlikely to kill, and therefore Vivienne must be guilty.

The show then brought in criminologist Dr Kathryn Whiteley, who worked in the United States and specialised in interviewing long-term incarcerated female killers. She said the crime was unlike anything she'd ever seen committed by a woman. The men on the panel seemed to shrug this off, even though their judgement of Vivienne was based on their experience of all their other cases. Apparently, that's something only men can do. (Dear Reader, that dripping sound you hear is sarcasm.)

At one point, Liz Hayes questioned Fergus's statement where he said Vivienne offered to leave him with the kids so he could move his girlfriend in to be their mother. Again, Dear Reader, you'll recall we've already laughed at the incredulity of this one.

242

Gary Jubelin had an interesting take on this. 'Going back to the standing that the Cameron family had within the community,' he said, 'the embarrassment of the situation, I can imagine him down-playing it: "Yes, I was having an affair, but we've come to an amicable arrangement that we're gonna separate", and explain [it] that way. It sort of diminishes the trauma of what his actions have caused.'

'So you give him a little benefit of the doubt?' Liz Hayes asked.

'There's room for, let's call it, error,' Gary Jubelin said. 'Whether it's deliberate or not, but ... that's the white noise around an investigation.'

In essence, Gary Jubelin reframed Fergus's account of events – that no woman would believe likely – and made it something almost gallant and courtly.

As for the early morning phone call to John and Robyn Dixon, Gary Jubelin said, 'The significant thing at the 3 am phone call is that she's telling Robyn Dixon she's going to the hospital. Now that's a lie. At that point in time, she had formed some sort of intent at 3 am, so she was up to something.'

So, according to Gary Jubelin, it's white noise when a man lies, but when a woman lies, she is 'up to something'.

It was at that moment that I felt I would likely be the lone voice for Beth and Vivienne. Things got clearer with each question from Liz Hayes. She said to Rory O'Connor, 'You'd been given information about an affair. You knew that Vivienne was missing, so did you go into that crime scene believing that Vivienne had murdered Beth?'

'Yes, yes, we did,' Rory O'Connor said. At the same time, he was also clear that the level of brutality wasn't something he'd witnessed before. 'Horrific scene. It really was. When you consider the damage that was done to the woman's body.'

'And what kind of killer did you think you were looking at here?' Liz Hayes then asked.

Rory paused for a moment then conceded, 'Well, definitely [it] was more than you'd think a woman would have done to another woman.'

'Why do you say that?' Liz Hayes pressed.

'It's the most brutal attack I've ever seen, and I've seen attacks that men do to men but this, this was horrific for a woman doing it to another woman.'

At that point, Dr Kathryn Whiteley weighed in on the matter. 'It's almost like I'm seeing a very masculine male killing as opposed to a female killing.'

*

In a filming break, the producer Danielle Collis came over to me and looked apologetic that I had ended up being one of the only dissenting voices present in the studio. But she was young and I am older and being a dissenting voice has become a default setting. 'This is good,' I told her, 'because now people will see how detectives think when they approach crimes. And they will see what we are up against when we try to question their conclusions.'

And at the end of the episode, one by one, Liz Hayes asked us all if we were on the jury and Vivienne Cameron were on trial, would we find her guilty or not guilty. Of course, I said not guilty because the evidence threw up so much reasonable doubt. Not surprisingly, Gary, Rory and Val were quick and unequivocal with their guilty verdicts. On the evidence of her state of mind (according to Fergus), the phone call to John and Robyn Dixon where she lied, and the vehicle found near the bridge, they all declared Vivienne Cameron guilty. That means there was no reasonable doubt at all. End of story, case closed.

To be honest, it was fascinating to watch in real time.

After filming had finished, a member of the crew came over for a chat. 'Every time those detectives spoke,' he said, 'I was watching all the women in the crew and you. You all rolled your eyes.'

The astute see everything.

And I guess, in a nutshell, he identified the problems in looking at this case. There is a certain type of man – we all know them and #notallmen – who invest in their beliefs a certainty that cannot be shifted. They believed the answer lay in the most logical theory. Vivienne Cameron did it. You didn't have to consider anything else but the basics, the easiest route from A to B. Guilty. Guilty. Guilty. Lock her up. Throw away the key.

At one point during the show, I mentioned the issue of the blood at the Camerons' house not matching the story. It was Vivienne's blood and there was lots of it, even the drag marks of it on her bathroom floor, but somehow there was no transference of blood to the Land Cruiser from a killer who'd surely be dripping with it. That didn't make the final cut, which meant that there was little ambiguity in the episode.

When it went to air, the overwhelming reaction I saw on social media was one of anger. You see, people who'd read the book and listened to the podcast understood the case's complexities. When the show simplified it down to the Vivienne-did-it suggestion, those who'd joined the fight for justice were understandably furious.

But all was not lost. Regardless of whether Channel 9 and the producers got it right or not, the airing of that episode of *Under Investigation* opened the floodgates once again.

CHAPTER 31

THE PROFILER

One person who reached out after the episode aired was a woman called Kris Illingsworth whom I'd interviewed years ago for another story. Kris is a retired New South Wales detective and FBI-trained criminal profiler known for her work on some of Australia's most complex and disturbing cases. I interviewed Kris about the 1999 rape of an elderly woman in a little town in New South Wales called Wee Waa. Kris profiled the offender and devised a questionnaire for men in the town to fill out as they volunteered their DNA for the purposes of elimination. The offender was eventually caught and he fit Kris's profile to a T. The last time I saw Kris was at a crime writers festival. She was in the audience and during the break I introduced her to a bunch of other crime writers who were thrilled to meet an FBI-trained profiler.

After she saw the *Under Investigation* episode, Kris got in touch and we spent hours on the phone discussing the case. Talking to experts like Kris Illingsworth, learning more, and soaking up their expertise and insight, is one of my favourite things about crime writing. Firstly, we examined the pictures of the Camerons' spare bedroom where Fergus said he went while he was bleeding following Vivienne's attack. The anomaly of course was that the blood on the floor, the bed and the chest of drawers was not his. It was Vivienne's.

'All those papers spread out on the bed from the leather folder, they look like they might be important,' Kris said. I had looked at the photo a hundred times, but I was concentrating on the fact that no one seemed to have sat on the bed like Fergus had claimed, rather than what was actually on those papers.

The next thing Kris looked at was the straw matting on the floor, which was dotted with Vivienne's blood. 'Could she have been flicking a hand that was bleeding?'

We both pondered those dots of blood.

Like me, Kris had trouble imagining how Fergus's back injuries could have occurred. One stab wound, sure, that could happen, but three? In a tight little cluster? If someone stabs you once, wouldn't it be your natural instinct to leap out of the way? Kris thought the small, shallow cluster of three wounds high on the upper-left side of his back appeared inconsistent with a violent attack, because they were shallow and superficial, and oddly clustered together. They and a single superficial linear scratch extending upwards from the cluster looked like they'd been inflicted with the tip of a knife, but without much force, given their lack of depth and breadth.

'These injuries don't look like any glassing injuries I've ever seen,' Kris said. 'His back injuries are inconsistent with what is seen in homicide knife attacks. The glass story doesn't stack up without any broken glass recovered, and I'd question whether the back injuries could be caused by jagged glass anyway, which

I would expect to create jagged gashes and tears in the skin and perhaps leave glass remnants in the wounds.' Kris felt the injuries' appearance simply didn't gel with an attack from behind. But in his statement to the police, Fergus clearly said, 'I turned my back away from her and she hit me two or three times with the broken glass.'

Kris then examined the crime scene photos taken at Beth's house. She called the murder scene 'behaviourally rich'. 'It's not a stranger,' she said. 'And whoever did it is comfortable in the house, knowing they wouldn't be disturbed, so they're definitely known to her.'

And this is where our talk turned to the possible 'staging' of the crime. Not surprising, since this crime scene never looked consistent. I asked Kris more about this. She felt the staging began once Beth's body had been dragged from the bed onto the floor.

'The cutting of her throat on the floor and the carving on her chest were in all likelihood inflicted post mortem, evidenced by the pathologist who was comfortable with saying only the chest stab wound occurred ante mortem. Behaviourally, this makes sense with the rest of the scene and injuries.' Kris was confident that the letter A was carved after Beth died. The photos held the key. 'You can see in the autopsy photo of the chest carvings the lack of inflammation and redness along the edges of the cut skin. This is from a lack of bleeding, which is because she was dead, which means post-mortem cutting. This wasn't a frenzied attack because the attacker stopped after inflicting the stab wounds to her chest while she was on the bed. The staging aspects, which occurred on the floor, by using the gruesome post-mortem cutting aspects to distract and misdirect the investigation, were likely done to protect the offender's identity.'

Kris then noticed something else I had never noticed. On the floor by Beth's bed are a box of tissues and an open magazine. I always assumed the tissues were there because Beth was unwell. I imagined she'd read her magazine and set it on the floor when she went to sleep. But Kris pointed out that the box of tissues and the magazine were both out of reach of the bed. They looked out of place, their positioning possibly the result of a struggle or scuffle in that space. Or had someone moved them? Were they part of the 'staging' of the room? Because even if Beth had tossed the open magazine on the floor, by the time the police photographer captured the crime scene on film, there was a blood-spotted white pillowcase partially on top of it. So who had put it there?

'What do you think of the covering of the body?' I asked Kris. 'If Vivienne did it out of revenge, why would she cover the body? Why not leave Beth uncovered for Fergus to find?'

'I think they covered the body to reduce the sight of it,' Kris said. 'They didn't want to look at it because they knew Beth.' She studied the pictures of Beth's bed and noted the blanket seemed to have been straightened. 'It's the same with the blanket, pulling it up over the sheet. They don't want to see it.'

I had always imagined that Beth's throat was cut by her killer standing behind her, like you might slaughter a sheep, but Kris wondered if it might have been done while Beth was lying on her back because she saw no signs of gravity bleeding below the neck wound – just oozing onto the carpet beneath her head.

And what about the smearing of blood over Beth's arms, abdomen and legs?

'The smearing is probably to make it look worse,' Kris said. 'It likely serves a functional purpose, not a psychopathological reason, to create a visual image to conceal what originally happened.'

Another thing that Kris thought might be significant were what she termed 'hesitation cuts' in the making of the letter A on Beth's chest. 'Why hesitate with the A?' she mused. 'That's not consistent with a rage attack. You just do it; you don't muck around. Was there blood on the underside of the doona? Because if there was, then it was put over her at the time, or soon after the murder, while the blood was still moist. A passage of time would speak to staging.'

I immediately checked the scientific report. The doona is listed as 'Item 4' on the evidence list. I cross-referenced it with the rough sketches made by Dr Bentley Atchison, and saw on the sketch that it was heavily stained on the underside, particularly near Beth's neck wound, meaning it must've been placed there soon after the injuries were inflicted. Of the eight samples tested from different areas of the doona surface, they all came up type O, PGM 1 – Beth's blood type.

Another thing that interested Kris was the fact that in the photo of Beth lying on the floor of her bedroom, there is virtually no blood *below* her knees. Did that suggest the killer straddled Beth while stabbing her? If that's the case, the clothing of whoever stabbed her would surely be bloodstained. But then Kris noticed some small cast-off drops of blood on Beth's lower left leg that suggested it was vertical when the blood landed because the blood drops ran downwards with gravity.

Kris explained why this was important. 'This direction is not consistent with her supine [lying flat on her back] position when she was found. Instead, this direction – and the general absence of blood from both lower legs – suggests her lower legs from the knees down were shielded from the bloodied attack. This aspect, combined with the majority of blood smeared on the front of her body, and the lethal stab wound to her chest, most likely indicates she was lying on her back on the bed trying to ward off the attack, and was quickly overcome by, the lethal chest wound.'

This was consistent with another of Kris's conclusions. 'Given the extent of heavy bloodstaining on the bedsheet protruding from around the blanket, and no staining other than light spatter on the perfectly positioned pillow at the head of the bed, Beth must have been sitting or lying across the bed, fending off the attack, when she sustained the stab wounds to her chest. Her lower legs would have been dangling down towards the floor. In this position, small amounts of cast-off blood could land vertically on her lower legs and run downwards. That the blood had dried while running down her legs shows there was a passage of time before her body was moved onto the floor for the next stage of the crime.'

Although photographs are not available of the bedsheets without the blanket covering them, behaviourally it is highly probable Beth's deceased body was dragged from the bed, onto the carpeted floor and away from the bed. Moving her was not about body concealment. It served another purpose.

One thing that Kris said that fascinated me about the staging of the crime scene was that it told you 'the what, the why, then the who'. If any part of this was staged to look like Vivienne was in a homicidal rage over a case of adultery, then that was *not* what this scene was really about.

The killer's clothes, hands and possibly arms, depending on the clothing worn, would have been heavily bloodstained during the attack. But there was no evidence of anyone showering at Beth's, no evidence of bloodied marks on the floor from someone stripping off a blood-soaked outfit; there was nothing but a faint watery drip of blood on one of the taps in the basin in the bathroom. The owner of that blood could never be identified.

Naturally, our next topic of discussion was the Camerons' Land Cruiser and the lack of any kind of transference of evidence.

'The offender driving the vehicle,' said Kris, 'had cleaned themselves of blood before getting into it. If it was Vivienne, that would mean she washed herself, and changed her bloodstained clothes, and destroyed them, as none were found. With no blood in the vehicle and no bloodied clothes retrieved elsewhere, the suicide theory doesn't hold up on the physical evidence alone.'

If Vivienne planned this murder, then planned to end her life, why go to all the trouble of bringing a change of clothes to the crime scene, and destroying or concealing them? If you left a letter A behind, carved into your victim's chest, you were pretty much declaring your guilt. Why not leave her blood smeared all over the Land Cruiser as well – what would it matter? Because if you really were heading to the bridge to jump, you would have had nothing to lose.

Our discussion then led to the biggest question of all: was Vivienne the likely killer?

Kris felt that the violent and gruesome nature of the murder was entirely *inconsistent* with Vivienne's victimology. No one just 'snaps'; there are always risk factors for targeted violence, including homicidal or suicidal thinking; 'last resort' thinking, where the person feels there is no other option but violence – Vivienne had a plan to leave; and psychopathy, psychosis, or fixation on a target – Vivienne was not known to have displayed any of these violence risk indicators. To the contrary, she seemed to abhor violence, as evidenced by her interactions with friends, her community work, her devotion to her children, her lack of mental health or substance abuse history, the lack of any displayed interest in violence or weapons, and the absence of any known threats or approaches towards, or stalking of, Beth Barnard.

I considered this list of attributes. Of course, I never knew Vivienne Cameron and cannot speak to each attribute with certainty. But what I do know about are the suggestions of violence that Fergus made about Vivienne. But even while Fergus described three violent outbursts from his missing wife, most of the other elements were missing. According to Vivienne's friends, *all* of the elements were missing.

Kris outlined her conclusions in an email.

There is a pathway to targeted violence which begins with grievance. While Vivienne had reasonable cause for griev-ance (the affair and humiliation), there is no indication she was engaged in violent or suicidal ideation as a means to resolve the grievance. Such ideations would need to be attached to the grievance and therefore become step two along the pathway to targeted violence. But there is no such indication she was moving in that direction, based on the information you've given me.

*

More people continued to get in contact. One woman wrote and said that she knew Vivienne from visiting the Community House with her mum. Her mum used to go there for counselling and the woman remembered sitting outside waiting for her to finish. She told me that when it was hot, Vivienne would appear by her side, giving her a drink or an icy pole. In her memory, Vivienne was kind and gentle and she noticed things that others didn't, like overheated little girls who needed something cold on a hot day. 'People like that don't change,' she told me. 'They don't suddenly become violent murderers.'

One man I spoke to had been asked by Beth's dad to do a quote for some repairs at the Barnards' farm. The man had a spare half hour and popped over to the McFees Road property unannounced. He saw the Camerons' Land Cruiser parked out back. When he pulled up, Fergus and Beth emerged from the house, both with wet hair. The man I spoke to said it looked like they'd just had a shower. Neither looked ill at ease with being caught out. The man said Fergus was 'bold as brass'.

'What did Beth look like?' I asked him. 'Was she embarrassed?'

'Nope,' he said.

Another time he saw the Land Cruiser was a bit of a puzzler. It was on the morning that Beth's body was found. He'd driven past it on the crest of the park near Forrest Avenue in Newhaven around 9 am. He reckoned his brother saw it around 5 am, but it wasn't near the park, it was on the *opposite side* of the road near what is now the bakery, but used to be a place called Dutchie's.

'What do you think that means?' I asked him.

'It means that someone moved it,' he said.

This was not the first time I'd heard this theory, but tracking down where the Land Cruiser was at what time is like trying to hold quicksilver.

At the same time, people started to message about others who they thought might want to talk. That hadn't really happened before. It was hard enough for one person to come forward, and no one came forward in pairs. It seemed like pals were getting together and deciding that this had all gone on for too long. It was like a veil had been lifted and suddenly people saw that this case wasn't about protecting those left behind; it was about two women whose lives had been lost and any hope for justice was fading. Suddenly that meant more than politics and friendships and old family allegiances.

And then I got a message from a man with a disturbing story.

Hi Vikki, heard your podcast and have something interesting to tell you about Fergus. My mum had a property [near the Camerons] in the 1980s. She had a beautiful standard poodle whom she loved dearly. One day she called me to inform me Fergus turned up at her house with [the poodle] in the back of his ute having just shot her. He said he'd seen the dog on his property and killed her then realised it was Mum's pet. Poor Mum was hysterical but he drove off. To this day I'll never forget that and how Fergus . . . dumped Mum's pet at her house. Mum never recovered. Wouldn't you recognise a poodle as not being some savage wild dog?

I need to put this message in context because there will be farm folk out there who say they wouldn't hesitate in shooting a dog on their property because it could harm their sheep or unsettle their cattle. I get that, but the thing about this instance was when I rang the man to discuss the issue, he told me that his mum knew Fergus. He would often call in to visit her. He knew her poodle. And even if he didn't recognise it and shot it, why would he load the dead dog onto his ute and drive it to the poor woman's house and dump it on her driveway?

As much as shooting dogs is not a nice topic of conversation, I followed this up with a farmer acquaintance who had experience with this type of thing. His own dog was shot by a neighbour. The neighbour did not say anything to him until the man asked him about it several weeks after the dog went missing, at which point the neighbour confessed to shooting the animal and ploughing its remains into his field. There was certainly no dumping of dogs on driveways. The man I spoke to explained that yes, dogs could be a problem for farmers, but he'd never heard of anyone loading a shot dog onto their ute and dumping it on the owner's driveway.

Yes, Dear Reader, these are the conversations I have with people in order to find you the truth.

CHAPTER 32

THE HOUSE OF CARDS

I always remember how long it's been since the Phillip Island case because it happened the year I got married: 1986. In idle moments, I think about how on my wedding day in February of that year, Beth and Vivienne were still alive. If I knew then what I know now, I could have gone to them and told them both to leave, to run like hell and get off the island.

But that didn't happen and they died and we can't bring them back. Even though powerful people have conspired to keep this case closed and quiet, there's something so strong about the memory of these two women and what their deaths represented, that the case has never died. Just when there was a hiatus and I hadn't thought about it for a while, someone would get in touch with new information and it would start all over again.

After the podcast and the episode of *Under Investigation*, I decided to write this book. I think it was my way of exploring this case through the 35 years that I had been looking at it. I was very young when I started and then I blinked and had turned 60. I know a lot more about life now, and I needed to look at the case through a feminist lens. It became clear that all of the people making decisions about both the investigation and the inquests were men. Men were investigating this case about women and deciding the outcomes with 'man-thinking'.

I knew I was on the right track because I was berated by so many of them. Before I made the podcast, one man in the police cold case unit read the file at the request of a friend of mine who also happened to be in the police force. I'd offered to speak with the cold case officer, but he didn't call until after he'd read the files. Our subsequent interaction was most unpleasant. He spoke to me in a tone I imagined would be used by a wife beater and literally spat his words. 'I don't know what you're on about! I've looked at this case. I've read the files. There's nothing wrong with the findings. I don't know what statements you're looking at because the ones I've got show me it's perfectly clear.' On and on, I listened to the rant, unable to get a word in edgewise. When I tried to answer his questions, he would cut me off. He'd say in a voice dripping with contempt, 'Will you let me finish!' And then of course I stopped trying to speak because, like all women, I knew even if I could get a word in, it would fall on deaf ears, blocked with the earwax of the patriarchy that tells men they are right and women are wrong and weak and don't have anything worthwhile to say.

Then there was that retired detective who said to me in that condescending tone that women know so well, 'Well, Vikki, her husband had just left her, what else did she have left?'

What I wanted to say was: *Are you for real? Do you honestly believe that without her husband, a woman might as well just die? Seriously.* As a side note, I did rather wonder if every case this retired cop ever worked on needed to be re-looked at if this was the kind of thinking he brought to his investigations.

Another man I spoke to used the exact same venomous tone as the cold case cop. 'Who do you think you are to question authority? And if Vivienne Cameron didn't do it, who do you think did? Come on. Bet you can't answer that. And anyway, I know Vivienne did it because she always read crime novels.'

I object on behalf of all crime readers who don't go down the slippery slope to murder. The man's tone was easy to recognise so I heard it coming and prepared for the assault. Don't worry about me, Dear Reader. I've worked in private schools and I am well used to being spoken to like that by the men in charge and have developed an armour of sorts. But I also have a mind suspicious enough to know that when men shut down women with such textbook nastiness, we must be onto something.

Ah, yes, aggressive, patronising men, we figured you out a long time ago.

Anyhow. Enough of that.

I always knew that there was an answer to the Phillip Island case, and I always suspected what it was, but part of being a good crime writer is ensuring you only put forward evidence-based conclusions. I tried to avoid the wild and often defamatory speculation that regularly popped up on social media. It is not enough to point the finger willy-nilly based on a gut feeling or a suspicion; you need hard evidence. Police won't consider anything less.

And then one day, it came.

But before we get to that, let's reconsider for a moment what retired homicide detective Rory O'Connor said to me:

So our main suspect – because of the evidence we've got – will always be Vivienne, but if someone can come up with something that says, 'It could not possibly have been Vivienne because I saw Vivienne at another particular place' – not phone calls, not this, not that, but on that night at that time – then you'd have to look somewhere else.

Most of the time, you'd have to look at other people that are involved.

Turns out, that's easier said than done.

Back to that hard evidence. On 17 July 2023, I received a message from a man called Andy:

Just wanted to touch base with you on a small piece of info that may or may not be helpful in the family murder incident where Vivienne Cameron went missing.

I was with Vivienne at the Cameron house . . . just before the incident all went down. I was working for [Fergus] Cameron with two other carpenters doing some work on the old control tower and ablution blocks on the old racetrack.

I was waiting with Vivienne until Fergus got home from working at the Penguin Parade. He was going to pay me and my two co-workers for the week. I had a cuppa with Vivienne but Fergus was a no show. From memory I believe it all went down just after I left the house.

Andy signed off his note by saying he'd be happy to talk. By the time I'd opened his email, it was too late to call, but the following morning, I rang him. Naturally, the first thing I asked was why it had taken him so long to come forward. His answer was simple. He didn't know there was anything to come forward about. The day after he stopped by the Camerons' farmhouse, the story broke about Beth's murder and Vivienne's disappearance. Andy's story was always, 'And to think I was there the night all this happened!' Because the Camerons and their friends never spoke publicly about the events that had taken place, none of their official accounts ever saw the light of day. So Andy had no way of knowing what Marnie said in her statement about sitting with Vivienne in the Camerons' kitchen drinking wine, waiting for Fergus to come home from the Penguin Parade.

Andy and his wife moved away from Phillip Island in 1988 and he became a police officer in New South Wales. He did not know there had been a book or a podcast, nor did he know of any of the other media we'd done on the case over the years. It wasn't until he was on a surfing trip in Timor and happened by chance to be camping with people from Phillip Island that he found out. The topic of the murder came up in conversation and Andy told them his story about being at the Camerons' farm-house just before it all happened. The islanders told him to get in touch with me. As soon as he got back to Australia, he sent me the above message.

I don't think Andy realised what he told me was so crucial, or that his story contradicted the official narrative. Because if he was waiting with Vivienne for Fergus to come home from the Penguin Parade, then Marnie Cairns wasn't. And that set in train a domino effect. If Marnie wasn't at the Camerons' house, then we naturally have to question Fergus's account of arriving home and finding his sister there. And while we're questioning those narratives, we must question Marnie's account of Vivienne's agitation about Fergus being late. Andy said Vivienne was mildly puzzled about Fergus's failure to appear, but good-natured about it, not worried.

Andy and I talked a lot over the following days, and I think he was in shock; he couldn't believe that his story might be so important. But that wasn't all. Something else he said gave me pause. Andy said that when Fergus didn't arrive home, Vivienne said that she'd pay him and his two co-workers the week's wages and square it up with Fergus later. Andy reckons it was around $1200. It made me wonder if Vivienne had been squirrelling money away for a rainy day. All the stories I've heard about the Camerons' farm during this period suggested that money was tight. Was Vivienne saving up to leave? Was that why she had such a large sum? But it's a long time ago, and while Andy said his work at the racetrack was a cash job, he couldn't be certain Vivienne didn't write him a cheque.

I looked for the millionth time at the crime scene photos taken at the Camerons' house. In one shot there are two coffee cups and a pewter wine goblet on the kitchen sink. In their statements to the police, Marnie and Fergus both spoke about alcohol being drunk, but the only drinking vessels on the sink are the cups and the goblet. The photo would seem to corroborate Andy's story of him having a cuppa with Vivienne.

And as if that all weren't enough, the plot thickened even further.

Andy told me I had to speak to his friend Rod, who still lived on the island. Turned out Rod had his own critical piece of information to add. I rang Rod immediately and he told me that he had driven past Donald Cameron's farm around 3 or 4 pm on Tuesday 23 September 1986, the day the story broke about Beth's murder and Vivienne's disappearance. Rod had been surfing in Kitty Miller Bay that morning and at the time he drove past the Cameron farm, he hadn't yet heard the news.

Driving along unmade road, flanked by Cameron farms on both sides, Rod saw Donald Cameron and a backhoe operator called Rod Patton. They were over by a small dam on Donald's property. Thinking they might need a hand, Rod parked his car on the side of the road and beeped his horn. He got out and waved at the two men, but they didn't wave back and didn't acknowledge he was there.

Rod wondered why they were digging such a deep hole so close to the dam; he figured the backhoe arm was around 10 feet in length and when it was lowered, it was completely hidden in the ground. Rod knew that such a large hole could very well destabilise the dam wall. The only reason you'd dig close to a dam wall was if you were connecting a relief valve, but Rod couldn't see any pipes or equipment. He stood and watched them for a while and then got back in his car and drove off.

The news of the murder and disappearance broke later that day.

My heartbeat quickened as Rod spoke. If what he said was accurate, it would mean that Donald Cameron discovered Beth's body, reported it at the police station, gave a statement to detectives, signed it at 12.50 pm, then drove home and organised a guy to dig a really big hole in a weird location on his property.

And then Rod told me something else that was curious. The next time he saw Rod Patton, the backhoe operator, he asked him what he was doing at the Cameron farm digging so close to the dam that day. Rod Patton's reaction startled him.

'The first time I asked him about it, he just scowled at me and walked away. Wouldn't even offer an answer. And I just asked him quite honestly, "What were you doing down there?" and he scowled at me again and walked away. Over the years since then, I've asked him a few times, and he just swears at me. Won't talk about it.'

*

Months later, on a visit to the island, Rod and Andy took me to the spot where Rod had stopped near Donald Cameron's farm that afternoon on Tuesday 23 September 1986. Rod pointed out the location and said something I'll never forget. His voice was tinged with sadness. 'Every time I drive down this road, I always look at this spot and wonder if that's where Vivienne is buried.'

We stood by the side of the road for a little while, talking and taking pictures of the area. The small dam was adjacent to a copse of trees on otherwise empty grazing land.

'Those trees weren't there back then,' Rod said. 'They were planted after. The hole they were digging was right where those trees start.'

It made me wonder if the copse of trees was intended to camouflage where the hole had been dug.

Andy and I had long talks about how to best get all of this information to the police. First, I emailed a detective at homicide. Here's the response I received:

I have spoken with investigators at Cold Case – they have informed me that this case is now currently inactive, meaning that there is no one actively looking at this job at the present time. I will submit this information however, so when it does get looked at again, the information will be with the file.

I read it and took a minute to say rude words and make a nice cup of tea, then my brain switched into a default setting that I'd learned many years ago interviewing a man who'd been lost in the high country and wasn't found until he was near death. Every day he would ask himself, *What can I do next that would be most helpful?* And he survived, so it worked.

I recalled what my friend Detective Pete had said when the family who'd seen the Camerons' Land Cruiser cross the bridge at 1.30 am the night Vivienne disappeared came forward. 'It's an open case. It's a murder where no one has been charged. If someone comes forward with new information, the police are bound to investigate. They *have* to take his statement.' I wish Pete was back in homicide. Or a Pete-like detective.

I suppose part of the reason why no one was looking at the case was because of the coronial finding that Vivienne killed Beth, then suicided. That means, officially, there was nothing to look into.

Whenever Andy tried to talk to the police or called Crime Stoppers, he got fobbed off. It seemed his story about being with Vivienne the night she disappeared – along with his friend Rod's story about a really deep hole being dug at Donald Cameron's property the following day – didn't warrant further investigation.

It's enough to make a crime writer need a second strong cup of tea and a lie down.

So what to do with the information?

Because you're reading this book, you know things didn't go well with the official channels. First, I turned to the Coroners Court. I had some documents and statements, but over the years I'd lost others. A lawyer I spoke with who'd been at Beth Barnard's inquest told me to apply for the inquest transcript. He added that he didn't think Fergus Cameron had anything to do with the deaths of the two women.

'Oh?' I said, interested in his man opinions.

'I asked him outright at the inquest, "Sir, did you kill your wife?" and by the way he reacted, I could tell he was an innocent man.'

Always amazed by the power of man-conclusions, I asked him how he could possibly tell this.

'He immediately went very pale when I asked him that question. That means he's innocent.'

Okay.

*

In September 2023, just after Andy and Rod got in touch and shared their information, I spoke to a number of Vivienne's cousins and we decided to make an official application to view the coronial briefs. Because Vivienne's inquest seemed to piggyback off Beth's inquest – in that it didn't seem to have been held at all – we needed Beth's coronial inquest file and if there was a transcription, we needed that too.

We filled out the requisite form at the Coroners Court and lodged it through the correct channels. Then we waited. The protocol in applying for files of this nature is that the family involved has to be notified and their permission sought. I explained in our submission why the Cameron family might not wish for us to access the file, but that there was significant public interest in the case that justified our request. I'd recently seen a *Four Corners* episode where a journalist cited a death where the coroner had released the file in the public interest. So we know it *could* happen.

We waited some more. Months went by. And then a year. I would send regular, polite nudges to the coroner's office but the wheels of bureaucracy turned at a snail's pace. From our application for the coronial brief in September 2023, let's fast-forward almost two years to June 2025. After countless emails following up on our application, I finally received a reply:

> Thank you for your email and for your ongoing patience regarding your application.
>
> Judge Cain has completed his review of your application and has approved release of the findings into the deaths of Elizabeth Barnard and Vivienne Cameron (both attached).
>
> His Honour has determined not to release the coronial briefs for these matters.

I already had copies of the two single pages sent with the response. Dear Reader, I think I need a pillow to scream into. Although, if I had one, I wouldn't use it. My response is to go to my laptop and pour my words onto the page. It's therapeutic. I imagined writing a letter to the coroner. My words would go something like this:

Dear Mr Coroner,

Thank you for your consideration of our request for the Cameron–Barnard file. While I accept your decision not to grant us access, I wanted to explain the reason why we asked. When the police notified Beth Barnard's family of her death, they said Beth was killed by Vivienne Cameron because she was having an affair with Vivienne's husband Fergus. It was clear the case had been decided, even though, at that stage, Beth's body was still lying in situ on the floor of her bedroom on the island while crime scene examiners worked around her. Only one member of the extended Cameron family had given a statement, and no evidence had been examined. For police to tell the Barnards this conclusion so early suggests a tunnel vision that continued through to the inquest.

The police seem to have ignored or have been unaware that even though Fergus Cameron claims to have been attacked by his wife with a wine glass, the blood splattered around the Cameron house is Vivienne's not his, and that there is in fact a drag mark in her blood across their bathroom floor.

Beth Barnard's inquest was held in 1987, a year after her murder. Coroner Barry Maher found that Vivienne 'contributed to the cause of death'. A year later, 1988, the same coroner concluded about Vivienne that he was 'satisfied that she is dead and that she leapt from the bridge into the water' – even though the evidence to support this conclusion was that a family vehicle was found half a kilometre from the centre of the bridge.

Here's why these coronial findings matter so much today. Because Vivienne Cameron was declared to be responsible for Beth Barnard's murder, then declared dead, the file was effectively closed. This means that when I got in touch with Victoria Police to pass on information from two new witnesses who had come forward – one who said he was with Vivienne Cameron on the night of the murder, directly contradicting one of the family member's statements, and the other who said he witnessed Donald Cameron on his farm with a local backhoe operator digging a deep hole on the day Vivienne Cameron went missing – Victoria Police can refuse to investigate or even take their statements because in 1988, a coroner made a decision that had no strong basis in evidence.

I just needed you to fully understand what you are saying no to.

But I didn't send it. By that stage, I had become jaded, convinced that men in power just didn't want to know about this case. Had I sent it, I would have included a picture of the bridge marked with an X to show the distance from where the Camerons' Land Cruiser was found, and I would have included a photo of the drag mark in Vivienne's blood on the Camerons' bathroom floor.

CHAPTER 33

LOOKING FOR A SIGN

In several ways, 2025 was a bastard of a year. My dad died in February. A couple of months later, we had to put down our 17-and-a-half-year-old dog, Muffin, when she stopped eating and started shaking. Then I lost a friend, Rory, to cancer. Unaccustomed to loss, I found out it was accumulative. The thing about loss is you lose the routine around those you lose: the visits to Dad in aged care, or Muffin always greeting me at the door even though she was deaf and couldn't hear me coming, or Rory, whom I messaged late at night, and he usually answered because he kept the same hours. I would drive past the street where my dad's aged-care place was, and my eyes would fill with tears. I kept one of his shirts and it sat on my laundry bench for months because I wasn't ready to find a place for it, but my breath would catch just looking at it. I missed him.

Then when Muffin went, our house didn't have a dog. Muffin was a herder; she liked all her humans to be where they should be. She wouldn't go upstairs to bed until I did, and I write long into the night. The first sign that the end was near came a month before, when she stopped following me upstairs and stayed asleep on the couch. Then came Rory. He sent me a message of condolence on the Saturday when I posted about Muffin. 'Oh Muffin! Such a little sweetheart whenever I visited. And my condolences to your whole family.' And that was the last I heard from him, because on the Monday, he woke up without cognitive function, went to hospital and was sedated, and then days later, his grieving husband Carsten told me he had passed.

Dear Reader, I'm not telling you all of this for any other reason than I want you to know that I was exhausted and sad. My PhD was nearing the end, which meant I was heartily sick of the sight of it and wanted it to be over. I couldn't remember the last time I'd had a day off. So one morning, the Phillip Island case came to mind, and I felt the weight of it. For the first time in three decades, I questioned whether I had any energy left for it. I'd been working on this book for years and my agent had pitched it but hadn't heard back from the publisher. I wasn't sure I could keep doing this. So many brick walls. So little interest from the officials who could make a difference. In a moment of exhaustion, I looked at the ceiling and whispered, 'Vivienne and Beth, if you want me to keep going, you need to send me a sign.'

The next day, I was driving to my morning aqua class at the local pool when my phone rang. It was Barry Gibson, retired head of the Victoria Police search and rescue squad. When I saw his name come up on my car console screen, I thought, *Ah, this is the sign.*

'G'day Vikki,' he said.

'G'day Barry! So lovely to hear from you!'

I first met Barry around 2004. He was a senior sergeant at search and rescue, and he told me a story which I think well illustrates his character. In 1981, when he was a young senior constable, there was a diving fatality near the Port Phillip Heads, not far from Western Port Bay. While it's a large bay, it narrows at the opening between Queenscliff and Portsea to a width of around 3.5 kilometres, which reduces to about a kilometre through the centre. The heads are the three headlands – Point Nepean, Point Lonsdale and Shortlands Bluff – that frame the narrow entrance to Port Phillip Bay.

While exploring the wreck of a scuttled submarine just outside the heads, a diver had gone missing. Barry was instructed to walk up and down the beach in case the diver's body washed ashore. Search and rescue were not allowed to look for the missing diver because the team was only trained to dive to a depth of 20 metres; the diver was lost around 40 metres below the surface. Divers from the military and navy were eventually brought in, but it was too late and the body was never recovered.

Barry vowed that if he was ever in a decision-making position, he would train a team for deeper diving. And that is exactly what happened. In 1997, history repeated itself. A diver exploring one of the scuttled submarines outside the heads failed to surface and was presumed drowned. Barry got to lead a team of police search and rescue divers to the site, and after a treacherous dive, the diver's body was recovered so she could be returned to her family.

When Barry retired, his squad gave him a plaque that read *Barry 'One More Dive' Gibson* because he never wanted to stop until the job was done. In short, Barry was a good copper. Then he retired and moved to Phillip Island. After seeing the episode of

Under Investigation, he got straight on the phone. When I asked Vivienne and Beth for a sign, what better sign than Barry Gibson?

Barry told me he knew the head of the homicide squad from years back and offered to approach him for me.

'Oh Barry, that would be awesome,' I said. 'All I need is an hour of his time.'

'Happy to come with you,' he added, because he knew as well as I did that the presence of a retired male copper might help.

My hopes lifted.

I told Barry I'd heard from quite a few people that Fergus Cameron was ill. I'd heard different diagnoses and none of them sounded good. People didn't pass this on to share idle gossip; they told me because it made the fight for answers and justice all the more urgent. With Donald Cameron's death in 2019, and Fergus being ill, that only left Marnie and Ian Cairns who were involved in the case back in 1986.

A couple of days later, Marnie Cairns died.

She was a good 15 years older than Fergus and almost 90 when the time came. Again, my phone pinged with messages from people on the island who wanted to keep me updated. Online, I found a funeral notice and an announcement that the service could be viewed on the funeral company's website. It was 16 May 2025, the same day I was leaving for London to do a Casefile stage show in Leicester Square and to meet with my new UK agent and publisher for my fiction, and to do lunch with a movie producer – not to boast, but rather to illustrate the wild new directions my writing career had taken, and also to say that while part of your year can have precious ones taken from you, it can also give you startling gifts too. Luckily my flight was late evening, and the funeral service was mid-afternoon. It felt voyeuristic to click on the link, but at the same time, I had spent so many years thinking about all these people and what they did on Monday 22 September and Tuesday 23 September 1986 that there was a familiarity.

The minister announced that Marnie's daughter and son would do the eulogies. I never knew Marnie and Ian had children. I guessed that since they were so much older than Fergus and Vivienne, there would have been a gap in the ages of their kids, and their kids may have been grown up and gone by the time the murder happened. Marnie's son and daughter spoke glowingly of their mother and her strength and her devotion to family. I watched with tears in my eyes because it had only been three months since I had stood in front of a congregation and my own father's coffin to give a similar speech about the dad I adored. I felt their pain.

They also spoke about Marnie and Ian's decision to return to the island in the early 1980s to work on the family farm. This meant they'd only been back a couple of years when Beth was murdered and Vivienne vanished. I wonder if they wished they'd stayed away. It made me sad that the shadow of Fergus's affair with Beth and her murder and Vivienne's disappearance would always follow Marnie. It was a pity, because this was not her doing. I listened closely to the eulogies. For all the talk of Marnie's steely resolve and unconditional love of her family, I wondered just how far she would have gone to protect them.

Fergus was there in the front row, flanked by his new wife and older son. Whenever the church service required the congregation to stand or sit, Fergus's wife and son had to hoist him up. At the end of the service, as he walked out of the church, he required a family member on each arm. And I realised that whatever struck him down had moved quickly, because in some of the pictures in the funeral photo montage that seemed fairly recent, he looked more robust.

So first there was Barry's call and then Marnie's funeral, all in the same week. Talk about signs. This case never quietens for long before it pokes at me to pay attention. And so I kept writing.

*

Shortly after the funeral, Barry called back and told me that the head of the homicide squad had agreed to take another look at the file.

'If he needs to talk to me, I'm happy to share what I know,' I offered yet again, realising as I said this out loud that the likelihood of anyone in homicide wanting to talk to me was remote. This is based on years of personal experience of homicide detectives not wanting to talk to me. The exceptions being Detective Senior Sergeant Jeff Maher, who visited me for tea and cake after the *Sensing Murder* show went to air. And then, after the podcast, the two lovely female detectives who came to my house and gave me several hours of their precious time and listened as I outlined the case to them. In words that were not spoken but rather hinted at through raised eyebrows or incredulous murmurings, I knew they could see the things that I could see, but I also knew that the decision to look at the case did not lie with them. It lay with men. As always.

CHAPTER 34

FORTY YEARS ON

So did he get back to you? I hear you ask, since we have moved on to a different chapter and you're still wondering if the head of the homicide squad called. You ask because you're newer to this than I am. You ask because you still have hope in truth and justice. You believe in common sense that of course a homicide detective would call an author who has spent 35 years collecting evidence about a case, talking to people and following up leads.

I'll let you down gently, Dear Reader, because you are not as used to disappointment as I am. No, he didn't call. Now, let's put on our big-girl pants and finish this story.

The search for Vivienne Cameron was never just a physical one; it was always about finding out who she was, because in all of this, she was lost. Lost to her boys. Lost to her friends. And given the island embargo on public conversation about her, she was lost to silence.

Having tried for two years after Andy and Rod came forward to get officials to talk to them and take their statements, we were at an impasse. The state coroner refused to help and all my attempts to get the police interested had failed. But then one day Andy *did* get a call back from Crime Stoppers and spoke to a detective. When Andy left the island, he joined the police in New South Wales so he speaks fluent cop. He tried to appeal to the detective who contacted him. 'Come on, mate, you need to take a look at this.'

'But her car was found near the bridge,' said the detective, which left Andy to wonder that, of the two people in the conversation, was only one of them smart enough to know that if a car is found parked near a bridge, anyone could have parked it there.

So still an impasse.

I then called Rod for an update. 'Did the police ever get back to you?'

'A detective called,' he said.

My hopes went up.

'It was a very short conversation,' he added.

And my hopes went back down to where they belonged.

'What happened?' I asked him.

'Well, I told him what I knew and what I saw and he said he wouldn't be able to justify to his superiors to hire an excavator, and get permission from the property owners—'

'I don't think police need permission if they're searching for a body,' I said. 'I reckon they'd need a search warrant, but not permission.'

'He reckoned you've really got to have some good evidence to do it. And even with an eyewitness like me, it would be expensive and might turn up nothing.'

But it might turn up something, I thought.

'Bit disappointing, to be honest,' Rod said. 'He said that with both Donald Cameron and Rod Patton dead, it's a dead end.'

'Bloody hell,' I said. 'Why did the detective go straight to talking about hiring excavators? Why couldn't they just come to the island and take your statement and maybe start by asking Rod Patton's relatives if he ever said anything about it?'

'Sounded like he was talking himself into abandoning it,' Rod said. 'He kept saying that he couldn't justify the expense and that the police were under the hammer with the financial guys. I felt so let down after than conversation, you wouldn't believe it.'

Oh yes, Rod, I *would* believe it. Welcome to my world.

What was truly surprising was that the detective didn't even offer to take Rod's statement. Surely they'd want it on record at the very least.

'I came away from the phone call with the detective thinking, *He just can't be bothered*,' Rod said.

Here's the thing. The detective didn't need to start with earth-moving equipment. He just needed to talk to people. One man I spoke to heard the same story from Rod Patton's cousin about Rod digging the hole the day Vivienne went missing. They could have started there. Or they could have brought in a human remains detection dog. Victoria Police doesn't have one, but I know a woman in Victoria with a certified dog that is trained to detect historical remains as well as recent ones. When I described the copse of trees planted on the site, she said if trees are planted near where a body is buried, the trees can absorb elements of the remains, and the dog can detect from the trees. It would be easy to send a dog and handler in, under police supervision of course.

So, even though Andy's story challenged Marnie Cairns's account of that night, and Rod saw Donald Cameron digging a hole on his property that was never searched on the day Vivienne went missing, Victoria Police would not act.

It's enough to make you weep.

*

The one thing for certain in the murder of Beth Barnard is the strong community code of silence that surrounded it, a code normally reserved for the criminal underworld, not a regular bunch of citizens. I never understood why this was, because when tragedy happens, it's human nature to talk about it. In the talking, we try to make sense of it. We try to learn from it. For those of us who have had some sort of tragedy in the family – which is most of us – it is all we speak of while we process it: the shock, the cause, the hope, the end, the guilt, the grieving, the lessons learned, the reconfiguring our lives to move forward to accommodate the loss. That's normal.

So why was talking about the case forbidden on the island? I saw it when I went there five years after the murder, and things haven't really changed three decades on. When I recently posted on social media about making a visit to the island, someone contacted me asking if I would be interested in doing a talk at the local library. My trip was the following weekend, and there wasn't time to organise anything formal, but I offered to meet with anyone who wanted to talk about the case. The person suggested a local café owned by some friends of theirs. We set a date and time, then they got in touch again. Sorry, apparently the café was closed on Saturday. Maybe another time? I knew the café wasn't closed because I had googled it. I knew what had happened. The person had mentioned it to the café owners, who panicked: 'You can't have her here! If people find out we've hosted her, our business will suffer!'

Perhaps it's a mark of my own stubbornness that when someone else asked to meet while I was on the island, I suggested *that* café. The irony is that the woman I met there wanted to tell me the story of starting a business on the island, then one day asking the 'wrong' person casually about the case, then having that person spitting in her face with fury, then suddenly having customers stop coming to her business until the business eventually failed. The latte I drank at that café on the day it was supposed to be shut proved the fear is still very real. And as the person I met there constantly scanned the other patrons over my shoulder, looking nervous, I knew nothing had changed.

But why?

Who are these people who shut down conversations with almost violent reactions to people talking about the case? Or say things like, 'Think of the children/grandchildren/Vivienne's family'? That question is rhetorical because I know *exactly* who they are. Their names come up constantly in the stories of people who contact me. Why are they so afraid of full and frank discussion? Don't they realise that shutting it down only makes people more interested? Or is it more an exercise in flexing their power?

It goes beyond the polite sensitivity type avoidance. I've spoken to people who have been screamed at by locals for even mentioning the case. One man brought it up with a health service provider on one of his regular weekly appointments and was never able to book there again; suddenly, they were booked out.

I recently spoke to a group of women who told me of three different workplaces that had forbidden any mention of the case. This
is how widely the silence is still enforced. Mentions of the case
in local news were minimal, and when there was a feature article
about it in *The Sunday Age*, the newspaper was not available on
the island that day, adding censorship to the silence.

The power and influence of the Phillip Island establishment
has long, cold tentacles. There are stories of it affecting businesses and job prospects. To those not from the island, it's hard
to imagine. This is why I've always admired the courage of people
like Sue Chadwick and Anne Davie, who chose to speak up even
though they were part of the community. I think that took more
courage than anyone imagined.

*

On 22 September 2024, the anniversary of the night it all began
38 years earlier, I received an email request to speak at a library
on the mainland some *50 kilometres* from Phillip Island. In the
lead up to the talk, I got another email. I've removed the name of
the library because I don't want to be mean.

Dear Vikki,

On behalf of the Friends of the Library, I wrote to you
a few weeks ago expressing our delight that you will be our
guest speaker, but also expressing our concern regarding
your book and podcast on the Phillip Island murders.

I apologise if I am imposing, but we really do need to
hear from you about our concerns. Most of the committee

are not long-term residents and so are not very familiar with the history of those events. We now know that local residents who were closely related to Vivienne Cameron are well known, work in the area and have children at the local school. My original letter was a request by the Friends of the Library committee to please not mention this book or the podcast in your presentation as respect for this family. We would also appreciate you not selling that book on the night. Of course please feel free to bring copies of all your other books. We are confident that you too will be mindful of hurt that may inadvertently occur.

I would appreciate your response to this letter, and, with all our committee members, very much look forward to your presentation.

The committee then rang me to reinforce the gag order. You could have knocked me over with a feather. Nothing like this had ever happened before. I told them I never intended to cause offence to anyone and, as a natural reaction to their impassioned pleas, agreed not to talk about the book – which I hadn't intended to talk about anyway.

But what would happen if someone asked a question about the Phillip Island case during my talk? 'Oh, you could just say, "I'm not answering that!"' laughed one of the women as if I could joke my way out of it. The whole thing was very weird. But then I started to stew on it. How could I hurt people 'and their children' when those people surely would not be at the event? There was something fishy about this. As you know, the 'think of the children' line had a long history.

True crime authors, by and large, are excellent researchers. And my researching skills had ramped up several notches since I'd begun doing my PhD. Who *were* these 'Friends of the Library'? I googled the committee members and immediately saw the connection. One of the women had hosted Vivienne and Fergus Cameron for a business dinner the week before Vivienne disappeared. During the dinner, her husband had told a story that resonated with the Camerons. Here's what Fergus told Detective Senior Constable Alan McFayden:

> Last Saturday night I went to dinner with Vivienne to [name]'s place in Cowes to discuss the future possibilities in a business venture and during the evening [he] cited a case of a friend of his who virtually started off with nothing and worked his way up; in doing so lost his loved ones on the way. This statement Vivienne drew on later.

During my research for the podcast, I contacted the woman to see if she could offer any insight since she had spent time with Vivienne on the last Saturday before she vanished. I wanted a woman's perspective on the social dynamic between Vivienne and Fergus, the tensions, or how Vivienne had reacted to the story about the man who 'lost his loved ones on the way'. Anything that could help piece this all together.

She never replied.

As for the 'Friends of the Library', I did what any self-respecting author with hurt feelings would do. I wrote a post on my Facebook page asking people who followed me what they suggested. In record time, 250 people told me in no uncertain terms to decline. A man called Matthew had the perfect response: 'Tell them to piss off.'

While not using Matthew's exact words, I wrote back to the woman I'd spoken to:

> I've given your request a lot of consideration today and I feel that while I can control the content of what I talk about, I cannot control the questions from the audience. If someone asked about the Phillip Island case as they would be sure to do, I would be placed in too awkward a position by refusing to answer it. Given the restrictions you require for my talk, I feel I am not a good fit for the Friends of the Library and must now respectfully decline your invitation.

Which I suppose is just a polite way of saying, 'Piss off'.

The 'think of the children/grandchildren/Vivienne's family' argument can certainly stop people in their tracks. Until you give it some thought. I have grandchildren and they are curious about their world. They are also curious about those family members who came before them. And if an ancestor were accused of murder, surely, one day, they'd want to know the truth. With my grandchildren, we can talk about relatives they never knew, and the grandkids ask intelligent questions about who and what and why.

So naturally, the mention of 'children' in the email from the Friends of the Library had a predictable echo. But all I've ever wanted was truth and justice for Beth and Vivienne. To suggest that the pursuit of this was going to damage people connected to Vivienne was incorrect. I've met with many of Vivienne's relatives over the years, and they are as keen to see justice for her as I am.

Days before this book was heading off to the printer, I got a message that Ian Cairns had passed away on 3 November 2025. He was 93. His funeral was held 17 days later at St John's Uniting Church, the same place where Marnie's service had been conducted in May. In the eulogy, his daughter talked about Marnie and Ian coming back to the island in 1982 to join the family farming business. She said they retired in 1986 and left the island. We know that at the end of September 1986, they were still Fergus and Vivienne's farming neighbours. So if she is correct about the year, some time in the following three months after the murder, they packed up and left the island. I knew they left afterwards, but I didn't realise it was that quickly.

Having said all of this, I feel like this book represents my last go. My writing has moved to fiction, which offers me the chance to address huge issues about violence against women and the way so many men escape the consequences of their actions. I don't have to be careful about treading on toes when I make up stories. So I need to let Phillip Island go now. I need to walk away, knowing that with the original book, the podcast, and now this new book, I've done everything I can to try to find the truth about what happened on that cold September night back in 1986.

But of course . . . if – like Andy and Rod – you have information about the case and the police won't listen or take your calls, find me on my Facebook author page or Instagram or my website and send me a message.

You know I'll listen.

Beth and Vivienne deserve that much.

ACKNOWLEDGEMENTS

This story has taken 35 years to write. It *made* me a writer. The first person I must thank is Paul Daley, then a journalist at *The Age*, who was my co-author for the original book, *The Phillip Island Murder*. It was at his side that I soaked up the craft of writing. I watched him redraft words I had written and turn them into something special. If you watch the magic closely enough, you too can become a magician. I have tried to emulate this over the years in turn by helping other writers.

To the publishers along the way who believed in the book. John Kerr in the beginning and Lindy Cameron since, and now, Ben Ball, thanks for keeping the story alive.

People had approached me about making a podcast about the Phillip Island case before, but until the Casefile host came along, the idea didn't get off the ground. He said, 'Do it with us!' And I did. *Casefile Presents: The Vanishing of Vivienne Cameron* was born. I owe the greatest debt of gratitude to the Casefile host, not just for taking on my podcast, but for trusting that I could do it when I had never made a podcast before. He will never know how much that trust meant to me. It is a rare person who welcomes a stranger so readily into the folds of their success.

I am especially grateful to have shared the investigative journey with some very special people. Vivienne Cameron's cousins, Lesley Avery and Pat Hammond, have offered much support and research. And then, unexpectedly, the women from the North Carolina Justice System who heard the podcast and got in touch to offer their incredible investigative experience, all in the name of justice. Lauren McCarthy and Stephanie Williams, the world feels very small when the hand of friendship reaches across an ocean. And to all the people over the years who contacted me to share their story or help piece together the puzzle, you all made me feel like I was never alone in this.

To Kris Illingsworth and Dr Mayumi Purvis, thank you for your measured and insightful professional opinions. I'm so lucky to have experts like you to call upon. To retired cop Barry Gibson, thanks for the chats in between your golf games. And to my beautiful friend Jacqui Hawkins, who offered to read this manuscript before anyone else in the world had seen it, your feedback and encouragement were very welcome.

And lastly and most importantly, there is family. Only the ones who live with and love a writer know that sometimes when they say something, the writer is *there*, but her mind has floated away to inhabit the world of her story. To Steve and Stacy who shared the journey. My parents Helen and John (lost in 2025) have delighted in my writing career. My mum is my greatest proofreader and champion. If you see a woman who looks like an older version of me sitting in a café with one of my books prominently displayed in front of her like a living ad campaign, that will be Mum. Stop and say hello.

ABOUT THE AUTHOR

Vikki Petraitis is an Australian true crime author and podcaster. Her first book, *The Phillip Island Murder* (1993), was co-written with Paul Daley. Since then, Vikki has written numerous true crime books, including her bestseller *The Frankston Murders* about Frankston serial killer Paul Denyer, and two acclaimed crime novels. Vikki is also a renowned podcaster with *Casefile Presents* with over 10 million downloads. *The Vanishing of Vivienne Cameron* podcast was released in 2020.